MW01291371

"*Rollie Peterkin left a glide path to Wall Street wealth for the bloody, gritty, impoverished life of a South American cage fighter. This sounds crazy. But what's crazier: Quitting an uninspiring job to chase a dangerous dream? Or how most of us live and die in cages of our own making—never thinking to fight our way out? I left this tale of competition, adventure, and primal fear feeling inspired to live a bigger and braver life.*"

JONATHAN GOTTSCHALL, PHD,
Distinguished Fellow, Washington & Jefferson College. Author of
The Professor in the Cage: Why Men Fight and Why We Like to Watch

"*Rollie's life is much like his wrestling style: wide open, contrarian, and unorthodox. But having coached Rollie, I am rarely shocked by his bold and daring adventures. This book speaks to how a single decision can cause a ripple effect in your life. One minute you're sitting behind a desk on Wall Street crunching numbers and the next you're stepping into a cage (in Peru, no less) to fight someone wanting to rip your head off. Truly a story of staring down fear and having the courage to follow your happiness and intrigue.*"

KENDALL CROSS,
Olympic Gold Medalist, NCAA Champion, and Distinguished Member of
The National Wrestling Hall of Fame

"*Rollie and I have unknowingly been living parallel lives. We were born wrestlers, graduated to become professionals, and then left the professional world for the allure of mixed martial arts. Though I've only known Rollie for a short time, our shared passion for wrestling, fighting and Spanish has created among us a strong bond and mutual respect. His life was meant to be transformed into a book. I mean, really, who leaves Wall Street and an Ivy League education for South American cage fighting?!*

CHARLIE "THE SPANIARD" BRENNEMAN,
UFC Veteran and Author of *Driven: My Unlikely Journey from Classroom to Cage*

ROLLIE PETERKIN

THE

CAGE

ESCAPING THE AMERICAN DREAM

ISBN-13: 9781514294208
COVER/INTERIOR DESIGN BY: ERIN TYLER

CONTENTS

ROUND ONE

ROUND TWO

ROUND THREE

My mother and father, thank you for everything.

ROUND
ONE

" *Most men and women lead lives at the worst so painful, at the best so monotonous, poor and limited that the urge to escape, the longing to transcend themselves if only for a few moments, is and has always been one of the principal appetites of the soul.*

ALDOUS HUXLEY, *THE DOORS OF PERCEPTION*

CHAPTER

1

The dull roar of the crowd echoed in my ears as I fell to my knees in the middle of the mat. I couldn't breathe. I couldn't move. The realization of what had just happened tore through me like a bullet. I was finished.

It was the last wrestling match of my college career and I had gotten pinned. If I had won, I would have been guaranteed a spot on the podium as an NCAA All-American. It was something I had always dreamed about, and this year was my last chance. I had beaten many top-ranked wrestlers during the season, but now, for the third year in a row, I was eliminated in the final round. I had fallen short and now I was done forever.

I got up, shook my opponent's hand, and staggered off the mat in a daze. I stumbled into the concourse of the Wells Fargo Center and collapsed against the cold concrete wall. And I cried.

I sobbed and sobbed until snot ran down my face. I sat with my head tucked between my knees, still sweaty and shirtless. I struggled to catch deep breaths of air between hysteric outbursts. Other wrestlers and coaches passed through the concourse, but I didn't care. I was in a different world.

When I finally caught my breath, I stood up and rushed through the concourse to meet my father. I kept my head down and wiped the tears from my eyes. When I saw him, I fell apart again. We hugged and I cried into his shoulder until his shirt was soaked in tears. He held my head and tried to comfort me.

"Rollie, I'm so proud of everything you've done."

Whenever I lost a match as a kid, he would always say, "You did a great job!" I would reply, "No I didn't! I LOST!" This time I didn't say anything. I had no words.

I thought about all the sacrifices my parents had made for me over the years. I knew they always wanted the best for me, but now I felt like a complete failure. I erupted in another bout of tears as my entire wrestling career flashed before my eyes.

Seventeen years earlier, I was doing handstands in the driveway when a neighbor commented that I would make a good wrestler. The next week, my parents enrolled me in a local youth program. After the first practice, I knew right away that this was the sport for me.

From that day forward, I rarely missed a practice. As the years passed, I started winning tournaments and traveling further around the country. By this time, I had quit soccer and baseball because I hated team sports. I didn't want to rely on other people. Winning was so much more fun when it was just me out there. And losing, as I was discovering, was that much worse. When I lost, I couldn't blame the goalie or the quarterback—it was me and only me out there. And the losses tore me up.

In high school I became a three-time Massachusetts state champion. In summer competition, I won nationals twice. For my last two years of high school, I went to a boarding school in New Jersey called Blair Academy, which was famous for its wrestling program. During my first year, we won a national title as a team. Wrestling was a religion at Blair and every day I trained with the most elite athletes in the country.

I was recruited to wrestle for UPenn and I qualified for nationals three consecutive years. Each year, I beat many of the top competitors during the season. I won over 100 collegiate matches, which was a notable achievement by itself. But that didn't help me at the NCAA tournament, where I suffered heartbreak in the same round for three years in a row. I had been working towards this moment for the previous seventeen years of my life and it all came down to one day in

March. And I had failed.

That final year, the NCAAs were held in Philadelphia, so UPenn alumni and supporters flocked from all corners of the globe to attend. They had rented out the entire top floor of the Loews Hotel for the celebrations following the tournament. There were speeches and toasts and everybody was having a good time, but I just wanted to shrink away from it all and disappear.

I spent the remainder of my senior year wallowing in anger and self-pity. I drank a lot, and that sometimes helped. Other times I would wake up in the middle of the night, panicked and sweaty, with the image of that last match searing my memory.

Eventually, I chased the feelings of pain and resentment into the remotest corner of my brain, and sealed them off, brick by brick, like a spiteful Poe character. I could talk about that moment, and maybe even joke about it with a few friends, but I couldn't let myself actually feel it.

Throughout my whole life, wrestling had always been there for me. No matter how crazy my personal life was, I went to practice each day and checked those feelings at the edge of the mat. Now, I was beginning to realize, I would no longer have that. I hadn't just lost the tournament, but I was losing the sport that had been so important to me.

My friends would try to console me by shifting the focus to the future. "You're lucky," they said. "You have a great job offer that people would kill for." I bit my tongue and nodded.

CHAPTER
2

When I moved into my new apartment in New York I was, in many ways, fulfilling my destiny. During my junior year of high school, I read a book called *Ugly Americans* by Ben Mezrich, which tells the story of a group of Ivy League graduates who worked for a hedge fund in Japan. They had outlandish adventures and became immeasurably rich by exploiting the Asian financial markets.

I was hooked right away and I began to read every book about finance that I could get my hands on. I read *Liar's Poker* and *Barbarians at the Gates* and *When Genius Fails.* I tried to read the *Wall Street Journal* every day.

Since I had won nationals in high school, I was widely recruited by college wrestling programs. After visiting many schools, I finally committed to the University of Pennsylvania, mostly because The Wharton Business School was ranked as the best finance program in the country.

The summer before I enrolled, I got an internship as a clerk on the floor of the New York Stock Exchange. I didn't do much that summer beyond taking lunch orders, but I was happy just to be there, witnessing the gears of the financial markets cranking.

During my sophomore year at UPenn, I contacted a former Penn wrestler named Clinton Matter who worked for a hedge fund on Wall Street. He helped me get an internship at a mutual fund in Philadelphia. It was the summer of 2008, and I realized I was lucky to have a job. In March, just before I started, Bear Stearns had been bailed out by the Federal Reserve. The bond trader I worked for that summer would pull me over to his seat. "Look at this," he would say. "You will never see something like this again for the rest of your life." The chart spiked down miles away from the steady, consistent line it had once traced. He would print out the graphs and hand them to me. "Hold onto that one." Months later, after I returned to school, Lehman Brothers went bankrupt, and the entire financial system teetered on the brink of apocalypse.

The following summer, Clinton hired me as an intern at the Royal Bank of Canada (RBC). He worked in the proprietary trading group as the head of their high yield bond strategy.

"I'm going to turn you into a financial ninja," Clinton said as he sat me down to talk over my first project. My assignment was to research the finances of a large casino operator and to present an investment idea at the end of the summer. I read everything I could about the company and their finances. I wrote a 40-page summary and built a financial model in Excel. In the end, the group invested several million dollars in a credit default swap on their bonds.

The next year, I came back to RBC and worked in the Equity Volatility group. They traded products that tracked the volatility of the market, from options to more complex derivatives. It was very different from what I had been doing the previous year. "A financial ninja has to know a broad array of instruments," Clinton said.

I went back to school for my senior year and focused solely on wrestling. When I got eliminated from NCAAs, I tried to take solace in the fact that I had a lucrative career waiting for me.

In September 2011, I entered RBC's rotational program, where I had the opportunity to sample different groups before finding a permanent position. It was a bit like speed dating: if I liked them and they liked me, we would get matched up. Eventually, there was an opening in the Investment Grade Credit group and I was hired.

My boss was a former Marine named Brian who liked to remind me that, at my age, he was commanding a rifle company. He was tall and athletic with a deep voice that oozed authority.

There were also two other guys on the team: a trader named Steve and a research analyst named Dan. Together, they managed a large fund of corporate bonds.

I was eager to learn everything I could. I arrived every morning before seven and I would read research reports until it was dark outside. The vernacular of the trading desk was entirely new to me. At first, I had trouble keeping up with the phones that rang incessantly all day. I would have to deliver messages to the guys as they came in. They would reply with things like, "Hit him through one-eighty if he bids them there, then whack out of some IGs." It may as well have been Chinese to me.

I noticed right away that I wasn't very good on the phones. I was awkward and I mumbled a lot. One day Brian let me execute a forty-million-dollar trade in treasury bonds. To a more seasoned trader, it was a fairly routine trade ("rolling the hedge" in the trader parlance). I was nervous as I picked up the phone. I talked slowly and tried not to confuse the large numbers. When he told me the prices, I shouted them to Brian.

"That's a good price," he said and gave me a thumbs-up.

"Done," I said into the phone.

When the trade tickets came through, I noticed that the prices were slightly different. I had given Brian the wrong prices and screwed up my first trade.

"I knew you would fuck this up," Brian said. He took out a calculator and started punching away then held it up to my face.

"Two thousand dollars," he shouted, "that's how much you just cost us." He talked loudly so that the entire floor knew I had made a mistake. Later, he asked Steve, "What do you want to get for lunch today?"

"It doesn't matter to me," Steve replied.

"Well, I was going to suggest sushi, but Rollie cost us all that money."

Everyone laughed but me. Later, he pulled me aside and explained that it wasn't a big deal. "Just don't let it happen again," he said.

One day, I was on the phone doing a trade with a junior salesgirl at JP Morgan and we both fumbled through the details. Brian was listening, and when I hung up he said, "Jesus, you sounded like two people having sex for the first time."

A few weeks later, our research analyst quit and Brian called me over to his desk. "You're going to get a lot more responsibility," he said. "I expect a lot out of you. It's a good opportunity for you, so don't screw it up." I began to stay even later each day, trying to figure out all of the complex computer systems. We had a massive spreadsheet that ran our daily profit calculations, and now I was in charge of it.

Even though Brian busted my balls sometimes, he did teach me a lot. He was respected as one of the savviest traders on Wall Street and he always had his finger on the pulse of the markets. He would stare at the screen all day as numbers scrolled across like *The Matrix* and he never missed anything.

Plus, it was exciting to get this close to the action so early in my career. With just three people, we managed a portfolio of several hundred million, or at times up to a billion dollars. But things were about to ramp up even more.

"Steve quit," Brian told me one morning as I sat down at my desk. "Things are going to be different around here for a while. We may eventually hire another trader, but for now, you're going to have to pick up the slack."

Without Steve around, it was a nerve-wracking summer. Most days, it felt like I never put the phone down. Just a few days after Steve left, the market started to take a turn for the worse.

"Sell everything!" Brian shouted. We split the bonds up and started calling brokers as fast as we could. After the flurry of action, we were both exhausted, but we had completed our mission. We avoided losing a lot of money and that was what mattered. Brian gave me a nod as he packed his bag to leave. "Good work today."

Brian respected the ability to make money above all else. Whenever he talked about other traders, his first question was always, "Does he make money?" It was his yardstick for measuring a man. He often reminded me that I wasn't a valuable contributor to the group because I wasn't actually producing any revenue.

In August, we hired another trader named Mike Bellini. He was from New Jersey and was quick to let you know that he was Italian. Bellini was riotously funny and could entertain a whole room full of people with his constant banter.

"I have a photographic memory," he told me the first time we met. "Remember that guy in college you hated because he never had to study? That was me."

"That's cool," I said, but I didn't actually believe him. When we started working together, I soon learned that his mind was a steel trap for information.

"How much money did we make yesterday?" Brian would say. Bellini would think for a second and then say, "$21,322." He could remember numbers and details like he had a stenographer in his head.

Bellini looked much older than he actually was. He used to ask people, "How old do you think I am?" and when they guessed way too high, he would reply, "Well, I am twenty-eight years old, but I look like I'm forty-eight, and my liver is sixty-eight."

We started going out to dinners and drinks three or four nights a week. I soon learned the true extent of Bellini's reputation: he could drink as much as any other two people combined. I tried keeping up with him at first, but I quickly learned that was a mistake.

Bellini could go out hard every night of the week and show up at seven in the morning ready to trade. He had close friends at all of the Wall Street banks, and he started inviting me out to gatherings. Through him, I was introduced to the cliquey trading desks of

JP Morgan and Citigroup. These guys were larger than life and it felt like they controlled the whole market.

I remember the first time I really impressed Brian with a trade idea. A large oil company had a pending legal settlement and all of the research reports said that the settlement would be less than expected.

"I bet a lot of people have that trade on," I mentioned. A popular trade would mean that everyone would be trying to sell their bonds at the same time, causing a bottleneck as they flooded the market.

"It does seem like it, doesn't it?" Brian agreed.

"I think if it rallies on the news, we should short them before everyone else unwinds their trades." By shorting the bonds, we could bet that they would drop in price and then we could buy them back for a profit.

Brian left work early that day but told me to do the trade if it felt right. When the settlement was announced, the bonds rallied as predicted. I waited until it lost steam and then shorted eight million dollars of bonds.

As the end of the day approached, the bonds started selling off as I had predicted and I bought the bonds back for a profit. Brian called and asked about the trade.

"Look at you go!" he said. "Making us money!"

Bellini did a lot to unite us and Brian jokingly named him our Social Chair. Sometimes when Brian was giving me a hard time, he would stand up for me. One time he told me, "You know Brian's just fucking with you, right? You can't let it get to you." That was just how it was on Wall Street: you had to have thick skin or you would get eaten alive.

Many days, the three of us would walk across the street after work to the Conrad Hotel bar. Brian would order a round of beers as we reviewed the day's activity. Huddled around a peninsula at the end of the long marble bar, we really felt like a team.

One night, a salesman brought us to Nobu and ordered dozens of platters of expensive sushi and fusion seafood dishes. They brought out large bamboo carafes of sake. We finished nine of them by the end of the night. Our group was getting rowdy, and inappropriate jokes flew around the table until we attracted the attention of the entire restaurant.

The waitress came over and tapped the salesman on the shoulder and whispered something in his ear. He laughed and shooed her away. "You guys will never believe this! Billy Crystal is sitting right over there," he lifted up his arm and pointed. "And that motherfucker asked them to tell us to quiet down!"

"What'd you say?" Bellini asked.

"Tell him to fuck off!"

The community of bond traders was tight-knit and I started making friends with other traders. Soon, I was spending most days of the week with my new friends. Now, not just my entire workday, but my entire life was starting to be consumed by my career.

I started having difficulty relating to my old friends who didn't work on Wall Street. Not only was I developing a whole new vernacular, but I also started spending money carelessly.

One day I went out with Bellini after work, and to my horror, I discovered in the morning that I had spent over $1,000. Bellini patted me on the back the next morning like a big brother consoling me after a Little League loss. "It happens to the best of us. Sometimes I wake up wondering if it was two or three. You just can't think about it."

Every summer, Bellini and his friends rented a shore house in Manasquan, New Jersey. He extended me an invitation to rent a room in the house for the three months from Memorial Day to Labor Day and I accepted immediately.

The first weekend, while most of us had gone to a bar called the Osprey, two police officers knocked on the door of our house holding one of our housemates under the arms. "Does this guy live here?"

"Uh, yes."

"We found him passed out on a neighbor's lawn. Could you please take him?"

The following weekend, another one of our housemates awoke Saturday morning on an unfamiliar couch. He was groggy and stumbled out of the room. As he entered the kitchen, he passed a family eating breakfast. He had come home to the wrong house.

That was the kind of pace we set. By some miracle, I made it back to my own bed every night. Now I wasn't just going out during the week, but I was also pushing my body to the maximum on the weekends. It was going to be a long summer.

CHAPTER
3

One weekend, my friend Kyle and I decided to enter an open wrestling tournament called the Northeast Regionals. We didn't take it seriously and made a joke out of it. After graduation, my training had come to a halt as I focused on my career. I didn't even belong to a gym.

The night before the tournament, Kyle and I went to eat at a steakhouse. We both ordered large steaks and beers—just to prove how little we cared. The next morning, we both won our first round matches decisively. When we won our second round matches, we were both a little surprised. We hadn't even warmed up. We were totally shocked when we both made it to the finals.

Kyle taught me about his theory of Flu-Like Symptoms. The idea was modeled after Game Five of the 1997 NBA Championships in which Michael Jordan suffered from "flu-like symptoms" before the game and almost didn't play. Although he started off the game sluggish, he picked up momentum and led the Bulls to victory with a spectacular performance. After the game, he collapsed.

"Sometimes when everything is going wrong," Kyle argued, "you're forced to rise to the occasion. Like today we've literally done nothing right, and yet it's working for us. It's Flu-Like Symptoms." When I thought back to some of my best matches ever, I was sick as a dog.

I had competed in the Northeast Regionals many times in my wrestling career and I had never won it. But today was different: we both won our weight classes.

When I returned to work on Monday, everyone was shocked. By winning, I had qualified for the World Team Trials. They were going to be held in Stillwater, Oklahoma and I decided to compete.

The World Team Trials uses a rigorous qualification process to select the top guys in the country. Somehow I had slipped through the cracks. In fact, it was almost comical that I had made the cut. Only thirteen guys had qualified at my weight of 145 pounds. Someone posted online the previous collegiate accomplishments of all the competitors in my weight class. But they didn't even bother to mention me.

KYLE BORSHOFF: 2 X ALL-AMERICAN

JASON CHAMBERLAIN: 2 X ALL-AMERICAN

JAMES GREEN: 2 X ALL-AMERICAN

ADAM HALL: 2 X ALL-AMERICAN

DREW HEADLEE: 1 X ALL-AMERICAN

KEVIN LEVALLEY: 2 X ALL-AMERICAN

BRENT METCALF: 3 X ALL-AMERICAN (2X NCAA CHAMP)

JORDAN OLIVER: 4 X ALL-AMERICAN (2X NCAA CHAMP)

CHASE PAMI: 2 X ALL-AMERICAN

KYLE RUSCHELL: 2 X ALL-AMERICAN

KELLEN RUSSELL: 3 X ALL-AMERICAN (2X NCAA CHAMP)

PHIL SIMPSON: 3 X ALL-AMERICAN

I had never even been an All-American, and now I found myself in a weight class with three former two-time NCAA champions.

The morning of the tournament, I drew Philip Simpson in the first round. He was a three-time All-American from West Point at 149 pounds. I had wrestled at 133 pounds in college and he looked massive compared to me.

Simpson got an early takedown to take a 2-0 lead. Towards the end of the first period, I whipped him to his back for a 3-2 lead. Before the period ended, he got another takedown to go up 4-3. In the second period, it became clear that I was outmatched. Every time we tied up, he snapped me down with so much force that my face bounced off the mat. He used his size and strength in every interaction. He scored a flurry of takedowns and then turned me to finish 11-3 in his favor. I stood up and walked to the center of the mat and shrugged.

The next round, I faced the former University of Wisconsin wrestler and two-time All-American, Kyle Ruschell. I got crushed 7-0 in the first period. Again, I shrugged and walked off the mat.

It had been an interesting experience, but one that reminded me that I had a new life now. Although it had been fun, wrestling was a thing of my past and I was now a bond trader.

I returned to work with a renewed focus, and as things grew more serious, I stopped going down to the shore house as much. Bellini was disappointed when I didn't even come to the end of summer party on Labor Day.

Brian had given Bellini his own slice of the portfolio to manage independently, and he assured me that I too would also get my own portion soon. Bellini was trading Energy & Pipeline companies and I was going to trade some smaller, less volatile sectors: Railroads, Transports, Aerospace & Defense, and Utilities.

I was just two years out of college and I was going to have my own multi-million dollar portfolio to manage. This would mean that I could make my own decisions and be responsible for my own stream of revenue. Many young traders had to wait years before getting the chance to manage their own portfolio. And many other traders waited their whole careers without ever getting an opportunity like this.

When a trade makes money, it is a great feeling. But if it loses money, on the other hand, there are few worse feelings. A losing trade can have very real implications on your life. You can lose your job, your respect, and your pride. Older traders would talk about sleepless nights during a losing streak, or dark depressing days in front of the glaring computer screen. I had heard their stories, but I was undeterred. I liked the idea of being able to control my own destiny and I was eager to start.

But first, I was going on vacation.

CHAPTER
4

In October, I took a break from work and went to visit Peru. The vacation couldn't have come at a better time; I was beginning to feel burned out from work. I had recently begun to feel cooped up and antsy as I sat at my desk. I wasn't sure what was missing, but I thought I had found a solution: I was going to buy a motorcycle. The previous week, I went to the Ducati dealership to look at bikes. As I sat in the Newark Airport, I bought a motorcycle magazine from a newsstand and read about the various bikes.

I traveled with three friends from college. We had all wrestled to-gether at Penn and were going to visit our old teammate, Ben Reiter. After college, Ben had joined an educational charity and moved to a small village in Peru to teach English to impoverished children. It had been three years since any of us had seen him. He met us at the airport where he introduced us to his Peruvian fiancée, Fiorella.

We barely recognized the guy who greeted us. Ben had been the heavyweight on our college wrestling team. At that time, he weighed almost three hundred pounds. His fraternity pledge name was Stay Puft, after the marshmallow man from Ghostbusters. Now, he was leaner than we would have ever thought possible.

"Are they feeding you out here, buddy?" I asked as we hugged.

"Oh, you're funny now, huh?" he responded with a laugh. "You should swing by the gym. Maybe it'll do you some good." He had a point—I had gained a lot of weight since my days of college wrestling.

The next day we caught a flight to Cuzco. At 11,000 feet in the Andes Mountains, the thin air made it hard to breathe and I became light-headed as we walked to catch a cab.

At our hostel, an old woman showed us up a flight of stairs to our rooms. I was gasping for air and she looked at me pitifully. She whispered in Spanish to Ben and stepped into the other room. A few minutes later, she shuffled back carrying a steaming teapot and some cups. "*Mate de coca*," she said, smiling.

"*Gracias*," I replied. I had studied some Spanish in high school, but that was more than ten years earlier and I could only recall a few basic phrases.

Ben explained that the Incas traditionally chewed the coca leaves as a remedy for the altitude sickness. The tea tasted like grass clippings and did little to satisfy my demand for oxygen.

We left the hostel and went to explore the Plaza de Armas. As we stood in front of a statue of an Incan warrior, two men stopped Ben and asked for his autograph.

"So, you're kind of a big deal now, huh?" I asked.

"I guess so," he said with a laugh.

I knew the outline of Ben's story, but I hadn't done the best job at keeping in touch over the previous few years, so he began filling us in.

When Ben first moved to Peru, he lived in the southern city of Arequipa, where he began training at a local Muay Thai kickboxing gym.

One day, he decided to try his luck in the world of mixed martial arts (MMA), a form of no-holds-barred cage fighting that was becoming mainstream in the Unites States with the growth of the Ultimate Fighting Championship (UFC). In MMA, you could win by knockout, submission, or a judge's decision. With Ben's elite wrestling background, he would be able to take guys down and control them more easily than most other fighters.

After several months of training, Ben accepted an amateur MMA fight in Lima, a 16-hour bus ride from Arequipa. In the first round, he caught his opponent's arm in a submission called an Americana, torqueing it until he tapped out.

While Ben was learning about MMA, his passion remained in working with children. He encountered a girl named Katy who had a severe medical disorder known as Treacher Collins Syndrome, which causes deformity of the jawbone. It hindered her ability to breathe, speak and even close her mouth. The proper surgery could fix her condition, but her family didn't have enough money. So Ben set about raising it. He hosted seminars and donated the money to help with Katy's surgery.

At the end of June, Ben was offered his first professional fight in the Inka Fighting Championships (Inka FC). Instead of dipping his toes in the water, this time they were throwing him to the sharks. He was booked to face the reigning champion, Fernando "Zopilote" Roca. Zopilote, which means vulture in Spanish, was one of the most loathed and fearsome fighters in Peru with a record of 11-2.

"No one expected me to win," he said with his signature humility. Ben was supposed to be an easy fight for the incumbent champion. They fought at 205 pounds, which was a far way from Ben's 285-pound collegiate weight.

Before the event, they appeared on a nationally televised news program to promote the fight. Ben had only been in Peru for nine months and still struggled with Spanish in everyday conversation, much less in front of a national audience. But still, he used the opportunity to explain Katy's ailment and how he was going to donate his prize money to help with her surgery.

At the end, Zopilote assured the audience that he would "*destrozar a mi rival.*" Ben chuckled and said, "*Sí.*" The commentator looked confused and explained to Ben in broken English, "He will destruction you." Ben chuckled again and shook his head. "*Estoy preparado.*"

The news anchor asked both fighters to stand up for a staredown. As they got closer, Zopilote pushed Ben and almost knocked him off the platform.

Ben's poor Spanish came back to bite him again at the pre-fight press conference. As Ben stood in front of the cameras, Zopilote shouted something to him. Ben replied, "*Sí*," without realizing that had agreed to fight bare-knuckle.

The promoter was a man named Ivan "The Pitbull" Iberico, who was an icon of Peruvian MMA. Ivan approached Ben minutes before the fight and told him that he didn't have to fight bare-knuckle if he didn't want to. But Ben didn't want to appear weak, so he held his ground.

When the bell rang, they traded jabs and low leg kicks and circled around each other for much of the round. Zopilote's shoulders looked like he was wearing medieval armor plates and his lats seemed like they were about to sprout wings. He was barrel-chested and built like an armored tank.

At the end of the first period, Zopilote shot in and threw Ben to his butt. Ben fought up to his base and rolled into a dominant mount position just as the period ended.

Zopilote stayed on the ground, clutching his knee in pain. He didn't get up and Ben thought he had won the fight. In MMA there are no injury timeouts—an injury means you lose. That is the whole point: to injure your opponent so that he cannot continue.

Ben circled the cage, waiting for his opponent to get up. The Peruvian crowd started chanting for Zopilote. Slowly, he got to his feet and they started again.

Moments into the second round, Ben shot in and brought the monstrous Zopilote to the ground. He pinned him against the cage and started hammering his bare fist against Zopilote's face. Ben didn't relent until the referee jumped in and stopped the fight. He had defeated the reigning champion by technical knockout.

After the fight, a local news station in Arequipa aired a story about Ben and his charitable initiatives. They met with Katy and her family and discussed the surgery she would need. Ben made a plea on air for all those watching to help support her. A few days later, the television station came back with good news. They had found a clinic that was willing to sponsor her entire surgery. Katy was able to go in for weekly treatments at no cost, thanks to the clinic's generosity.

Through Ben's growing fame in Peru, he launched various fundraisers under the name *Luchas Nobles*, or Noble Fights.

By the time we arrived in Peru, he had already amassed an impressive MMA record of 12-0-1. As Ben carved out a name for himself in Peru, he grew closer to Ivan "Pitbull" Iberico. Eventually, he decided to move to Lima so that he could train with Ivan full-time. In Lima, Ben met Fiorella, and, along with her young daughter Ghaela, they eventually moved in together.

Fiorella joined us in Cuzco and served as our local guide. She took us to some bars that night, and in the morning we left for Machu Picchu. After driving through the dizzying Andean roads, we reached Ollantaytambo and boarded the train to Aguas Calientes. From there, it was a quick bus trip to the top of Machu Picchu.

The ancient city stretched out in front of us, and the surrounding mountains were shrouded in mist. We walked through the stone walls and grassy terraces. In every direction, I saw enormous peaks covered in thick green foliage. It was beautiful, but there were so many tourists that I felt like I was back in Times Square.

Back in Cuzco, Ben found us a cheap hostel for the night. "This is gross," I said. "You guys can do what you want, but I am going to get a real *ho-tel*." I walked down the street and booked a room at a four-star hotel. I had worked hard all year so that I could afford things like this. What was the point of making money if I wasn't going to spend it?

When we returned to Lima, Ben brought us to the gym where he trained. A large billboard announced that we had reached the Pitbull Martial Arts Center. Ben introduced us to his teammates.

His coach, Ivan, had a stout, compact build and a swarthy complexion. Ivan's brother, Hector, looked just like Ivan, but wore a square patch of gauze over his nose. A kid named Claudio introduced himself to us in perfect English. He was only seventeen years old and already had a professional MMA record of 3-0. When Ben mentioned that I had wrestled, Claudio bombarded me with questions about wrestling techniques.

Ben encouraged us to train with his teammates. I began grappling with a fighter named Zury Valenzuela who was around my size. As we wrestled on our feet, I dug in for an underhook and trapped his shoulder. I grabbed his far ankle and pushed him over and he fell to the mat.

"Good takedown!" he said. I pulled him back up to his feet and taught him the move, called an ankle pick. He landed on his back in jiu-jitsu guard.

I had trained jiu-jitsu a few times with friends and was familiar with the basic positions. In jiu-jitsu, the dominant position was on your back with your legs wrapped around your opponent's torso. The uninitiated often remarked that it looked like missionary position, often with a slew of giggles. But it was a dangerous position for experienced competitors.

"Be careful," he cautioned as he wrapped his foot around the side of my head and transitioned into a submission called an armbar.

After that, Claudio and I started to wrestle. After taking him down several times, we drew a small crowd. Ben came over and grabbed me.

"They want you to go with Ivan. He knows wrestling and has trained with the Cuban Olympic team."

Ivan had the weathered face and swollen ears of someone who has been fighting for many years. There is no mistaking the face of a veteran fighter; it boasts the violence of a hundred punches like the rings of a tree.

We tied up and pushed against each other, but he was so compact

I could barely budge him. I dropped my level and shot in to his legs. He sprawled and dropped his weight on me, but I turned the corner and caught his ankle. He tried to kick out but I trapped his other ankle and took him down. He stood up with a grin and we started grappling again. I snatched a single leg and threw him to his butt for another takedown.

When we stood back up, he tightened his stance and kept his hands down. I shot in, but he fended me off. This time, Ivan peppered me with shots. He shot in and wrapped his arms around both of my legs. I backpedaled and tried to squirm free from his clutches, but he was too deep.

In desperation, I grabbed both of his triceps and sagged my weight down to meet him chest-to-chest. I locked my arms around his and threw him through the air. His back smashed down on the mat. As he got up, he shook my hand with a demonic grin.

After we broke, Ben came over and said, "Ivan wants to take you guys out for drinks before you go." We only had a few hours before our flight home but we accepted his invitation. We arrived at the bar and found a long table in the back.

"Ivan wants to know what you guys want to drink," Ben said. "Whiskey or vodka?"

"Whiskey," I responded quickly. Apparently that word translated perfectly because Ivan's face lit up and he reached out to shake my hand. He grabbed the waitress and ordered two bottles of Johnny Walker Black.

When the waitress brought the bottles, Ivan filled everyone's glasses. After filling my glass, he topped off his own. He raised his glass and we all took big sips of whiskey. I let out a hiss and Ivan laughed at me. He started speaking to Ben in Spanish.

"Ivan says that he was impressed with your wrestling today. He says that you have heart. He was wondering if you ever thought about fighting MMA?"

I laughed and shook my head. "No way! I'd get my ass kicked in the cage."

"I think you'd be surprised," said Ben.

"I can't even imagine getting punched in the face. I have tons of respect for you guys, but I'm really not tough enough."

Ben translated our conversation to Ivan, and then turned back to me.

"Ivan said that you would be able to figure it out quickly. He said he could tell that you miss competing."

"I definitely do," I said, "but it's not really an option. I have a good job and don't have the time to train. Did you tell him that I work on Wall Street?"

Ben translated and Ivan stared blankly at me before muttering something else.

"He said you could come down here to train with us," Ben chuckled. "He is really persistent. You better watch out, Ivan is the one who convinced me to start fighting. It sounds like he really wants you to fight."

Through Ben, Ivan told me a story. When he was launching his career, MMA in Peru wasn't very competitive. When he won a tournament, he left the prize money with his wife and his newborn son, and went to Brazil to train. He knew that if he wanted to reach the next level, he had to train with the best.

"That's badass," I said, "but I don't think he understands. I have a really good job."

Ivan filled his glass to the brim, and then he filled mine. As we touched glasses, he looked directly into my eyes. He tipped his back and finished the whole thing. I knew the game and matched his every move. Ivan was smirking like child who was proud of his own mischief.

"Ivan said that he can tell you still have the itch to compete."

I thought back to my final college wrestling match. I usually tried not to think about it, but now the memories flooded my brain. I did miss competing. I had locked these feelings away for years, afraid to let them see the light of day, and now, after meeting Ivan for the first time, he had stared into my eyes and discovered them.

Ivan raised his glass again and we both tipped them back. The next thing I remember, I was on the plane back to New York.

CHAPTER
5

I returned to work on Monday and put the vacation out of my mind. Brian said I would be able to launch my portfolio at the end of the year, so I had three months to prepare. I began studying the companies and industries that I would be trading.

Brian asked me to put together a presentation that outlined my strategy for making money. I wrote some bullet points and sat down with him in the conference room.

"Maybe I didn't explain this right," Brian said. "I wanted a full presentation, in the style of a pitchbook." I needed to outline the industry and present specific trade ideas. "We'll have another meeting, and hopefully you'll do it right this time."

Brian was right: I hadn't put much effort into it. I should have been ecstatic about the opportunity, but for some reason, I couldn't get excited about it. I was about to get the opportunity to manage my own multimillion-dollar portfolio. This had been my dream since I first became interested in finance. Many people waited their whole careers for this opportunity. I had leapfrogged all of that. I had met and surpassed all of my own goals. And now, all I had to do was put together a small presentation.

As I watched thousands of numbers flash across my computer screen daily and I began to realize that I just didn't care about them anymore.

Upon returning from Peru, I had signed up for jiu-jitsu lessons. Now, every day after work, I went to train at Renzo Gracie Academy. They put me in the beginner class because I had no experience, but I soon learned that I could use wrestling techniques to transition into effective submissions. I was getting in shape again and started losing weight. One day I called Ben.

"You think Ivan was serious about that offer?" I asked.

"Are you really thinking about this?" he asked. "Well, I don't want to push you into it. It's not for everybody. It's a tough life."

The truth was I did want it. I was growing more frustrated at work and had trouble focusing on even the most mundane tasks. I grew antsy and reached out to Ben again.

"Did you talk to Ivan?" I asked.

"Yeah, but here's what happened. A few of the guys on our team lost recently and were cut from the team. Remember Zury? He lost and they fired him. So be careful, because there is a lot of uncertainty."

I had been gazing into the abyss and it had grabbed ahold of me. As I struggled at work, my mind had begun to cling to the idea like a life preserver.

I was first exposed to MMA as a senior in high school when I watched a documentary called The Smashing Machine. It told the story of Mark Kerr, a former collegiate wrestler who fought in the early days of MMA. I couldn't believe any person would willingly enter a cage and face such bloody brutality.

MMA arrived in the United States with the launch of the UFC in 1993. At first, it marketed itself as an organization with no rules. Competitors were allowed to do just about anything except for eye gouging and biting. The sport was rooted in the vale tudo ("anything goes") tradition in Brazil, where the Gracie family had pioneered their own brand of submission grappling: Brazilian jiu-jitsu. For years they had challenged any doubters to fight them in the ring, and they soon became the most fearsome family in the world.

At the first UFC event, Royce Gracie shocked the world by winning the eight-man tournament against significantly larger opponents. No one knew what to expect, as boxers squared off against wrestlers, and Muay Thai fighters against jiu-jitsu practitioners. They were trying to answer the age-old question of which martial art would be the best in a real fight.

At first, fighters tended to be specialists. Some guys came from striking backgrounds such as boxing, Muay Thai, or kickboxing. Others had jiu-jitsu or judo training. But as the sport grew, fighters were required to become masters of every style.

Since the early days, MMA had evolved in many ways. They dropped the "no rules" mantra in favor of a more restrictive rule set. They prohibited striking to the back of the head and kicking an opponent on the ground. And they adopted small fingerless gloves to appease athletic commissions as they made a push for mass-market acceptance.

In college, I watched some of the big fights on television. I was always appalled yet intrigued by the violence. "I could NEVER do that," I would say.

I didn't understand what drove people to fight. It certainly wasn't the money, because only the top fighters in the world made good money. The rest of them struggled to feed themselves. There were much easier ways to make a living than cage fighting.

As I sat at work, I imagined what it would be like to get in the cage with another fighter. I was terrified by it, but I couldn't seem to shake the idea. Ivan was right—I did miss competing.

Now, I was teetering on the edge of wealth and success. I had wanted to live in New York City since I was a child. I even broke up with my girlfriend when she wouldn't move to the city after college. "I am going live in New York until I die," I told her.

A battle raged inside my head. My career was extremely important to me, but I began to feel like I was missing something. There was a whole world out there that I didn't know about. I had always viewed myself as adventurous and here was my opportunity to prove it. Ivan had barely known me but he already believed in me. Maybe I could even learn Spanish, like Ben.

I reached a point where I couldn't turn back mentally. I felt like I was tunneling out of prison, planning everything secretly and not even telling my closest friends. I wanted to make sure that everything was ready to go before I told anyone. That way, they wouldn't be able to stop me. I started emailing Ben every day, trying to get a sense of what I needed to do to prepare.

In my head, I ran through all of the reasons why it was a bad idea, but it didn't matter. I had made up my mind. The more I tried to talk myself out of it, the more I was convinced that there was no other way.

As it got closer to becoming reality, I began telling my friends about it. They reacted in different ways. Some thought it was the coolest thing they'd ever heard, whereas others lectured me about how I was ruining my life. Some simply didn't believe me. "You can't actually leave your job, are you serious?" And my parents were not thrilled.

"My dream for all my children, is that they be happy," my dad chose his words carefully. "While this is not what I want, you are an adult and can make your own decisions. But please be considerate of us. Your mother has been crying a lot over your decision. Please bear that in mind."

Over the next few weeks, I started to listen to other people talk. Everyone had a secret dream they harbored as they slaved away at work. "I would love to teach high school gym class," one friend told me. Another told me his dream to run a charter fishing boat in Florida. "In three or four more years," they would say, "when I save up a little more money, I will leave."

"But aren't you worried it'll never happen if you don't do it now?" I would ask. "In three or four years, maybe you'll have a girlfriend or a mortgage. I feel like I have to do it now or I never will."

I still had to put together a presentation for my new investment strategy. I tried to get my deadline pushed back, but eventually ran out of excuses. Brian suggested I give it the following week and I reluctantly agreed. That weekend, I came in to the office on Saturday and Sunday and put together a PowerPoint slideshow with detailed charts and graphics. I put everything I could into it.

When I gave my presentation, I outlined each sector, presented trade ideas, and created a model portfolio. After I finished, Brian spoke up, "That was really good, Rollie. You made big strides since the last time."

It was one of the nicest things he had said in the two years I'd been working for him. At the end of the day, Bellini and I walked out of the office together. "Good job today, Rollie." Even though it felt great to have succeeded, my heart wasn't in it anymore. I'd had enough.

On Monday, January 6th, I took the elevator up to the 14th floor as I had been doing for the last two years. I was nervous and uncertain. I had never quit a job before, I didn't know what to expect. When I arrived, Brian and Bellini were already busy at work.

"Hey, Brian can we talk?"

"Sure, can it wait?"

"Not really."

We sat down in a conference room.

"I am quitting." He looked confused, but he didn't say a word. "But I'm not going to a different firm. I'm leaving the industry." He started to open his mouth but then he stopped as I kept talking. "I'm moving to Peru to train and fight MMA."

"What?" he said. I explained it again.

"Don't do this," he said, almost paternally. "You don't want to do this. Look, I know it can be frustrating. When I first started, I hated my boss and I thought about leaving the industry. I know I can be tough, but that is no reason to give up on finance. If you want to go to a different firm, that is fine, but don't ruin your career over this."

"I have a one-way flight booked for three weeks from now. I am doing this," I replied as calmly as I could.

I stood up, shook Brian's hand, and walked back to my desk. After speaking with several other coworkers, Brian walked me out of the building. Before we reached the elevator, he pulled me into another conference room.

"Rollie, please be careful," he said. "Seriously, if you ever need anything, do not hesitate to reach out to me. Anytime, for whatever reason, I am here for you."

Everyone seemed to be concerned for me, but I was more confident than ever. I walked out the door and onto the New York sidewalk. The air smelled different.

ROUND
TWO

" *People say that what we're all seeking is a meaning for life. I don't think that's what we're really seeking. I think that what we're seeking is an experience of being alive.*

JOSEPH CAMPBELL, *THE POWER OF MYTH*

CHAPTER
6

I didn't know what to expect as I stepped off the plane in Lima, but I was excited at the possibilities. I would be moving in to the apartment with Ben and Fiorella. Ben took me down the street to get a copy of the key. An old man with a small cart clipped the key into a machine with a metal wheel, which he turned by hand to carve the grooves.

Ben showed me around the neighborhood of Barranco where we would be living. We walked to the main plaza, where large black buzzards perched high in the lanky palm trees. There was an old yellow Spanish-style cathedral at one end and an equally old library at the other. The walkways were lined with white canvas tents containing different local brands of pisco, a clear liquor that reminded me of light rum or tequila. Ben and I ordered pisco sours and sat on the edge of the stone fountain. It had been cold when I left New York, but now it was summer in the Southern Hemisphere.

"How do you feel about donating blood?" Ben asked.

"I've done it a few times. Not a big deal, I guess," I replied.

"Not even blood, just platelets."

The previous Christmas, Ben had visited a children's leukemia ward to distribute toys they had collected and learned that they have a chronic platelet shortage so he set about using his name as a fighter to encourage people to go donate. He would bring crews of fighters once a month to donate.

"I haven't even been here for twenty-four hours and you're already roping me into your charitable endeavors?" I teased him.

"It's a serious thing," Ben replied. "Medical care and access not the same here as in the States. Every little bit helps these kids a lot."

"Of course I'll help, Ben."

The next morning Ben had to go to teach a class at the gym. I hopped on the back of his motorcycle and we drove to the Pitbull Martial Arts Center. As Ben taught the class, I trained on the side of the mat with Daniel "Heiana" Aspe, an accomplished amateur boxer. Ben had beaten Aspe early in his career, but now they occasionally trained together. Heiana put me through drills to work on my form.

He didn't speak any English, but he would smack me with a foam pad every time my elbows came out. He showed me the footwork and instructed me to shuffle across the mat. He grabbed both of my wrists in his large hands.

"No, no, no," he said and shook his head. He adjusted my hands like a rockstar shifting a microphone. "*Así.*"

Some of the Pitbull fighters were competing the following day in a grand prix tournament so after training we drove to the press conference.

I sat on the back on Ben's motorcycle and held on tight. It had been one of the worst winters on record when I left New York, but now we cut through the warm air. The street was lined with palm trees and I could smell the salt water blowing off the ocean.

At the next light, we pulled alongside a troupe of three Lima police officers on motorcycles. They were decked out in heavy riding gear and looked like a cross between the Hell's Angels and a SWAT team. One of the officers pulled up beside us and shouted something to Ben. He pointed to a parking lot one hundred feet ahead.

"Are we getting pulled over?" I asked Ben.

"It's just routine, they want to check my papers."

The officer puffed his chest out and strutted over to us. "*Documentos!*" Ben handed him the registration and his license. After reading them, the conversation started to escalate. I couldn't understand the Spanish, but it was clear there was an issue. Ben was growing argumentative. I kept my head down and stared at the ground. The shouting in Spanish would have been comical had I not been involved.

"What's happening?" I asked.

"This guy is saying I can't drive a motorcycle, only a car—apparently because my New York ID isn't a motorcycle license. But I've been pulled over before and they didn't say anything."

The ruckus continued. Ben was getting more angry and emotional by the minute. I could hear him pleading, his voice strained with frustration. He muttered a stream of curses under his breath.

"They're trying to tell me the fine is eighteen hundred soles," he said. At 2.80 soles to the dollar, that was 640 dollars. In my novice Spanish I translated him saying, "I could buy a new bike for that!"

It only escalated from there. The same arrogant officer strutted around like a razorback. The shouting rose higher and I got worried he would lash out.

Then it suddenly stopped and everything became eerily calm. Ben got back on the bike and I followed.

"What's going on?"

"They want me to pay them, but on the down low."

"How much?"

"One hundred and twenty soles." Forty-three dollars.

We rode fifty yards ahead and one of the younger officers signaled us to pull over. Ben took out the cash and tucked it under his license.

"Do you need any cash?" I offered.

"No, and don't take your wallet out. I told them I only have a hundred and twenty soles."

"*Documentos!*" said the young officer. The other two officers idled in the distance. Ben handed it over and the officer made a big fuss. He waved his arms and rattled off some Spanish. Then he handed Ben's license back and they sped away.

It was my second day in Peru and I was already having run-ins with the police. These were exactly the kind of adventures I wanted in my life.

We arrived just in time for the press conference. Ivan was on stage and called each fighter up one-by-one. A highlight reel played on the giant screen in the background and photographers snapped pictures. People came from every corner to pay respects to Ben.

The grand prix tournament was held the following night. There was an eight-man bracket of 145-pound fighters with a cash prize of $5,000 for the champion. Two fighters from Pitbull were competing in the tournament. One of them was named Jose Paico, but he was an alternate. If he won the preliminary fight, he would fill in as a substitute if someone couldn't continue. The other was Enrique "El Fuerte" Barzola.

They began the tournament with Paico's fight for the alternate slot. Paico was one of the best wrestlers in Peru and he had represented his country at the World Championships and the Pan American Games. He was forty-two years old and it was hard to believe he was still competing.

In the eight-man bracket, the champion would have to win three fights in one night. Each fight was fifteen minutes, so he could potentially spend forty-five minutes inside the cage. That was a grizzly prospect to me.

"How often will I be fighting?" I asked Ben.

"You should be fighting just about every month at the start."

"Every month?"

"Yeah, that's basically what I did."

I got butterflies in my stomach as we watched the action. Paico pressed his opponent against the cage and shot into his legs. He took his opponent to the mat easily, and won the bout when he locked up a rear-naked choke.

Next, my new teammate Enrique "El Fuerte" beat Marco Anatoly with a second round TKO. After that, Adilson "Godzilla" beat Fabio

"Gasolina" by decision. A short but stocky Brazilian fighter named Fernando Bruno beat Victor Nunes. Bruno "Crocop" defeated Diogo "Sinistro" by decision.

They took a short break before commencing the next round of fighting. It shocked me away that they would be fighting again so soon. I knew that in the early days of the UFC, they had one-day tournaments, but I thought that was a thing of the past.

Even though Bruno "Crocop" had won his first fight, Ben informed me that he was throwing up in the back room due to a violent concussion, so Jose Paico stepped in as the alternate.

Paico squared off against Gasolina and controlled all three rounds. Again, he utilized his wrestling to take his opponent down and he won by unanimous decision. He had gone from an alternate to a finalist.

In the other semifinal bout, our teammate "El Fuerte" faced Fernando Bruno. Fuerte fought hard, but lost by decision.

To give the finalists a break before their bout, they featured another match. The seventeen-year-old Claudio Puelles, aptly named "El Niño" won his fight with a quick first round rear-naked choke.

In the finals, Paico lost to Bruno by a first round submission. Bruno threw his arms in the air in triumph. The Brazilian had just won $5,000.

It had been a fun night, but I shuddered at the thought of actually getting into that cage myself.

CHAPTER

7

O ver the next few weeks, I worked with Ivan every day to improve my boxing. Although I had trained a bit of boxing in New York, I still knew next to nothing. Until recently, I had never even put on boxing gloves.

Each morning, Ivan would pull me off to the side of practice to do drills. He taught me the proper footwork. I would shuffle across the mat and hit the pads as he called out combos.

He didn't speak any English and I barely spoke any Spanish, but we didn't really have any problems communicating during these sessions. He would grunt and smack my arm with his padded hand if my elbows were too far out. I shuffled across the mat and he would lift his fists up in front of my face, signaling me to mimic his posture. "*Manos arriba!*" he called. "Hands up!"

It was difficult to break my old wrestling habits and I learned slowly. "*Manos arriba!*" he said again.

He put a foam pad under my right elbow and asked me to clamp down. He then held a pad up and had me jab with my left hand while keeping my right arm clamped. He moved around the mat as I shuffled after him, jabbing spastically. He smacked my arm away and mimed the motion of a punch for me. He corrected just about every motion I made.

He took the foam pad away and held his other hand up, instructing me to throw only straight right punches. Each time, I gritted my teeth and slammed my fist into the pad with all my force. After hitting the pad a few times, Ivan held up both hands and put them on my shoulders, signaling me to relax. In our nonverbal conversation, I filled in the blanks with my mind.

I tried to relax and hit the pads. He pointed down to his ankle and pivoted it. When you throw a right, he was saying, pivot your back foot like you are squashing a bug. It helps to align your power behind the punch. I concentrated on pivoting my foot, but inevitably Ivan stopped me every time to correct something else I was doing wrong.

It was clear that boxing wasn't coming naturally to me. I didn't even realize how much I didn't know until I started learning. Like fixing a car, fighting is one of those things that men are just *supposed* to know. But now, I was realizing for the first time how little I actually knew about throwing a punch.

I felt like I wasn't getting any better, but Ivan seemed to believe in me because he continued to work with me daily. He was a legend in Peru and I felt lucky to have the chance to work with him.

Ivan grew up in a poor barrio called Breña. As a child, he trained karate and fought on the streets. At age fourteen, he discovered wrestling and took to it right away. After just three months, he made the national team, where he got the opportunity to travel and wrestle at tournaments in Colombia, Venezuela, and Cuba.

Although he loved wrestling, he needed a way to supplement this income. So when he was offered a chance to fight MMA, he accepted. He was just eighteen years old when he had his first fight. Back then, it didn't resemble the sport that we see today. A bar in Lima had set up a boxing ring in the back and participants competed in *vale todo*. This no-holds-barred fighting quickly captured Ivan's interest.

Unlike modern MMA, there were barely any rules. You could head-butt, soccer kick an opponent on the ground, grab hair, or kick him in the balls. Also unlike modern MMA, they fought with no gloves and no time limits. Without a submission or knockout, the fight would continue until someone gave up. Sometimes Ivan fought four times in one night. "The winner at the end of the night got a thousand dollars," he explained, "and the rest of the fighters got a free beer."

By this time, he was developing a reputation and they started calling him "The Pitbull." He was still wrestling, but soon his coach started to take notice of his fights and gave Ivan an ultimatum to choose one or the other. He chose to pursue a career in MMA.

One day a Brazilian fighter named Alexandre "Pequeno" Nogueira came to Peru for a fight and invited Ivan to come train in Brazil. Ivan had just won a tournament, so he left his prize money with his wife and newborn son and set off for Brazil. He began fighting at events in Brazil and his career skyrocketed from there. By the time I met him, his self-proclaimed record was 42-2. Although, because many of his early fights were unsanctioned, his official record was 13-2. He was quick to add, "I've never lost to a Peruvian fighter."

I soon learned that Ivan's name was synonymous with MMA in Peru. He had almost single-handedly brought the sport to the place it was today. Sometimes I would chat with a cab driver and explain that I was fighting MMA and he would respond, "Like the Pitbull?" Even people who knew nothing about the sport knew his name.

At the end of my first week, it felt like I had been there a month already. We trained twice a day and I lost no time jumping into the mix. One night after practice, Ivan called over one of his younger students, a small child who couldn't have been more than sixteen years old. He strapped boxing gloves on both of us and told us that we were going to spar. I looked over at Ben for clarification.

"We're just going one hundred percent in boxing?" I asked.

"Yeah, sparring."

"I've never done this before, are you sure?"

"He's just a kid, you'll be fine."

"Uh, okay."

I strapped the gloves on and walked to the center of the mat and faced him. We circled each other a few times. I reached out for a jab and he easily blocked it. I jabbed again, but still nothing. He poked me with a jab and I tried to bring my hands up to block, but it slipped through and I felt the glove against my face. It stung a little bit but it didn't hurt.

"*Manos arriba!*" Ivan called out.

I raised my gloves up over my face, but I grew impatient. I shot forward with a jab, but when I pulled back, my left hand dropped to my chest. The kid immediately exploited my mistake and came in with a heavy right hand that caught me square on the chin. It was the first hard punch I had ever taken. It was like the cartoons. Everything went black for a second and I saw stars. Kapow! Kablaam! Pow! Boom!

I knew that I had to pull myself together fast so I got my footing and raised my hands to cover my face. He came at me with a barrage of punches, which I fended off by closing up and backing away.

I was embarrassed and felt like I had let Ivan down after the faith he had put in me. I started to get mad and I came after the kid with a hard jab. He anticipated my punch and sidestepped it, brushing my fists away casually. I didn't stop though. I came at him with one after another, windmilling my arms recklessly through the air. I didn't have any plan, or any technique. I pushed forward, and each time, he circled away and planted one on my face. I missed another swing and he cocked his fist and blasted me with an uppercut.

He was backpedalling and I was chasing him, but each time I paid the price. Eventually Ivan called me over and delivered a message through Ben.

"Ivan says that you let that first punch get to you and then you got emotional. You have to control your emotions. After that, he said your form sucked. You dropped your hands and took wild punches. You have to be a little more patient and wait for your opportunity."

I was embarrassed by the whole fiasco.

"But he says that he was impressed that you kept moving forward. A lot of wrestlers who come in to MMA get punched and then back away. He says that you kept pressing forward and attacking. Even though you don't know the technique, he says that your attitude is the most important thing."

CHAPTER

8

Before practice we rested on the bunk beds in the back room, which were laid out like barracks with fourteen beds between two floors. As part of the agreement with the gym, the professional fighters were required to live there during the week, in order to ensure they were always available to train. Ben and I were the exceptions. Ben was exempted because he had a family, and I was exempted because I lived with Ben.

Ben was the team captain and often took on the role of a dorm parent. He was always the first person ready each morning and arrived early to wake everyone up for practice. Whenever any of the fighters had a problem, they would come to him and he would listen patiently. When there was a problem, he served as intermediary between the coaches and us. He was quick to offer an encouraging word to a struggling teammate, but not afraid to lecture someone for cutting corners.

I immediately took a liking to the other guys on the team. Even after just a few days, they took me in as one of their own. I had grown up my whole life on wrestling mats, and I was glad to discover that the dynamic in this room was much the same. There is a certain non-verbal language that we all spoke—the language of sweat and blood. While waiting around before practice we would grab each other and start grappling lightly. Maybe it would start as a handshake and turn into a takedown. It was how we greeted each other.

When you spend so much time together in such a grueling environment, you develop an unshakeable bond and we horsed around like brothers. And then there was the teasing.

"It can get pretty brutal," Ben explained. "Ivan calls Fuerte 'Canoe Face' because he has such a big chin. And we all joke about how ugly he is."

Fuerte, looked up after realizing that we were talking about him even though he didn't speak any English.

"Look at that chin," Claudio agreed. "He is so ugly." Then he repeated his comments in Spanish, just to make sure Fuerte understood.

Fuerte just smiled and didn't seem to take their heckling to heart. He faked a punch to Claudio who lifted his hands to cover his face and then he slapped him in the stomach.

"In Peru," Ben explained, "they just refer to people by their dominant attributes. For instance, people will probably call you 'chato' which kind of translates into 'shorty' but it isn't offensive really."

"Interesting."

"Or take 'cholo' for instance. It's a kind of derogatory word for dark skinned people of native descent, but people use it to refer to each other all the time in a friendly way. It kind of depends on the context."

I began to notice this all the time after he pointed it out. The owner of our gym, Martin, was of Chinese descent. When Ivan saw him he would say, "Hola Chino." Or "Hey Chinaman." Martin would reply back, "Hola Chato." Or "Hey Shorty." Many people would refer to me as Gringo or Chato regularly. I once heard Ben's wife Fiorella refer to her overweight cousin as Gorda, or "Fatty." It was a cultural difference and rarely did anyone take offense.

When Ivan arrived we began practice. Ben led the warm-up and we stretched out. Ivan called out "Guantes!" and we retrieved our boxing gloves and hand wraps. We put on foam shin pads so we could practice kicks.

When everyone was secure in their gloves we paired up for a five-minute round of light sparring on our feet. I went with Fuerte first. I was still hesitant from my previous boxing fiasco, so I circled cautiously. If I had fared so poorly against a small child, how would I handle a professional fighter? I tried to focus on keeping my hands up to protect my face. Every time his momentum moved forward, I backed away.

Fuerte had been fighting for less than two years but had already amassed an impressive record of 7-1-1. A year and a half earlier, he had walked into the Escuela Pitbull in Breña, which was run by Ivan's brother Hector. At the time, Fuerte was twenty-four years old and had never played a sport in his life or displayed any athletic prowess. Hector began training him and immediately recognized his talent.

After just a few months of training, Hector came to him one day and told him that he was going to fight. "When?" Fuerte asked. "Next week," Hector said. He accepted his coach's wisdom and entered the cage, unsure of what to expect. For the first two rounds he got clobbered and his face was bloodied. Just when he thought he could take no more, he took his opponent down and locked up a submission.

He was encouraged and began training even harder. He had taken a beating out there and didn't want to do that again. He trained daily in boxing and began to spar constantly, like we were doing that day.

As he stood across from me, he moved with ease. His shoulders were relaxed and his gloves bobbed in little circles as he shuffled his feet. I could tell that he was going easy on me. He came in with a series of surgical punches, but he hit lightly enough that they didn't even hurt. His hands moved fast as he executed a combination of punches to my face, and when I covered up with my forearms, he threw a left hook into my ribs.

When I tried to hit him, he ducked and evaded my attack. I threw a jab and he came across and hit me in the chin with a light tap. He stopped me in the middle of sparring to mime out the error I was making. The message was clear: when you throw a jab, keep your chin down and right hand up protecting your face.

I was grateful that he was patient and took the time to correct my mistakes. Sometimes training partners have too much pride, and instead of helping their teammates, they just focus on beating them. Fuerte, I quickly learned, was a good teammate and a good friend.

As the five-minute session ticked away, he stopped being offensive, and instead just protected his own face. Again, he was letting me practice my own strikes and combos without fear of retaliation. He even intentionally dropped his hands at one point and left his face exposed. I hit him once on the chin and he smiled. I hit him again. Another one-two combo and he raised his hands back up. When the buzzer rang he patted me on the back.

For the next round, Ivan paired me off with Jesus Pinedo. He was only seventeen years old and had just won his professional MMA debut. Pinedo was a tall and gangly 145 pounder. The other fighters would call him *Momia* because he had the physique of a mummy, or *Mudo* for "Mute" because he didn't talk much.

Pinedo had a clear advantage over me with his reach. He moved like a cat, and whenever he wanted to, he would jab his long arms out and penetrate my defenses. Like Fuerte, he was going easy on me, but unlike Fuerte, he had a little more to prove. He was still the young guy at the gym so he let me have a few good ones before easing back when he realized my level was nowhere near his.

Next, I faced Claudio. Right away, we started hitting each other hard. I was determined to show him that I was tough. I came in with a jab and then a hard right, which he just brushed off and countered with a hook. He hit me and it hurt, but I remembered Ivan's comment about moving forward and I kept pushing.

Claudio faked a punch and cocked back his leg and kicked me. His shin smacked against my thigh with a pop and my skin burned at the impact. He could tell that I looked surprised. I had never trained kickboxing before and this had caught me off guard. He stopped me, like Fuerte had.

"When your opponent goes for a low kick, raise your knee up like this," he showed me. "And his shin will hit your shin instead of the soft part of your thigh."

"Doesn't that hurt? Shin-on-shin?"

"Yeah, but it's better than the other part of your leg. After a while your shin will toughen up."

When time ran out, Ivan instructed us to take off our gloves and pair up again. For the next hour, we grappled. I was usually able to get a takedown, but once on the mat, it was a different story. The two months of jiu-jitsu I had from New York was helpful, but I still had a lot to learn.

In wrestling, a takedown is two points and can make a huge difference in the dynamics of a match. In submission grappling, the goal is to submit your opponent, which can be accomplished from top or bottom position. Some guys would even pull you in to their guard, a position in which the bottom guy is on his back and wraps his legs around your torso to control you.

I grappled with Pinedo, and after I took him down, he locked his gangly legs around my neck and squeezed until it felt like my head would pop off. I tapped the mat and he released the lock, which was called a triangle choke.

Ivan started out on bottom against me. He ensnared my leg with both of his legs in his half-guard. I struggled and squirmed, but it just seemed to get tighter. Just when it felt like I was about to get control, he would flop over and trap me again. He stopped me to show me a technique called a kimura. If I just grabbed his wrist and threaded my arm through, he explained, I would be able to submit him with a shoulder lock.

After practice we all showered and congregated in the kitchen for lunch. We had a chef named Jordan who worked at the gym full-time and cooked three meals a day. It wasn't fine dining, but the meals were free. It didn't take a health inspector to realize how dirty that kitchen was. Behind the counter where Jordan prepared the food, everything was covered in grime. The floors were wet with black sludge and the counters were not much cleaner. All of the plates and glasses were washed by Jordan, or maybe just rinsed because they always looked dirty.

Jordan brought out plates for each of us at the wooden table in front of the counter. We ate boiled chicken with rice and sliced potatoes.

"Do you like the food in Peru?" Fuerte asked me.

"*Sí, está rico.*" I replied. "Yes, it is delicious."

"This food? No. This is garbage," he said, winking at Jordan. "The fat chef doesn't know how to cook for nothing."

"*Huevón,*" said Jordan from behind the counter. He pronounced it whey-vohn and emphasized the second syllable. I had never heard the word. I asked Jordan what it meant.

"It is something you say to friends," he said. "Every time you see Fuerte say '*Hola huevón.*'"

"*Hola huevón,*" I said to Fuerte and they all laughed.

When Claudio walked up the stairs and joined us at the table, I asked him what huevón meant in English.

"It's Peruvian slang, it's like a swear word. It doesn't have a good translation in English. Kind of like asshole, or dick, or douchebag. But we say it to each other all the time."

"Thanks, *huevón,*" I said and he smiled.

CHAPTER
9

One day Ben informed me that he was appearing on a game show later that night. "You know that Titanes show we watch in the back room all the time?"

In my primitive understanding, it looked like a mix between a game show and a reality show. There were two teams, Silver and Gold, and they competed in physical challenges. There were men and women on each team and all of the contestants were usually fairly attractive. The women wore nothing but sports bras and spandex shorts.

That night, Ben stood in the middle of an octagonal cage with two scantily clad girls on either side of him. He was refereeing a two-on-two wrestling match. Ben stood in the middle and occasionally shouted out "*Acción!*" I couldn't discern what their objective was but it didn't seem to matter.

Later on, I would meet Peruvians, and when I mentioned Ben, they would invariably say, "Oh yeah, I saw him on Titanes!"

A few weeks later, he made another appearance. This time the host was the popular Peruvian singer and model Tilsa Lozano. She kept grabbing Ben's hand and leading him around the set. He looked uncomfortable and tried to break hands with her. I was at home watching it with Fiorella and she giggled.

Another time, Claudio was invited to be on the program. One of the girl contestants flirted with him in front of the camera. She took him by the hand and talked to him the entire show. When he got back, his girlfriend was furious. His friends had taken screenshots of the scene and posted them online.

They invited Claudio to be a permanent member of the show. Ivan pulled him aside and told him, "Listen, you have to make a choice in life. You can be on television, or you can fight MMA. You can't do both." Everyone in Peru watched the show, even if they did make fun of it. He could be a celebrity overnight if he said yes.

"It would be fun," Claudio told me, "but Ivan's right, I have to focus on my MMA career." I was impressed by his maturity. At seventeen years old, I would have had a much tougher time with that decision.

Guys like Claudio inspired me. He once told me that he knew he was going to be an MMA fighter since he was twelve years old. He wasn't fighting for money or fame; he fought because he loved the sport.

It was hard to imagine that just a month ago I had been sitting at my desk in New York. There had been so many people who had doubted my decision, and so I set about proving them wrong.

Ivan would give me drills to do after practice and I shuffled across the mats shadowboxing. I put my boxing gloves on and hit the bag until the mat around me was covered in droplets of sweat. Each time I hit the bag, I let out a loud guttural grunt. Ivan instructed me to keep some distance from the bag, then leap in suddenly, throw my jab, and dart backwards. He was trying to teach me to get in, do damage, and get out of danger.

I slowly got back in shape and my body hardened. The old Wall Street pounds began to melt away. When I first came down, I weighed over 160 pounds. Before too long I was down around 150. I tried to eat to keep up my energy, but the food didn't always agree with my stomach. I developed a constant stomach bug. After practice I would pick at my food, but I never really finished a meal. My body wasn't used to training multiple times a day and I got aches and pains all over.

My whole life, I had worn wrestling shoes while practicing, but now we did everything barefoot. As I practiced punching, I pivoted on the ball of my foot so much that I soon developed a blister the size of a silver dollar. It became cracked and bloody and it hurt to walk. Since I didn't take any time off of training, it didn't heal for weeks. I tried wearing socks to ease the friction against the mat, but then I would just slide around. I showed Ivan the blister one day when I was struggling with my footwork.

"*Limón*," he said.

"Huh?"

He told me to slice open a lime and squeeze the juice onto the wound. I laughed, but that night at the grocery store I picked up a small bag of limes. This was all about trying new experiences after all.

I squeezed the lime onto the wound twice a day, and I was shocked when it actually started to heal. I told Ben and he laughed too.

"I think the citric acid kind of burns it closed," I speculated.

"It's kind of like how they cook ceviche," he replied.

"Exactly."

One day after practice, Ivan invited Ben and I to go out for ceviche with him. Ceviche was the specialty of Lima and you couldn't walk two blocks without passing a *cebicheria*. Because Lima is on the ocean, they pride themselves on fresh seafood. Their ceviche is served as a mountain of big fatty chunks of fish and monstrous tentacles jutting in every direction. It came in a stew of briny fish juices with chopped onions and a piece of *camote*, or sweet potato.

We sat down at a small table in the corner. The café opened up into the street and the warm summer breeze blew in. Ivan ordered a beer and asked me if I wanted one.

"No, gracias," I said, remembering the last time we drank together.

We all ordered a plate of ceviche. As I read the menu, I looked up at Ben. "What's *leche de tigre*? Tiger's milk?"

"It's like a fish stew. It's made from the juices of ceviche."

Ivan heard me ask about it and insisted on ordering it for me. I still had an uneasy stomach so when the plates arrived, I just picked at the chunks of fish. I didn't have an appetite. The *leche de tigre* came out in a small cup. I took a sip. It was salty and small chunks of fish floated in the mixture. I grimaced and Ivan laughed. I tried to have another few sips to be polite, but I just couldn't eat it.

Ben and Ivan were talking in Spanish while I stared at my food. They were talking about an MMA event coming up in April. Ben explained that they were bringing in a Brazilian for him to fight.

"That's the best thing about Inka, they bring in really good guys. No other promotion in Peru has the money to get guys like that. Ivan and Martin really want to take it to the next level and make it an international organization. That's why Ivan is excited to have guys like you, it gives Inka some international credibility."

"What's Ivan's role in Inka?"

"He and Martin own it. Martin puts up the money, but Ivan runs it. Martin has a few Ferraris and a Lamborghini. That kind of money. He also pays our salaries."

In 2006, Ivan decided that he wanted to start his own fighting promotion and created the Inka Fighting Championships.

One day, he met Martin at a party. Some of their friends started placing bets that Ivan could submit Martin in less than two minutes. When no one would take the other side of the bet, Martin realized that he was outmatched and backed out. The two became close friends and Martin developed an interest in MMA. He began supporting Inka FC financially and they brought in new talent from all over South America.

"He has a bunch of businesses," Ben explained, "I think he is involved with mining. And maybe real estate."

"Does he take a cut of the fighter payouts? How does he make money on MMA?"

"I don't think he does, he just kind of," he thought for a second, "throws money at it."

"Interesting."

"It's like this: Martin has racehorses, and he has MMA fighters."

I had met Martin a few times, although he still seemed an enigma to me. He was a fat man of Chinese descent who chain-smoked cigarettes. Occasionally he would come to practice and stand on the side of the mat. Even though he had very little background in martial arts, he liked to give advice to fighters. In a way, he had bought his status in the MMA community. Because he paid our salaries, people listened when he opened his mouth.

As Ben and Ivan spoke, I pushed my ceviche around the plate with my fork. Suddenly Ben smiled and he turned to me, "Ivan said he found you a fight." I choked a bit on the slimy tentacle I was trying to swallow.

"That's awesome—that's, uh, great," I gasped.

It felt like I'd already been punched in the stomach. My abs tightened, my fists clenched, and my pulse quickened instinctually. My mind began playing a bloody montage of flying fists and elbows. I could feel my heart beat in my throat. My brain swirled in the muck of the limitless possibilities. I pretended to be excited but I was actually terrified.

Since the day I arrived in Peru, I had pestered Ben, "Tell Ivan to get me a fight as soon as possible. I want to get out there!" I had left everything behind to come here and fight, and I was in a rush to prove that I could do it. Now that Ivan gave me the news, however, it hit me harder than I could have imagined. Now, for the first time, it was real. I finally grasped the reality of my situation: that I would be locked in a cage with another human whose sole intention was to hurt me.

I knew that it would be scary, but I had thought that somehow the fear would be more pure. When you watch gladiator movies or soldiers going off to battle, they are always so stately and dignified. I always thought that experiencing this extreme fear would somehow be cleansing.

I was terrified, but that was the thing that drew me to MMA in the first place. There was a Mark Twain quote that I had read as a child and had stuck with me over the years: "Courage is resistance to fear, mastery of fear, not absence of fear." It was nice and easy to quote something like that, but a whole different story to actually live it.

I had spent my whole life worrying about studying for exams or what job I would get. I worried about talking to girls at the bar. I worried about sounding stupid when I ordered a coffee. But how could I worry about such trivialities when confronted with legitimate danger? That was my logic anyway. I wanted to chase fear down the rabbit hole and see if I could not root out its most basic and primal form. Then once I discovered it, I wanted to conquer it.

I thought about it the whole day, and it occupied my mind non-stop. I tried rationalizing it a million different ways. But when I went to bed that night, my mind turned over and over in uncontrollable panic. What had I gotten myself into?

CHAPTER
10

When I decided to come to Peru, I knew the training was going to be tough. I knew it was going to take a lot of sacrifice and discipline. But somewhere in the back of my mind, there was the voice that said this was going to be like a vacation. I had packed nice dress shirts and shoes to go out in. And yet, I hadn't even been to a bar yet.

My friends from the gym were all the same way—they rarely, if ever, went out drinking. I had no social life anymore and I actually didn't miss it. Each night we practiced at nine o'clock and the next morning we were up early to train again. We had Sundays off, but I was so exhausted that all I wanted to do was rest. I coveted every bit of recuperation I could get.

I remember my first Saturday sparring session clearly. We arrived at eight in the morning. Everyone was very serious as we suited up for battle. We wore boxing gloves and shin pads. We warmed up on our own before approaching the cage at the end of the room.

I entered the cage with a fighter named Kike (short for Enrique, pronounced "key-kay"). He was slightly bigger than me and had a few professional fights under his belt. Every group of friends has a guy like Kike; he knew everybody in Lima and everybody loved him. He was always meeting people and helping people out. He drove a Jeep and was quick to offer a ride to a stranded friend. He spoke a very small amount of English, but often struggled and choked on phrases. "I...speak better...when I am drunk," he explained.

Unlike the rest of the fighters in the gym, he had a real job on the side and didn't train full time. This Saturday morning, he was not in peak physical condition.

When the clock started, I took an opening salvo of punches from him before dropping to his legs and planting him on the mat. He tried to tie my hands up, but I got my gloves free and punched him in the face. I looked up to Ben, who encouraged me to hit him more. "Ground and pound!" he yelled. I raised my posture to draw more force in my punches. It seemed barbaric to me. Kike was my friend. Unlike the friendly sparring I had done during practice, Saturday morning sparring was different. Once the cage door closed, it was an all-out battle for survival. I landed blow after blow on his face. I looked up again at Ben.

"Keep landing those!" he yelled. "Free your hands and then— good, exactly. Stay there! Keep him down!"

We were both exhausted when the second round started. Kike kept his distance and peppered me with jabs. I took the punches with increasing confidence until I was able to take him down again. I was too exhausted to do much from top and Kike used the opportunity to punch upwards at my face.

"You gotta keep working!" Ben yelled. "Free your hands!"

When the period ended, Kike threw in the towel. He wasn't in shape. I was dead tired too so I was happy it was over.

My wrestling, I was learning, gave me a big advantage, even over more experienced fighters. Now, I realized, I needed to work on my submissions.

Three days a week, Ivan's brother Hector came in to coach our afternoon practice. Both Ivan and Hector were black belts in luta livre. Although Hector had never competed in MMA, he was a specialist in submissions.

He wore a square patch of gauze over his nose. He had worn the same patch when I had visited the gym the first time and I assumed he had broken his nose or was recovering from surgery. I asked Ben one day, "When is his nose going to heal?"

"Oh, that's permanent. He's had that as long as I've known him."

"What happened to him?"

"No one really knows. It's one of those things you just don't ask about."

"You'd think he could get surgery," I thought out loud.

"Life is different down here, man."

Hector, like Ivan, didn't speak a word of English. As I got to know him, I grew to understand his unique sense of humor. He often teased me for my lack of comprehension.

"Repeat after me," he said one day. "*Pablito clavó...*"

"*Pablito clavó...*" I replied, confused.

"*Un clavito...*"

"*Un clavito...*"

"*En el culito.*"

The other members of the gym started snickering.

"What is he saying?" I asked Claudio.

"Oh it's a *trabalengua*. How you say it in English? Tongue twister?"

"Yeah."

"But it's a really gay one."

"*Huevón*," I said to Hector and everyone laughed.

I grappled with Hector many times in those first few weeks. Like Ivan, he would pull me aside and show me a technique. We would wrestle and he would often stop to show me submissions.

One day I was grappling with him and he shot into my legs. I draped over the top and grabbed his leg. As I fell to the mat, I hooked his far leg with my own and rolled him to his back. I began to pull his legs apart in a wrestling move known as the "banana split." I split his legs like a wishbone. Like Ivan, he had a short stocky build, and because of this, flexibility was not his strong point. I pulled harder and he tapped the mat with his hand. I had submitted a black belt with an old wrestling trick.

One afternoon, I practiced with Hector when no one else was around. When Ben or Claudio weren't around to translate, I struggled communicating in Spanish. After wrestling hard for an hour, he mumbled something that I didn't understand. I got the impression that he was talking about another student of his, but I didn't know.

He grabbed his car keys and told me to follow. Where were we going? I asked but I still didn't understand his answer. We got in his car and drove off. During practice, Hector and I were usually able to use nonverbal cues to communicate, but outside of the training room we were lost.

We met one of Hector's students, Diego, who thankfully spoke English. The three of us began to grapple. Hector told me to watch out for his ankle locks.

I should have listened because right away Diego trapped my ankle in the crux of his arm and leaned back. I winced and tapped the mat. We started over, and he quickly caught me again by the ankle. After he got me a third time, Hector jumped in.

They battled back and forth. When Diego locked up Hector's ankle, he squirmed and rolled like an alligator. When he couldn't roll anymore, he rolled back in the other direction. He thrashed about and I could see the grimace on his face. He gritted his teeth and made one last push to escape. Then he tapped the mat.

He walked off, shaking his head, and I started to roll with Diego again. I was able to avoid his leg lock for a while, but he eventually caught me in another one. I tried gator-rolling like Hector, but the pain shot up my leg and I tapped.

We packed our stuff up and got ready to leave. Hector said something and Diego turned to me, "Hector says that the two of us are the only people who have tapped him out in the last year."

CHAPTER
11

y ankle was still hurting when I showed up to the gym
Saturday morning. Ivan had given us the morning off
from sparring because the gym was hosting a series of
amateur fights later that day. Ben and I ran a three-mile loop around
the neighborhood. When we returned, Ben and Ivan started talking.

"Ivan says you are going to fight today." I wasn't sure if Ben was
translating poorly or if Ivan actually spoke in such certainties.

"What?"

"In the amateur fights later."

"When?"

"At two o'clock."

"That's in four hours."

"Yeah, you'll be alright."

"Um no. Tell him I don't want to."

Ivan furrowed his brow and looked at me. He didn't say anything,
but his gaze said it all. I pointed to my ankle, which had swollen after
Diego's leg locks. He continued gazing in my direction.

"I would think about it if I were you," said Ben. "It will be really
beneficial."

"I want to fight, but—my ankle, I can't."

My ankle did hurt, and running with Ben hadn't helped. The blister
on the bottom of my foot stuck with me at every footstep, it was still
raw and bleeding. But it wasn't just the physical pain that bothered
me: I wasn't mentally prepared either. I had arrived to Peru exactly
twenty days earlier. I wasn't ready.

We left the gym and caught a cab home. I looked out the window as we were stuck in traffic. I worried that maybe I was just making excuses because I was afraid. In college wrestling, it was rare to make it through a season without being injured. Most people push through a season with three or four nagging injuries. We were training hard and I realized that there would never be a time when I was feeling perfect.

I remembered Kyle's theory of Flu-Like Symptoms. Many coaches give a speech that goes something like, "You have to be comfortable being uncomfortable." That was one of the reasons I had come down here: to learn how to be uncomfortable. I wanted to plunge into the depths fear and danger, and see if I could swim. Here was my opportunity to prove I could do it.

I turned to Ben in the cab, "I need to buy a mouthguard."

"And a cup," he replied.

In the meantime, Ben explained the amateur rules to me. The distinguishing difference between an amateur and professional fight is, of course, the money. But it is more than that. Amateur fights don't count on your official record. Every professional fighter has an official record that you can look up in a central database.

This fight was more along the lines of what they would call a "smoker." A smoker is an unofficial bout between gyms. It falls somewhere between the realms of sparring and a standard amateur bout. The fights were held in the octagon on the far side of the gym. All of the local gyms were invited. The event was called *MMA Proyecto* and was created by Ivan to develop new talent.

The rule set was stricter than professional MMA. Once the fight goes to the ground you are not allowed to punch to the head or face. Striking with knees or elbows is prohibited. Instead of the normal 3 x 5 minute rounds, it would be 3 x 3 minute rounds. We wore boxing headgear and shin pads. We would use MMA training gloves, which are slightly more padded than regular MMA gloves.

When I arrived at the gym, I weighed in at 151.5 pounds. There were no weight classes, but the coaches got together and paired off fighters by weight. Ivan called out my match and I stepped forward to take a picture with my opponent, facing each other with fists raised.

I was nervous, but not about the fight. I was nervous about the ceremony and the etiquette that surrounded it. I had wrestled hundreds of times in my life, but this was different. I wasn't accustomed to wearing a mouth guard. It felt like I was choking, so I cut it shorter with a knife. I kept adjusting my cup awkwardly.

I was confident, but I still just wanted to get it over with. I would try to use my wrestling skills to my advantage. I might have to take a few punches, like I had against Kike, but I was ready for that. I would try to keep moving forward, like Ivan had said. I would have to be careful with submissions once I took him down.

Eventually, they called me up to the cage. When the bell rang, everything became crystal clear. My vision narrowed. He lunged in for a heavy jab. I lowered my level, shot forward, and snatched his left leg, driving my shoulder into his gut. Takedown.

I landed in his guard and he locked his legs around my waist. I buried my head under his chin, freed my arms, and pounded on his ribs from either side. Back and forth, back and forth. I wasn't going to end the fight here, but I wanted to make him hurt.

I tried to lock up a guillotine choke, but I fell off and wound up on bottom. I couldn't lock my hands around his neck with the headgear and the gloves. When his glove slipped off they restarted us in the same position. I quickly escaped to my feet and took him down again. I pounded his ribs until the period ended.

"Go for a hard right," Ben said when I went to the corner, "and if he gets out of the way, take him down."

When the second round started, I did exactly as Ben told me, pivoting my back foot and committing to a hard right to the jaw. Just as anticipated, he leaned back and I dove in for a single leg takedown. I pounded on his ribs again, but I got stuck in his guard. When he grabbed my headgear, it fell off. I looked at the ref, and used hand motions to signal my frustration. I finished the round on top and went back to my corner.

I didn't think my lungs would hold up through the third period, but my conditioning felt good. I was bouncing in my corner and even threw some jabs into the air. I wanted my opponent to see that I was ready.

"When you're in his guard, start to let him up a bit. If he gets up maybe something will open up and at worst you'll take him down again easily," Ben said. "Push yourself out there, you got him tired."

When the third and final round started, I saw the look in his eyes change and I knew he was about to mount an offensive. He moved forward with a blitzkrieg of flying lefts and rights. I caught one or two of them as I dropped my level and shot into his legs. I turned the corner and got a takedown.

I was getting frustrated with being stuck in his guard. "Let him loose!" Ben yelled. I remembered the feeling in wrestling of cutting someone loose and taking him down again; it demoralized an already tired opponent. I cut him loose and hovered over him, ready to pounce.

As soon as he got to his feet, I shot in. Just then, he cocked his fist back and caught me in the mouth with an uppercut. When the punch landed, I knew it was hard. I knew it was supposed to hurt, but I was surprised that it didn't. It was as if I was watching someone else get punched. My conscious mind told me that it hurt, but I just didn't feel it. I finished the shot and took him down. I was breathing hard at this point, and my mouth guard wasn't making it any easier. During one deep exhale, I sprayed blood on his stomach. When I noticed, I was proud. I had been punched hard and I still finished my takedown.

When it ended, I didn't need to wait for the judge's decision because I knew I had won. I could feel my swollen upper lip pressing against my teeth and I tasted the blood. When the cage doors opened, Pinedo came in with a towel and tried to wipe the blood from my face.

"No, no, no! I want to look tough in the pictures!"

CHAPTER

12

Sunday was our day off from training. The weather was beautiful and I decided to walk to the park in Barranco to do some reading and writing. I sat outside Starbucks at a small metal table and took out my laptop. A security guard was posted at the door and he watched me uncomfortably for several minutes before coming over.

"*Cuidado*," he warned me gently. "I have been watching people watch you. It is not safe with your computer." He motioned that someone would grab my laptop and run away. He seemed sincere so I decided to take his advice and put it back in my bag.

Robbery seemed to be the name of the game here. The night before, I was driving along the beach with a Peruvian girl. A few miles to the south, perched on top of a mountainous peninsula, a giant cross illuminated the night sky. I asked if it was possible to drive there. "Yes," she said, "but it's too dangerous." Her friends had been robbed there recently. "Maybe if you leave your valuables at home."

On my flight to Peru, an old Peruvian man next to me warned me of the dangers of taxis. "They're dangerous. *Cuidado!* They will take you, rob you and..." his voice trailed off and he made the universal hand signal for "shank you in the ribs with a sharp object."

Peruvians did not seem to have a very high opinion of each other. But I was learning that it could be a dangerous place. One time, Ben was on a bus that suddenly stopped on a country road. The doors opened and five bandits boarded, all wearing black ski masks and brandishing pistols. They lined up the passengers facedown on the ground and took everyone's wallets, cellphones, and watches. They even took Ben's shoes.

After leaving Starbucks, I decided to take a walk and explore my new home. I walked down the old stone stairs that cut through the cliff to the ocean. I crossed a footbridge to the beach and looked to the horizon. Four or five miles down the beach, I saw the giant cross that I had seen the night before and I decided to walk there.

The beaches were so packed that I could barely see the sand. The kids were on summer break and had flocked to the beach in droves. Small streams of water formed tide pools near my path, but they were littered with trash and debris. Little children splashed around in them, not seeming to care.

A few miles down, I neared the giant cross. The beach ended and I came upon an enormous jetty that shot out into the ocean. I began walking through the fish market at its base. The stench of fish invaded my nostrils. Mangy dogs hovered at the edge. A group of pelicans stalked aggressively. I'd never seen pelicans like this before. They were mangier than the dogs and bigger too. When they got too close to the fish on the table, a purveyor sprayed them with a hose.

I walked down the crowded pier. Little kids pulled at me from every direction, trying to sell me trinkets. I was most likely the only gringo in the crowd. Kids were jumping off the pier and climbing back up the barnacle-clad pilings. The last fifty feet was fenced off, with a woman standing at the gate. She shouted a bunch of Spanish at me. I nodded my head and pretended to understand. "*Sí, sí,*" I said.

She grabbed my arm and led me to the end of the pier and down a small staircase. There was a line of people boarding a boat. The woman turned to me, "*Remos o motora?*" I realized I had agreed to a boat ride. "*Motora,*" I replied. She pointed to a large motorboat with four rows of seats and about fifteen people on board wearing fluorescent orange life vests.

Just then, a guy pulled up to the dock in a ten-foot long rowboat.

It was rickety and wooden with long oars rowed by a shirtless middle-aged man. There was a bucket of bait in the middle. The woman indicated to me this was the other option for ten soles.

"*Por qué no?*" I said. Why not? I hopped aboard.

Before I could say anything, we shoved off. It became clear that we were having trouble communicating. I gathered that he was a fisherman, but I couldn't tell if he was taking me fishing. I didn't know where we were going or what we were doing. We navigated in and out of the moored boats that huddled in the bay.

Suddenly my mind started racing. It was pretty obvious that I was a stupid American. The guidebooks, had I read them, would have surely warned me against something like this. I was all alone. I didn't speak the language. Not a soul in the world knew where I was. As far as Ben knew, I was still in the park. No one would notice that I was missing for hours, if not days. Furthermore, my backpack contained my MacBook and my iPad. And I had $300 in my wallet. What did the guidebooks say about heading out to sea alone in a rickety boat with a strange man?

My heart was thumping and my stomach felt like I'd swallowed a cue ball. I hadn't eaten much and I looked down to see my hands shaking. Should I take my cellphone out and call Ben? Nothing says scared American quite like that maneuver.

He said something about another boat, and I think he was asking my permission. "*Sí, sí,*" I managed to say, trying to sound confident. We pulled alongside a bigger fishing boat with a group of dark dreadlocked men aboard. Please don't make me get aboard, I thought, I just want to get back ashore.

The three men hopped aboard our boat, and he introduced me as an American. The only thing going for me was that I couldn't see any cement among their belongings. Maybe they just didn't care if I floated ashore.

I was relieved when we headed back to the dock. He dropped the fishermen off and they threw him a few coins. We did this several more times, shuttling fishermen from their moorings to the dock. After the third one, he asked me if I wanted to go out to the deep water. *"Por qué no?"* I said.

This small Peruvian man stood up and threw his weight onto two giant oars. He introduced himself as Ivan, which was apparently a common name. It was a beautiful day and I leaned back, taking in the sun. I looked at Ivan, who was smiling ear to ear. He loved his life and you could tell. How had I been afraid of this man?

I asked him if he had any children. "Three daughters," he smiled proudly. He reached over the hull, rocking the boat slightly, and pointed to the side. The boat was named *"Mis Tres Amores."* My Three Loves.

He even let me row for a bit. I struggled and he corrected my technique. Keep the oars lower to the water, he said, relax and use your whole body. The old wooden boat was heavy and clumsy. There were no oarlocks. Instead, the oars were lashed down with a shaggy rope. He had made it look so easy.

The motorboat tour group passed us at one point and we reeled in its wake. Ivan looked over and scoffed. That's not a good way to do it, he explained. They just take you out and back and you don't get to see anything. I couldn't agree more, we were having a great time. Even with the language difficulties, we understood each other, and we laughed a lot.

After we picked up another fisherman, we headed back to the dock. This was the end of the tour, and Ivan nodded solemnly. I got off and took out my wallet. *"Diez soles,"* he said. I threw him a twenty and walked off, sad to be back ashore.

CHAPTER

13

The following Saturday night I returned home late after a long day of exploring my new city. Ben delivered some news. "Ivan just called and said you have to compete in a luta livre tournament tomorrow morning."

The main difference between luta livre and Brazilian jiu-jitsu is the kimono-like "gi." When the Gracie family pioneered jiu-jitsu, all practitioners wore a gi, the heavy fabric uniform that competitors wear in karate and judo. In jiu-jitsu, you can grab your opponent's gi and use it to gain control. It was meant to simulate a street fight where clothes could actually influence the outcome. At one point though, a group splintered off and stopped using the gi. They called their discipline luta livre.

In Portuguese, luta livre literally means "free fight," but it would be more accurately described as "submission grappling." Like jiu-jitsu, the purpose is to submit or choke your opponent through a series of techniques that apply pressure on the joints or the neck. In both disciplines, though, you don't actually put your opponent to sleep or snap their limbs because they will tap out first.

My wrestling skills would help me, but only to a certain point. I had spent my whole life learning how to control an opponent using the forces of leverage and pressure, but it wasn't just control that mattered. One wrong move and I could wind up submitted or choked. I had been training submissions for a few months now, but I still had many blind spots.

The event was being held at the Pitbull gym. I woke up at eight in the morning to weigh in. I arrived at the gym and I weighed in at 68 kilos. The weight class was 70 kilos, so I was 2 kilos (4.4 pounds) underweight.

"When does this thing start?" I asked Claudio.

"Not until noon. They have to do the whole Junior Division first."

I stretched out on a couch in the back room and fell asleep. I was startled when Fuerte barged in and shook me awake. "*Vas a pelear!*" I was up and they were waiting for me.

I stumbled down to the gym, rubbing my eyes. My weight class had only three people in it. They made us all come to the center of the mat. The ref took three sheets of paper, crumbled them, and dropped them on the mat. My two opponents reached down and each picked up one. I looked around confused, still half asleep, and then I picked up the last one. It said "*Vai.*" That meant I had a bye to the finals and the other two guys would compete first.

The guy with the brown shirt beat the guy with the blue shirt, so I was set to face brown shirt in fifteen minutes. I sat down on the mat and waited until they called me. The whistle blew and I stood straight up. I leaned back and left my legs completely exposed. He took the bait and dove in for a takedown. I sprawled and spun around behind.

Most bouts don't end in a submission, so there is a point system. You get two points for a takedown; two points for passing guard; four points for "full mount" (basically straddling your opponent's abdomen); and four points for "taking the back." I was on his back, but I hadn't taken his back in the technical sense. In order to score the four points, I needed to throw both of my heels ("hooks") around his waist and inside his legs. He turtled up and closed off so much that I was unable to get anything secured. I stayed on top for the entire five minutes. The score was still 0-0 even though I was in control the whole time. In the one-minute overtime, I got behind him again, but was unable to get the hooks. Because no conclusion was reached, it went to the referee's decision and he ruled in my favor.

I had won my weight class without scoring a single point. After I walked off the mat, I actually started to feel the adrenaline pumping. It had felt good and I actually wanted to compete again.

Then they announced the Absolute Division, where anyone could compete regardless of weight class or belt level, so I decided to enter.

There were eight guys in the bracket. My first match was against the guy in the blue shirt from my weight class. I won 2-0 when I passed his guard.

Next I had to face Fuerte. As teammates, we didn't want to compete against each other, but one of us had to win. We trained together every day so we knew each other's styles. We shook hands at the center of the mat and both cracked a smile. I took him down almost immediately for two points. When he got out, I took him down again and got his back. In the end I won 8-0.

I had made it to the finals of the Absolute Division. I was facing Tano Fernandez, a well-respected purple belt. Standing in the center of the mat, I heard my teammates cheering.

"TEAM PITBULL!"

"VAMOS ROLLIE!"

Above the clamor, I heard Claudio yell, "Pretend this is your last college match again!" I had told him about my heartbreaking loss at NCAAs and how it affected me. I looked over at him and laughed.

When the whistle blew, I circled around the mat. Tano jumped up and pulled me into his guard, using his weight advantage. Every time he squirmed for better position, I countered and maintained control. The small gym was filled with people surrounding our mat yelling. Most of the guys were cheering for Tano since he was Peruvian and they knew him, but the Pitbull guys cheered loudly for me to compensate.

I had trouble passing his tight half-guard because I was not accustomed to the unorthodox feel, and we were stuck in a stalemate for most of the match. We had a few scrambles, but each time, I wound up back on top. Towards the end of the match, I was about to take his back when he did a forward roll underneath and locked up a knee bar submission. He squeezed it to his chest. I tried to roll and wrench my leg free, but the more I resisted, the tighter it got.

The whole crowd hovered over the mat. The energy reverberated off the walls of the tiny gym. "OOOOH!" I heard the excitement rise. I took a deep breath into my lungs and tried to center my mind. I let my leg go limp and rolled in the same direction as his pressure. I sat up and pushed back into him. I took another deep breath and pushed forward, putting pressure on his arm. The crowd grew louder as they sensed the end was near. I looked up at them and waived them off. Then I stepped my foot out.

It was still 0-0 when regulation ended. "*Punto de oro!*" someone shouted. Golden point. Sudden death overtime.

He shot in on my legs and I spun behind to his back, but before I could secure anything, he rolled under again and I got stuck in his half-guard. I tried to pass his guard, but I was unable to get anything going before time ran out. It was 0-0 after overtime. When we walked to the center of the mat, the referee rendered a decision in my favor. I won the Absolute Division.

"That guy you just beat was really good," Claudio said. "That's crazy."

All of the Pitbull guys crowded around me and I hoisted my over-sized trophy in the air. It was almost two feet tall.

When things were wrapping up, I placed the trophy high on the shelf overlooking the gym. Everyone came over to congratulate me and I felt like I was part of the team. It didn't matter that I wasn't Peruvian; I was a member of the Pitbull gym. I had won it for them as much as me.

CHAPTER
14

I n two weeks, I was scheduled to have my professional MMA debut. I had been in Peru for just under two months and my body was finally getting accustomed to the rigorous training. I was ready.

Pitbull was hosting another amateur MMA event and Ivan wanted me to get one last amateur fight before my pro debut, as a last-minute tune up.

At the beginning of the week leading up to the fight, I got pretty sick, and was still running a high fever mid-week. I missed a few practices.

"You sure that I should fight so close to my pro fight?" I asked Ben.

"Yeah, whatever man."

Ivan checked in with me the day before.

"I think so, but…" he stood silently and awaited my response. "*Sí.*"

I had learned my lesson last time: Flu-Like Symptoms. I was ready for this, sick or not. Ivan just had a way of inspiring me. When I looked into his eyes, I just knew that no excuses ever held him back and I didn't want to let him down.

Ben and I showed up early and I went through the same routine as my previous fight. I weighed in and they matched me up with an opponent. I wasn't nervous this time because I had already been through the procedure and I just wanted to get it over with. They called me up and I started to strap my gloves on. Just then, Ben got a phone call and sounded worried.

He hung up and turned to me, "Fiorella just fainted at the house so I have to go home." He turned around and started walking out before

I could say anything.

I was on my own. Ben had been with me during every step, patiently guiding me through the obstacles. Now I was in a gym full of people screaming in Spanish and I was about to enter the cage. I tried not to panic. I found Martin, the owner of the gym, and asked him to corner me. He was the only person in the whole place who spoke English.

It felt weird stepping in the cage without Ben but I tried to put it out of my mind. The bell rang and we touched gloves. I got an early takedown and pinned my opponent against the side of the cage. I took his back, but he closed his arms around my bulky gloves and I couldn't lock the choke. From my corner I could hear Ivan yelling, and Martin translating into English. The referee stood us back up on our feet.

I faked a right and went for a single leg takedown, but he slipped his leg free. He cocked back for a hook, but I ducked down and shot in again. I wasted no time in throwing him to the ground. I got behind him and punched his ribs and stomach for the rest of the round.

After we traded blows at the beginning of the second round, I shot a double leg takedown and smashed him against the cage. I was getting tired from pounding his ribs so when Martin yelled, "Guillotine!" I spun around to the front and locked my hands around his neck. I squeezed hard, but the headgear made it difficult to finish the choke.

In the third round, I wanted to strike with him rather than just go for takedowns. We circled and I threw a hard jab to his face. As I was bringing my fist back, I left a gap open and he smashed his right fist into my face. Everything went black for a second and I felt a sharp pain radiate from my right eye and pulse outward through my face. Blood spattered across my field of vision. My eye instantly swelled up. I stumbled backwards in a daze. It felt like a movie scene where the bomb detonates and everything is in slow motion and silent.

I knew that all it took was a moment of hesitation—a moment of distraction—and my opponent could end the fight. I was swimming in confusion and my internal sense of balance was off. I saw my opponent coming toward me with fists flying. He appeared blurry through the blood and bewilderment.

I didn't have any time to think and my basic survival instincts took over. As he charged towards me, I dropped down and shot forward for a double leg takedown. I plowed through him and took him to his back, saving myself from certain defeat.

I saw that I was bleeding badly when my face brushed against his chest and left a bright smear of blood. I finished the period on top, but I was still woozy. When the bell rang, I got my hand raised.

I walked out of the cage and Ivan gave me a thumbs-up. Martin patted me on the back. But I didn't feel right. It felt like I had lost the fight. I blew my nose and wiped the blood from my eye. I rushed home to Ben.

Ben was tending to Fiorella, but helped me clean the blood from my eye. "You're a sight right now, man," he said as he tossed a piece of blood-soaked gauze into the trash. "One look at you and it's obvious you're a fighter." I didn't have much to say. I didn't feel very well. This wasn't just a fat lip; this was real damage. I had taken a big hit in a silly little amateur fight. Was I even prepared for my pro fight that was coming up in two weeks?

CHAPTER

15

My busted eye wasn't the only badge I earned from my developing MMA career. My ears were soon to become the next casualty.

I had wrestled for seventeen years without ever getting cauliflower ear. I knew many people who had sported it with pride, but it just wasn't something I wanted. In my early years of wrestling I remember kids who were excited when their ears swelled up into monstrous knots. The wrestling community abounds with stories of kids who would hit their own ear with a hard object in order to induce swelling. It was a badge of honor—a way to "make your bones" in the wrestling world. My teammates would sometimes tease me, "How can you consider yourself a serious wrestler without it?"

When I was younger, I remember thinking, "I don't want to be an adult around the office with mangled ears." Cauliflower ear is easily preventable, and my whole life I had worn the necessary headgear, so I had escaped unscathed.

It is caused by repeated trauma to the ear's cartilage. After enough bruising, the skin separates from the cartilage, the capillaries burst, and the flesh swells with fluid.

When it first occurs, the ear will swell up into a soft fleshy lump. I've seen some that looked like a golf ball sticking out of an ear. When it swells, you have approximately twenty-four hours to drain the fluid before it hardens. Once it hardens, the damage is irreversible (although I've heard there is corrective plastic surgery in extreme cases).

Cauliflower ear is not unique to wrestling and martial arts, because rugby players frequently get it too. But in the wrestling community, it's almost like a secret handshake, like how biker gangs wear their emblem across their vest so they recognize each other on the street. Prison gang members get tattoos, wrestlers get cauliflower ear.

The previous summer, I was with Bellini on the Jersey Shore and I stopped a big guy with mangled ears. "You wrestle?" I asked. It turned out that he had wrestled in college. I knew who he was and he knew who I was, but we had never met before. We drank together all night like old friends. "Typical Rollie," Bellini said, "he comes to the bar and picks up a wrestler." Secret handshake.

Another time I was walking through the ancient ruins in a medieval Italian town. I walked by a muscular Italian guy with grisly cauliflower ears and a shaved head. "You wrestle?" I asked him. He looked puzzled.

"How did you know?"

"Your ears."

We had a laugh and talked at length. The ears bridged the cultural divide and brought us together. Secret handshake.

They didn't sell wrestling headgear in Peru, so my ears were exposed every day in practice. The left and right hooks would land squarely on that soft spot of my ear. The worst damage came when we practiced ground-and-pound. One fighter mounted on top of the other with boxing gloves and would rain down blows on the bottom guy as he tried to protect himself. When fists are coming from every angle, you're bound to get hit in the ear. When my ears started to hurt, there was nothing I could do about it.

During a sparring session just three weeks before my professional MMA debut, my left ear swelled up. It wasn't a huge bulbous swelling, but it ran up and down my ear, making the flesh soft and squishy. It hurt when I touched it. I showed it to Ben after practice.

"Oh yeah, we're gonna have to drain that."

"Do I go to the doctor or what?" In college, the athletic trainer had always done it for my teammates.

"Nah, I'll do it."

"Wait, really? Is that safe?"

"Yeah, I do it all the time."

We walked to the pharmacy and bought a package of syringes. It was 1.50 soles for five of them. I did the math—that was around ten cents apiece.

"Don't I just need one?" I asked.

"No man," Ben laughed, "we're going to have to drain that sucker every day."

"Really? I always thought you just drained it once."

"Nope, especially because you are going to keep practicing every day. It will keep coming back."

I noted for the first time that I wasn't going to get any sympathy or days off for my ailment.

"How long will I have to drain it for?"

"It depends. Maybe if you take some time off after your fight it will go away. Maybe a month or so."

"And then it will go away completely?"

"Maybe," he said.

Back at the gym, Ben applied rubbing alcohol to the swollen area. The chill of the alcohol sent a shiver up my spine. I braced myself. He jammed the needle into the soft tissue.

"Argggg!"

He pushed it further in.

"Tsst. Tsst. Tsst. Tsst." I inhaled and exhaled in short bursts through my clenched teeth, like a woman in labor. The guys at the gym started laughing. He squeezed the swollen flesh and pushed the fluid towards the needlepoint.

"STOP! NO MORE!"

He pulled the needle out and handed it to me. It contained 2mL of my blood. I was sweating and panting like a dog.

Just as Ben had predicted, I had to drain my ear the following day. This time we did it at the apartment and Fiorella giggled as I grimaced in pain. The three-year-old Ghaela watched attentively. I gripped the edge of the table as he pulled back on the plunger.

It hurt to lay my head on the pillow at night, so I began to sleep on my right side. That worked for a while, but then my other ear swelled up one day in practice. I was two weeks away from my fight and now both of my ears were swollen.

I drained both of them every day—sometimes twice a day—but like the mythical Sisyphus, I awoke the next morning fated to repeat my punishment. My ears became pincushions. I would pester Ben after practice, "Can you drain them now?"

Sometimes he would miss the pocket of fluid on his first try and had to poke the needle around my ear. Other times, the needle would sink into the cartilage, and when he pulled back on the plunger, nothing came out. I would buy needles by the dozen from the pharmacist on the corner.

As fight week approached, we started to taper our training. We practiced just once a day and the training was light. I even managed to find some headgear. My friend Paico, the wrestler who had made the finals of the grand prix, had an old headgear that he lent to me. He had bought it while competing in the United States many years before. He handed it to me like it was a prized possession.

Between the headgear and the lighter training, my ear actually started to get better. But, as Ben reminded me one day, I would still have some permanent swelling in my ear. I wasn't going to make it through an MMA career, he said, without cauliflower ear. My whole life I had cared about what people around the office would say. Now, I wore it with pride, as a reminder of the new life I had chosen for myself.

CHAPTER
16

M y anxiety over my pro debut continued to escalate. About a week before the fight, I was riding home from practice on the back of Ben's motorcycle and we stopped at an intersection. It was the sort of mayhem you find only in Lima. There was a stoplight but it didn't seem to mean anything. Cars crossed whenever they could find an opening.

As we waited, my mind ran wild. "I hope we get in a crash and I get hurt," I thought. "Then I won't have to fight next week." The light turned green. "Nothing too serious, but a large abrasion would be enough. Maybe a broken bone at worst." Another voice chimed in. "But wait, that's crazy, Ben is on the bike too. I don't want him to get hurt, just me."

After we got home, I reflected on the idiocy of my thoughts. Surely a motorcycle crash would be worse than anything that could possibly happen to me in the cage. Was the pressure getting to me? I had been competing in high-pressure matches my whole life, but this feeling was different.

No matter how I tried to rationalize my way out of it, the cloud hung over my head. I started to doubt all the decisions that had led up to this point. Everyone else had freaked out when I decided to leave my job and move to Peru, but I never did. I had not allowed myself to have an *oh fuck* moment. But now I was having it all at once. What had I done? I had no business cage fighting.

I mentioned it to Ben one day and he laughed. "Yeah man, the mind plays some nasty tricks on you before a fight."

My opponent was Renzo "Nene" Mendez. He had a professional record of 1-2 and was just eighteen years old. Like Claudio, he had come from the generation young guys who were well-rounded fighters right from the beginning. In fact, his second loss had come from Claudio. They fought at 145, but then Claudio moved up a weight and Nene moved down.

My birthday was three days before the fight, but it came and went without much notice. What was another year anyway? I couldn't celebrate or even eat cake because I had to make weight. It was the first time in many years that I hadn't gone out drinking.

The event was being held at the Casino Atlantic City in Lima. The weigh-ins were scheduled for eleven in the morning the day before the fight. I showed up early to the casino, but no one was there. At eleven o'clock, nobody appeared. I started to worry that I was in the wrong location.

It was close to noon when the first people began to arrive. It was typical of Peru that something so official would start an hour late. Everything starts late in Peru, and they even had a phrase for it: *La hora Peruana*, or Peruvian Time. After everyone showed up, I made weight and we all got a cab back to the Pitbull center, where Jordan had prepared spaghetti. I passed the remainder of the day resting in my bed, trying keep my mind at ease.

The next day, I met the guys at the gym and we piled into two cabs headed for the casino. In addition to me, four of my teammates were fighting in the event: Pinedo, Fuerte, Claudio, and Ben.

On the way to the casino, we got stuck in the rush hour traffic. The mood was somber and nobody said a word, each of us stuck in our own minds, thinking our own thoughts, as we prepared for what lay ahead of us. We were headed to battle and each of us knew that tomorrow we would be different people.

All of the sacrifices we had put ourselves through would hopefully pay off. An MMA fight has a way of eliciting truth. There is no way to fake your way in a fight. There isn't even a way to lose gracefully. A loss in soccer might be upsetting and emotionally painful, but a loss in MMA is dark and physically debilitating.

You could get knocked out, which by definition is a traumatic brain injury. Getting a punch, a kick, or an elbow to the head literally shocks your brain into shutting down. The more times you get knocked out, the easier your brain shuts off each time. This is why they talk about older fighters "losing their chin." And after enough of these, they become punchy. Many veteran boxers suffer physical and psychological ailments as a result of the repeated trauma. But that's just one way to lose.

Any one of those vicious strikes could also cut the skin on your face. Thankfully, this alone is not ground for losing a fight. Fighters get cut all the time and continue fighting. Sometimes they stop the fight to clean up the blood. If they can't stop the bleeding, then they stop the fight and you can lose because of this. Usually when the fight ends the way, the afflicted fighter is left begging the referee to let him continue.

You could also get submitted or choked out. When a fighter locks up a submission and applies pressure, the other fighter will usually tap out. But there have been instances where stubborn fighters have refused to tap out and have suffered broken bones. One of the most famous instances of this was when Frank Mir got a kimura shoulder lock against Antonio Rodrigo Nogueira. When "Minotauro" Nogueira refused to tap out, his arm snapped at the elbow. It was a grisly end to the fight, but it highlights what a submission really is: by tapping out you are conceding that, if he wanted to, your opponent could snap your arm off. It works the same way with chokes as well: if you refuse to tap, you can find yourself unconscious. Sometimes the referee has to stop the fight and wait for the losing fighter to regain consciousness.

The fight could also go to a judge's decision after three hard-fought rounds. That's fifteen minutes locked inside a cage with another human being who is trying to do nothing but inflict pain on you. The more pain he inflicts, the better his chances of winning. And so you try to inflict pain back onto him. You kick and you punch. You want to make him hurt so that he can't continue. Then you win.

It is a frightening prospect, no matter how you look at it. Fighting has been around since before we even had a spoken language to describe it. Our first hunter-gatherer ancestors didn't settle disputes in the court of law. They had to protect their land and their families however they could. The difference between winning and losing a fight was life or death.

An MMA fight is a competitive simulation of this struggle. If you got knocked out in a fight to the death, your unconscious body couldn't defend itself anymore, and you would be dead. If, like Minotauro, your arm snapped, you would be flopping on the ground like a trout on the riverbank as your enemy ended you. The implication is that, by losing a fight, you would be dead.

We arrived at the casino and climbed the marble stairs to the second floor and made our way through the crowd. It was still early and many seats were empty.

Two warm-up areas were separated by a vinyl curtain, which was suspended from metal support beams. Each room had a mat and a television. On the television, we could watch the other fights as we waited. The fights would also be streamed online, and I had made sure that all of my friends in the United States were tuning in.

The first fight began around eleven o'clock. I sat in the corner of the warm-up room, trying to conserve my energy. Much as I tried to relax, there was a certain tension that permeated every corner of the building. I heard the light rumbling of the crowd every time the door opened. I saw my teammates pacing back and forth. I felt what they felt.

Pinedo was the second fight and he was getting his hands taped by Kike in the corner of the room. When he was finished, Kike called me over to tape my hands. I was the third fight of the night.

I had never had my hands wrapped with tape before, only with the fabric wraps that we used in practice. Kike applied a layer of gauze over my knuckles then wrapped the gauze around my palm. He applied several layers of shiny white tap on my knuckles.

Taping your hands serves two purposes. First, it compresses your hand and keeps everything tight. The conventional wisdom is that the bones in your hand are susceptible to breaking with a hard enough punch, and the wraps hold them in tight formation. The second reason is that it provides padding for your fist. With the extra padding, you can hit harder.

"How does it feel?" Ben asked.

"A little tight," I replied.

"Yeah, it's supposed to feel like that. It will loosen up as you move around."

"It's crazy that there's no one here to monitor this." The world of boxing is full of tales of cheaters putting metal objects or even cement in their hand wraps, causing a devastating effect on their opponents.

"Well, there is no athletic commission down here. In the United States they would have someone monitor the whole process. It's the honor system, I guess."

After he finished taping, I squeezed into the MMA gloves. They were stiff and rigid. I squeezed my fingers closed several times to test the range.

We gathered around Pinedo as he waited in the staging area to walk out into the cage. Claudio and Ben walked out into the arena to watch the fight, but I stayed behind and occasionally glanced at the small television.

He was facing a Muay Thai fighter named Victor Arata. Pinedo used his long arms to capitalize on his feet. Victor held his arms up defensively, but Pinedo pierced through his defenses with aggressive striking. He took him down in the second round but then I stopped watching.

I was up next and focused on my warm-up. I wore a heavy grey hooded sweatshirt and sweatpants. I stood in the middle of the mat and threw punches through the air at an imaginary opponent. I focused on getting my heart rate up. I was starting to sweat, and I shuffled my feet on the side of the mat. Ben came over and rubbed my arms to get the blood flowing through my muscles.

The nervous energy began to drift away as my fight approached. I clenched my teeth around my mouth guard. This was why I had come down here.

Pinedo won by decision and the organizers came back to get me. I draped an American flag over my shoulders. All of the Team Pitbull guys surrounded me and we put our hands in the middle. On Ben's three count, we yelled "PITBULL TEAM! HUA HUA HUA!" I was ready to go out. I had selected *'Till I Collapse* by Eminem as my entrance music.

The rhythm started slowly as I walked through the crowd. When the beat dropped, my adrenaline surged and my heart began pumping. This was it, kill or be killed.

CHAPTER

17

I walked into the dark room. Blue spotlights cut through the smoke machine near my feet. I shuffled down the concourse until I reached the cage. A man with latex gloves took a gob of Vaseline and applied it to my face to prevent cuts. I stripped down to my shorts and handed my clothes to Ivan.

I stared across the cage at my opponent and he stared right back at me. At that moment, my entire universe was locked inside that cage. The referee brought his hands together with a clap and started the fight. We approached the center cautiously and touched gloves.

We circled tentatively at first, and I tried to stay outside the range of his punches. Nene was a better striker so I didn't want to engage him up close. I stayed light on my feet, ready to dodge or strike at a moment's notice.

Nene stepped forward with an exploratory jab and then cocked back for a left hook. As his fist swung through the air, I dove in and grabbed his front leg. He dropped his weight onto me as I squeezed the leg tighter. When I started to feel his pressure rise, I straightened my back and lifted him over my head. I lifted as high as I could and slammed him down on the hard floor. There was a loud thud and the crowd cheered.

I landed in his guard, but I caught his legs and threw them to the side. I felt a wave of relief now that I had him on the ground. Now I wasn't exposed to his strikes. When I passed his guard, he rolled to his stomach. He tried to stand up, but I scooted underneath and pulled him into a guillotine choke.

I squeezed but I didn't have the right pressure. I didn't want to get stuck on bottom, so I rolled back on top and worked my ground-and-pound strategy. I planted my hand on his face and dropped all of my weight onto my elbow and forearm, smashing his face as hard as I could.

It was halfway through the five-minute round and I was already breathing heavy through my mouth guard. I tried not to think about how much time was left. When the referee stood us up, he came in with a left hook. I shot into his legs as he stepped forward and snapped him to his butt.

Even though I had gotten the takedown, I suddenly realized that both of my arms were trapped and he started punching me in the head. I tried to turn towards his legs but he wouldn't release my arm. Each punch hit me directly in the ear and I felt a dull pain. I was trapped and he knew it. He began hammering away at the side of my head.

He got excited and started to sit up so that he could do more damage, but his grip loosened just enough and I spun around and returned to the top position.

I attempted a choke, but my forearms were burning, so I released it and smashed my elbow into his face. When he tried to escape, I took his back and threw my hooks in. I was comfortable here. I tried to lock up in a choke, but it wasn't tight enough, so I punched him in the face for the remainder for the round.

When the bell rang, Ivan came in and placed a small wooden stool against the cage and I sat down. He rubbed my arms and yelled things in my ear in Spanish. I was too busy trying to catch my breath and take small sips of water.

"Good job Rollie. Breathe! Relax! Breathe!"

Before I knew it they called me back out. Nene cocked his leg back and swung it through the air, narrowly missing my face. He stepped forward and I threw my right hand at his chin. At the same time I shot into his legs. He turned away to escape the takedown, but I locked my hands around his waist and dragged him to the ground.

I got his back, and every time he tried to squirm out, I stuck to him like gum on a shoe. My lack of submission experience was showing, but I compensated with control. Instead, I started throwing my bony elbows into his soft lower ribs. As the final seconds of the round ticked away, I postured up and dropped my fists down on his face like a jackhammer. Another five minute round in the books.

Ivan shouted commands in my ear as I plopped onto the stool. I struggled to catch deep breaths of air, but it was never enough. In MMA, there is never a lull in the pace. Even when it seems like there is no action, every muscle in your body is taut, ready to explode into action at the slightest provocation. Your mind whirls in a frenzy as it tries to anticipate the surge of limitless hypotheticals.

If you lose concentration for a split second, it could mean a swift shinbone to your face. A monastery full of Tibetan monks couldn't achieve that level of concentration. It is impossible not to live in the present moment with such immediate threats to your survival. Adrenaline surges through your body and base instincts take over. Every cell of your body is magnetically aligned towards your opponent, just as every cell of his is aligned towards you. The outside world doesn't exist inside the cage.

I knew I had won the first two rounds so I decided to make him do the work to attack me in the third. He charged at me, jumping in the air to kick me. I jumped to meet him and threw my knee forward. We crashed into each other and fell to the ground. I scrambled to wrap my arms around his neck. I squeezed as hard as I could, but we were sweaty and tired from over ten minutes in the cage.

When Nene pushed against the cage, I lost my balance and fell to the ground. He stood up and came down to punch me in the face, but I grabbed his leg and held on for dear life. "How much time is left?" I wondered.

I clung to his back and pulled him on top of me, but suddenly he spun around and now I was on bottom. I was too tired to even care about the loss of my position. I grabbed onto him and pulled him closer. He started punching me in the ribs and the face, but I didn't feel it. I just wanted time to expire. When he shifted his weight, I rolled through and finished the period on top.

At the end of the round, the judges ruled a unanimous decision in my favor, and I got my hand raised. I was happy that it was over. I had done what I had come here to do.

When I saw Claudio in the back room, his jaw dropped. "Holy shit!" he said. "Wow! Your ear."

I reached up and felt my right ear. The entire thing was squishy like a water balloon and it was swollen shut. For the first time, I noticed that I couldn't hear anything out of it.

The fight doctor came to check on me. I pointed to my ear and he looked startled. He examined it for a minute.

"Well," he said after a few seconds of deliberation, "we're going to need a syringe." I ran over to my backpack and grabbed one.

"Oh," he said. "I come back after next fight, okay?"

I went over to Ben. "I don't think that guy has any idea how to drain an ear."

"Want me to do it?"

"Shouldn't you be warming up?" His hands were wrapped in tape already.

"It's fine, we can just do it fast."

Just a few weeks before, I hadn't trusted Ben to do it. Now, I didn't trust anyone else. Not even a licensed doctor. I sat down as Ben filled the entire 5mL tube with dark crimson blood. The doctor returned several minutes later to reexamine my ear.

"It looks better," he said.

"Yes, I already drained it."

"Oh yes, of course. Good."

I went out to watch Fuerte fight against Humberto Bandenay, who was known as a striker. Bandenay and Fuerte traded heavy blows on their feet, but in the second round Fuerte locked up a rear-naked choke to end the fight. Claudio continued the Pitbull win streak by downing a Brazilian fighter named Lander Alves with a unanimous decision.

In the co-main event Zury Valenzuela was defending his Inka FC championship belt against a Brazilian fighter named Gilberto Dias. This was one of Zury's biggest tests yet, as Dias was a well-respected fighter who sported a 14-2 record. They fought at 125 pounds, just one weight class below mine. While Zury now trained with Hector, he was still considered a member of our extended family. Zury shot in but Dias punched him in the head repeatedly. Before he could react, the referee stopped the fight. Zury had lost the belt.

The main event pitted Ben against a Brazilian fighter named Danilo Pereira, who had more than thirty fights under his belt. I sat cageside and yelled until my voice was hoarse. Ben won with a unanimous decision, capping off a perfect night for Team Pitbull.

CHAPTER

18

didn't win my fight because of my striking abilities—I won it despite my shortcomings. I knew that I had been lucky to take Nene
down so easily. We had traded some punches and kicks on our
feet, but for the most part the entire fight had been on the ground.

I had been working with Ivan on striking before and after practice.
He would pull me aside and hold the pads for me and try to correct
my many mistakes. But striking wasn't Ivan's specialty, and it would
take someone with a higher level to correct my shortcomings.

I found that someone in Romulo "Agulha" Correa, a sprightly and
enthusiastic Brazilian amateur boxer and coach. Agulha was always
smiling ear-to-ear and had a boundless energy that was contagious
to all around him. He had a small wiry frame, but a mature face that
made him look older than his actual age of thirty-three. His receding
hairline and short thinning hair betrayed an intricate blue tattoo on
the back of his scalp. His head bobbed up and down as he studied us.

We were all lined up on the practice mat as Ivan introduced him.
He led us through the warm-up and then he assigned each one of us
to a heavy punching bag. He mimed out a combination on the bag:
jab, cross, switch feet, low left kick. We repeated the combo on the
punching bags that hung from the ceiling.

He came over to me and put his hands on my shoulders, indicat-
ing that I should slow down and relax. When I gritted my teeth and
kicked the bag, he stopped me again. He put his hands on my hips
and I kicked again slowly. He rotated my hips and turned my body.

Agulha lived in the back of the gym, so he was always around. He began to coach us every day and would even jump into our sparring sessions. He was around my size so he was a good training partner for me. When we traded punches, he would hold back and let me work my technique. He was patient and would stop to adjust my errant fists or show me the finer points of footwork.

He was often the first one up in the morning and he would wake everyone by yelling to the top of the stairs, "*Vamos meninas!*" or "Let's go little girls" in Portuguese.

That Saturday during sparring I was paired off with Fuerte and we got in the cage. I tried to box with him, but before I knew it he had me pressed against the cage. I covered my face for dear life as he unloaded a series of punches to my face and body. I was desperate and dropped down and shot in to his legs, but he anticipated it and trapped me beneath him as he blasted away at my head and ribs. The second and third round weren't much better. He shut me down in every way, and I couldn't breathe or think straight. After the round, I collapsed on the mat.

Agulha came over and lifted me up. He told me to put my boxing gloves back on. I looked up at him pathetically, but he just nodded. "Take five minutes to recover," he told me. He held the pads as I hit various combinations for thirty minutes.

Agulha brought some much-needed levity to the gym and his sense of humor lifted everyone's spirits. He started calling Fuerte "Monstro." The name stuck, and as usual Fuerte just smiled and laughed along.

Ben had left to visit his brother in California and would be away for a month, so I was fending for myself. I began spending more time with the guys on the team. My Spanish was improving enough that I could joke around with Fuerte and Pinedo between training sessions. We would sit on the couch and talk about our favorite MMA fighters.

Fuerte would sometimes try to sing songs in English and scramble the words up beyond recognition. He and I went for a run together one day. "*Yup round world,*" he sang at the top of his lungs. I told him that I didn't understand what he was singing. He said the line again, but with slightly more melody.

"Ohhhh," I said, "*Uptown Girl.*"

"*Yupton yurl?*" he said.

One day in practice, *Another One Bites the Dust* came on the stereo. "*Yotherun rights sabust,*" he said slowly.

"Noooo," I corrected him, "Another…One…Bites…the…Dust." He worked on the pronunciation for weeks and weeks, but he could never say it properly. "*Anozor run bize tidstus.*" I began to think maybe he was messing it up just to be funny.

Another time, Fuerte brought a wooden flute to practice. He played the Mario Brothers theme song and *Imagine* by John Lennon. I sat listening to him play tunes for a half hour. Fuerte and I came from just about as different upbringings as you could have, but we may as well have been brothers.

There was another Inka FC event coming up at the end of May and Ivan informed me that I would be fighting against Gonzalo "Diamante" Vallejo, a two-time Peruvian Muay Thai national champion. He was a powerful striker with vicious low leg kicks, but he only had one MMA fight: a draw against Fuerte. Still, this was a massive challenge for me.

Agulha started working with me on defense to low kicks. I had a bad habit of turning my hips away from the kick and exposing the soft fleshy part of my hamstring to my opponent's bony shin. Instead, I was supposed to lift my knee up and meet it with my shin.

Muay Thai utilizes many leg kicks where bone meets bone and they actually develop a resistance to the pain. Some young Muay Thai fighters will even go outside and kick their shins against a tree in order to kill the nerve endings and build an armor of scar tissue.

Agulha had me train this defense hundreds of times. Fuerte would put shin pads on as we sparred lightly. After throwing a few soft punches, he would low kick and I would raise my leg up to meet it. No matter how many times we drilled it, it still felt unnatural. Whenever we sparred, Ivan would call out for my opponent to kick me. Often, I still turned away and felt the sting of his shin on my hamstring.

Most days Ivan would send me off to the corner to work with Agulha while the others practiced because I had the weakest striking skills of anyone. I was lucky to be getting so much personal attention from a coach like Agulha. Little by little my striking began to improve. He even tailored the training to my wrestling style. He taught me how to come in for a hard right and drop down to a shot. I drilled it hundreds of times with him.

Ivan announced that Agulha would also be fighting at the upcoming Inka event against one of Hector's students, Jorge "Karateca" Cuenca. It was unusual for one of Ivan's guys to be fighting against one of Hector's since our gyms were so friendly with each other and Hector came in to train us twice a week. Either way, Agulha started training harder. I tried to repay him by teaching him some wrestling.

One Saturday morning sparring session, Hector's students came in to train with us. I was excited to spar with Zury because he was actually my size, unlike the other Pitbull team members. He was coming off of his recent loss of the Inka FC belt. He had begun his career with Hector, but switched to Ivan's gym when they offered to pay him a salary. After he lost an important fight, Pitbull kicked him out and he returned to Hector's gym.

Whenever I made a conscious effort to stand firm and trade punches with a sparring partner, I usually abandoned the plan when confronted with a flurry of punches. I just didn't have the confidence to exchange punches when I always had an easy alternative with my takedowns.

This time, however, I vowed that I would try to stay on my feet with Zury. We circled each other and darted in and out with probing jabs. I pressed forward and threw my weight behind a jab. He covered up with his forearms and I jabbed again, pushing him back against the cage. I began to unload on him. He turned and circled out and fled to the other end of the cage. Now that I had him on the defensive, I dropped down to his legs and tackled him to the mat.

I tried to apply the new striking techniques that Agulha had taught me. Each time I landed a punch, I could hear Agulha yell, "Isso!" When we finished three rounds, Zury was collapsed on the mat. I walked out of the cage and Agulha patted me on the back.

CHAPTER
19

Have you ever tried to drop ten pounds for beach season? Or maybe shed the freshman fifteen? Imagine having to lose that in one week and then stepping in a cage to fight the next day. That is what we did.

In my sedentary Wall Street days, with the fancy dinners and binge drinking, I had gotten up to 170 pounds. Now, after the rigorous training and constant stomach bugs, I was down to 145. My last fight was at 135 pounds, but my teammates insisted that I was still too small for the weight class. They insisted that I should drop down to 125.

The strategy was to lose as much weight as possible in order to fight against a smaller opponent with less muscle mass. If I fought at my natural weight of 145, my opponent would likely be coming down from at least 160. Most of the weight we lost was water weight, and it was common for fighters to gain ten to fifteen pounds in the twenty-four hours between weigh-ins and competition.

Now, Ivan started pressuring me to fight at 125 pounds. I hadn't made 125 since my junior year of college five years earlier. Vallejo was also pretty big and had fought against Fuerte at 145 pounds.

"He'll have a tough time making weight," Claudio insisted.

"But so will I."

"It will be worse for him," he said.

"Okay, fine. I'll do it."

That night I went for a long run along the beach. I had two weeks to lose twenty pounds. I hadn't lost this much weight since college and I wanted to do it the right way.

Over the years, many people have asked me, "What's the secret to losing weight?" My response never changes: eat less and work out more. And that's what I did. I started dieting and drastically cutting back on calories.

I struggled to keep up in practice every day and I was totally drained of energy, but the weight slowly started to burn off. By the end of the week I was down to 140 pounds. Just fifteen pounds to go. I knew I could lose ten pounds of water weight in the last few days, but I wanted to slim down first.

I walked out of my bedroom one day and Fiorella gasped, "*Flaquisimo!*" So skinny! My pants didn't fit me anymore and even the smallest loop on my belt wasn't tight enough. I became grumpy and irritable. Sitting around the gym between practices, I would get annoyed by little things my teammates said. I would put my headphones in and try to tune them out.

Most of my teammates would lose fifteen to twenty pounds for each fight, so they knew how to do it. They've all done it several times. They all had tricks that they swore by.

"You have to eat coconut, it helps burn fat," said Alfonso.

"Sure, okay," I nodded.

"I'm going to go pick you up some watermelon," said Kike. "It's a *diurético natural.*"

"No thanks," I said, trying to be patient.

The day before weigh-ins I was weak and having trouble even getting up to walk. Agulha ran into the kitchen and came back with a hardboiled egg. "Eat this!"

"No thanks," I said.

"You need it for energy," he insisted. "Just eat the white part."

"No!" I said, but he continued to lecture me. Some of my other teammates began chiming in with their own opinions.

"GUYS!" I yelled in English. "I wrestled for seventeen years. I have cut weight hundreds of times. I know what I'm doing!" Claudio was the only one who understood me, but they understood the message.

I felt bad about losing my temper, but at least they left me alone in my misery after that.

In college, we would weigh in one hour before the match. In one hour, it can be difficult to rehydrate and replenish nutrients. Sometimes I would eat too much and feel bloated when I stepped on the mat. In MMA, however, we weighed in the day before, allowing us plenty of time to recover.

The NCAA also didn't allow the use of saunas or rubber suits to lose weight. Of course, we never obeyed that rule, but at least now I didn't have to be secretive about it.

The night before the weigh-ins, I barely slept. When I awoke, my mouth was completely dry and my stomach empty. Every movement, not matter how small, required my full mental exertion. And I still had four more pounds to lose.

I met my teammates at six in the morning and we left for the sauna. Each of them had several pounds to lose also. The weigh-in was at eleven in the morning so we had a few hours.

We arrived at the sauna and I immediately got to work. First, I rubbed Albolene all over my skin. Albolene is a makeup remover and moisturizer that supposedly helps you sweat more by opening your pores. I got in the sauna and started sweating right away. It was going to be a long morning.

I watched the sweat drip down my chin and splash onto the dry floor below. Each drop weighed some tiny fraction of a pound and brought me that much closer to my goal. The sweat tickled my back and I toweled off my body. I stayed in the sauna as long as I could, until my lungs burned and my skin felt like it would melt.

When my skin couldn't take it anymore, I walked out and breathed in the cool air like a glass of lemonade on a summer day. I didn't want to stop sweating so I went into the steamroom. It wasn't very hot but I just wanted to keep my sweat flowing. Sometimes steamrooms are overpowering and you can't breathe, but this one was perfect. The sweat continued to pour off my body. Or was that condensation from the air? I could never tell in steamrooms.

I went back in the sauna and then back to the steamroom. I did two more cycles of this. After the last one, I stayed in the steamroom for longer, hoping to keep my sweat going. I got out and checked my weight on the scale and my heart sank. I still had 1.5 pounds to lose. I had already wrung out every last drop of water that I could. Hector offered me a stick of gum. "I can't," I told him, "my mouth is too dry." I had no saliva left and my tongue sometimes stuck to the roof of my mouth. I really didn't want to get back in the sauna.

I lay across the tiles and breathed deeply. My fingers were interlocked on my stomach, rising and falling with each breath. My waist had shrunk so much that each breath felt embellished. I knew I had to get back in the sauna but I wanted to enjoy this brief pause on the cold floor.

"Claudio!" I called out and he walked over. He wasn't fighting, but he had come to support us.

"I need you, bro."

He helped lifted me off the floor and walked me to the sauna. I was going to do one final push.

"It will be over soon, Rollie."

In the sauna, my skin burned and I was dripping with sweat.

"Final push, man," Claudio shouted. "You can do this!"

I stood up with my final ounces of my energy. I was way past fumes.

"Think of your opponent. He is probably hurting way worse."

I started shadow boxing. My feet dragged against the dry floor and left footprints of sweat. Each movement hurt but I continued. I thought of all the water I would be able to drink, of the food that would be in my stomach soon. I did jumping jacks. The sweat flew from my fingertips onto the sauna wall.

I couldn't take it anymore, but I knew I hadn't lost enough weight.

I stepped out of the sauna and immediately put my rubber suit on.

Sweat is the body's natural cooling system. As sweat evaporates from your skin, it takes your body heat with it and cools your skin. An impermeable rubber suit prevents this process from happening, trapping the heat and moisture inside.

I covered my rubber suit with sweatpants and a sweatshirt and lay on the tile floor with the heat of the sauna still trapped inside. I wanted to keep my sweat flowing as long as possible. If I was still overweight, I was fucked. I couldn't go back in that sauna anymore. I just couldn't do it.

"This is the last time I am making 125," I said to anyone who would listen. "Never again."

When I finally cooled down and stopped sweating, I got up and peeled the layers off. I toweled myself off to make sure there wasn't any residual sweat and I walked to the scale. I stepped on and held my breath as the red digits clicked into place. I was on weight!

I shared a cab with Claudio back to the gym. When we arrived at the weigh-in, my opponent wasn't there yet and I had to wait for him. When he finally arrived, he looked sickly and pale. I stepped on the scale and made weight, but Vallejo was still 1.8 pounds over.

"Is there a sauna around here?" his coach asked Ivan.

I gulped down a red Powerade and I left them to figure it out. I went into the back room where I had stashed my food and drinks.

Shopping for food the night before a weigh-in is a timeless ritual that requires immense discipline. They say you're not supposed to go shopping when you're hungry, right? Well, imagine when you're literally starving and dehydrated. When I was younger, I used to buy everything in the store. But over the years you learn that, after drinking a few Gatorades, you get full really quickly. During the weight cutting process, your stomach shrinks, and even though your body needs nutrients, your stomach can't handle it. With a full stomach, you begin to feel queasy and all that stuff you bought the night before now seems unappetizing.

Ivan had hired a nurse to administer intravenouses to members of our team. This helps solve the problem of having a full stomach when your muscles are still begging for nutrients. An IV sends the nutrients directly into the bloodstream and muscles, bypassing the digestive system. It helps you recover much faster.

Four of my teammates were already lying down, slumped over in bed with tubes coming from their arms. The nurse was putting a needle into the arm of Sergio. He kept flinching as he contorted his face in terror. She missed the vein twice. He was yelling at her and she was blaming him for moving too much. After the third miss, she gave up and came over to me.

She wrapped a piece of elastic rubber around my bicep and tied it off with a snap. She studied my veins and then jammed the needle in and connected the tube to the clear plastic bag that hung from the top bunk of the bed.

I watched each clear drop of solution fall from the bag into the chamber and down the narrow plastic tube. Drip by drip, the bag slowly drained. I could feel the cool liquid flowing through my body as I came back to life.

Jordan had prepared spaghetti and I devoured it in minutes. When the IV finished, the nurse came over and attached another one.

"I only wanted one bag," I protested.

"This is a different type," she explained, "That was *salina*, like water. This is *solución electrolítica*."

When I finished the second bag, Claudio and I walked to the grocery store. On our way out, we saw Vallejo weighing in. "Wow, he looks terrible," Claudio said. He was having trouble standing up straight.

I bought some drinks to rehydrate. When we returned to the gym, Claudio recognized my opponent's coach sitting outside our living area. "I wonder why they're still here," Claudio said, then added, "I hope he isn't getting an IV from *our* nurse."

When I walked in the door, my teammates looked up with the guilty look of a toddler sitting next to a puddle of milk. Vallejo sat on one of our beds with an IV snaking out from his exposed arm. I walked up the stairs to the other bedroom where I took a nap on the couch.

Vallejo's coach told Claudio that Ivan had allowed him to take one of our IVs, which seemed strange to me. I felt betrayed that Ivan would allow my opponent into our den. I took a nap, and when I awoke he was gone.

The next morning, at the gym, Ivan called a meeting. His face became disfigured and he started yelling. He pointed to me, then to Claudio. He was angry with the team for letting Vallejo receive an IV from our nurse. When confronted, the other coach had said that Claudio gave him permission.

"We weren't even there!" I defended Claudio. We had been at the grocery store.

"Any one of you guys should have stopped him," Ivan said. "Or you could have called me. Why would you think I would approve of something like that? You shouldn't have even let him in this room at all. Why would you let the enemy in? This is where we live. This is where we eat. This is where we train. This is our house!"

CHAPTER
20

As if the pressure of fighting my second professional fight wasn't enough, I would be fighting in front of one of my idols. I had heard the rumors for a while, but a few weeks before the fight Ivan confirmed that Jon "Bones" Jones was coming to Lima. Jon Jones was the best pound-for-pound fighter in the world—and maybe of all time.

Jones was sponsored by a supplement company called Muscle-Tech and they were sending him on a tour through Colombia, Peru, and Brazil to promote their brand. He was scheduled to visit various gyms and promotional events, and thanks to Ivan's influence, he would be in the audience for the upcoming Inka FC event.

About a week before the fight, I passed a supplement store and noticed a life-sized cardboard cutout of Jon Jones in the window. I stepped inside and an employee began to show me some of their products.

"You're a fighter, no?" he asked.

"Yes."

"And you are fighting in the event with Jon Jones, no?"

"Yeah, how did you know?"

"I recognized you from the poster." He pulled up the poster on his computer and pointed to my picture.

Jon Jones was a member of MMA royalty. In high school, he had won the New York state championship in wrestling, beating my college teammate Jack Sullivan in the finals. Jones won after a controversial last second penalty against Jack. They had faced each other several times and were 2-2 in total.

When Jones started training MMA, he won his first six fights in less than three months—all by a decisive stoppage. In his UFC debut, he defeated another talented prospect named Andre Gusmão by unanimous decision. Next, he defeated Stephan Bonnar, who was already a big name in the sport. He beat Jake O'Brien with a second round guillotine choke.

Jones's next fight against Matt Hamill was the sole blemish on his record. Jones controlled the action early and even dislocated Hamill's shoulder. After taking Hamill down, Jones landed punches and elbows so hard on his face that they broke his nose. Jones lifted his elbow up high and brought it down on Hamill's face several more times. When the referee stopped the fight, Jones celebrated a victory. But the ref had stopped it for different reason: Jones had used an illegal technique. It shows just how far that the sport had come since the early days. Jones had used illegal 12-6 elbows, meaning he came from twelve o'clock down to six o'clock, like a jackhammer on his opponents face. Because Hamill was unable to continue, the fight was ruled a win for Hamill by disqualification.

After the fight, neither competitor was happy with the outcome. Hamill later said, "He definitely didn't lose this fight, and I definitely didn't win, but I guess the rules are there for a reason. It is what it is."

Jones continued his assault of the division, beating Brandon Vera, Vladimir Matyushenko, and Ryan Bader in rapid succession. When Jones beat Mauricio "Shogun" Rua with a third round TKO, he became the youngest UFC champion in history.

Since then, he has defended his title against some of the toughest fighters in history. He beat Quinton "Rampage" Jackson with a fourth round rear-naked choke. He choked Lyoto Machida unconscious with a standing guillotine. He beat Rashad Evans, Vitor Belfort, Chael Sonnen, Alexander Gustafsson, and Glover Teixeira. Already, at age 26, many argued that he was the greatest fighter to ever step inside the Octagon.

The news spread quickly through the MMA scene in Peru and everyone was talking about his arrival. It wasn't every day that such a celebrity came to Lima. Ivan was more excited than anyone.

The morning of the fight I got a message from Ivan to meet at the Pitbull center at 11:00 a.m. because Jones was coming to visit our gym. We waited for hours until word came that he would be arriving at 1:00. I guess Jones had already discovered Peruvian Time. When 1:00 arrived, it became 1:30. Then 2:30. By now more people had trickled into the gym. The news had gotten around and there were at least fifty people waiting.

I was annoyed since I was going to be fighting that night and I was burning a lot of nervous energy waiting around. Finally at 3:00 p.m. a black SUV pulled up. Jones walked in, flanked by a large entourage of professional-looking men.

Being one of the few people in the room who spoke English, I was in a unique position to talk to him. We all lined up for pictures with him and I forced my way to the front.

"Hey man," I said. "I'm a wrestler from the United States."

"Oh, cool," he said and smiled at the camera.

"And I was college roommates with Jack Sullivan."

He turned to me in surprise. "No way!" Then he thought for a second. "So you went to Penn?"

"Yeah."

"Oh man, that guy was my arch nemesis! I always hated wrestling him!"

"Yeah, but you beat him in the state finals, right? Apparently it was an epic match."

"Yeah, yeah. He used to do this thing where he would fake like this," Jones thrust his hands forward, low to the mat. "Then when I reacted, he would post my arms and blast through me. Did he ever say anything about me? Did he hate me?"

I wasn't sure how to answer. Honestly, Jack hadn't talked much about it. "He just said you were tough, I guess. But you guys didn't really know each other personally, right?"

"No, no. But I always hated him. He was tough."

"Yeah, he was." The people in line were shifting anxiously, waiting to meet the champ, so I excused myself.

Soon, it fell into complete chaos. Everyone stormed him, trying to get autographs or photos. The crowd of tenacious fans eventually pressed Jones into a corner. An older guy in his entourage with a black polo shirt came and grabbed him by the arm. "Jon, we gotta get out of here."

"Okay, give me a minute." He was smiling and signing autographs. I was impressed by his composure amidst the chaotic scene.

CHAPTER
21

I t was a thirty-minute cab ride to the Coliseo Chamochumbi in the district of Magdalena. Much like the last time, the mood was somber. Before a fight, the world becomes a different place, seen with different eyes. We had been distracted all day, but now for the first time, the grim reality set in.

We would be fighting in an open air soccer stadium—a rarity in MMA. The warm-up area consisted of two small rooms equipped with a 10x10 foot mat. The bathroom stalls had no doors and the toilets were all clogged and smelled terrible. There was no toilet paper. I asked one of the guards if there was another bathroom that, perhaps, had toilet paper. "No, sorry," he said. Thankfully Fuerte had brought some.

I stretched across the mat and tried to relax. I was the third-to-last fight so I was going to have to wait a few hours. Soon the fights began.

I watched Agulha battle back and forth against Karateca. Ivan and Hector sat on the opposite sides of the cage. It just didn't seem right. When Agulha caught Karateca with a stiff punch, his mouth guard went flying out and the referee stopped the fight to replace it. Agulha threw his arms in the air at the injustice. He felt that he could have finished him if the ref hadn't paused the fight. In the end, Agulha lost by decision. I tried to remain unemotional, but it was tough. I gave him a hug when he got back to the room. He was loudly protesting the call.

I never knew what to say to someone after a loss. Some people don't say anything and some people say too much. I personally always wanted to be left alone, so I tried to give that respect to others. But everyone is different.

An hour before my fight, I began to warm up. Claudio held the pads as I fired off combos. Suddenly there was a commotion by the door as Jon Jones entered the room with his entourage. I tried to focus on warming up, but he was right by the door signing autographs. One of the administrators came into our warm-up room and said we had to leave.

"What?" I thought I had misunderstood. The other fighters started gathering their belongings and moving out of the room. I couldn't get a straight answer out of anyone. They placed a group of chairs on the mat and Jon Jones and his crew sat down. A group of security guards formed a barrier, blocking me from my own warm-up mat. We were instructed to use the other room, which was not only jam-packed, but my opponent was warming up in there.

I jogged in place off to the side of the room where Jones sat. Jones was in a heavy conversation with one of his entourage. That night, there was a UFC fight between Daniel Cormier and Dan Henderson, and Jones would probably fight the winner.

"Anyone got an update on the fight?" Jones asked and looked around.

"It should be up any minute now," said one of his guys.

I imagined being in his shoes. He was being mobbed everywhere he went and had no privacy. He had come back to our locker room because people where climbing over the bannisters to get into his box. I almost pitied him.

One of his handlers explained that he had to win two more fights before he could be, without any doubt, considered the greatest of all time. I listened intently at first, but I felt weird eavesdropping, so I returned to my corner and focused on my warm up. I began sweating even though I couldn't move around very much. Just as I was finishing, Jones and his entourage stood up and went back to the arena.

When it was time for me to walk out, I draped the American flag over my shoulders and slapped high fives with all my teammates. My entrance music began to play. I had chosen *Empire State of Mind* by Jay-Z because Jones was a New Yorker and I hoped to get his attention.

I walked down the cement concourse above the rows of seating. The sky was dark, except for the lights over the cage. I shuffled my feet to the rhythm of the music and bobbed my head to the beat. I looked into the video camera in front of me with a scowl. It had been lightly drizzling that night, but thankfully they had covered the cage with a canvas roof supported by tall metal pylons.

I descended the cement stairs between rows of screaming fans. Just as I reached the bottom, the song's chorus blared. "*In New York... Concrete jungle where dreams are made of...*" I ran up into the cage. It was time for battle.

When the bell rang, my opponent came in with a low kick to my left leg. I shook it off and tried to maintain distance between us. Just then, an idea popped into my head. I didn't want to engage him at close range because of his powerful striking, but I also needed to get close to take him down. I sprinted across the cage and jumped into the air. I aimed at his head with a flying kick. When my foot met his face, I had lost much of the momentum and it hit him lightly. But I had achieved my goal of closing the distance.

I landed on the ground and immediately spun around and grabbed his legs. As I took him down to the mat, he snaked his arms around my neck in a guillotine choke. He squeezed my neck and suddenly I realized I was trapped. This wasn't supposed to happen. He was a Muay Thai fighter by training. I hadn't anticipated that he would even have any submissions, and now, suddenly, I couldn't breathe. I panicked at the thought of being submitted by a Muay Thai fighter. I pressed both of my hands against his face and pushed, hoping to pull my head out. The harder I pulled, the tighter it got and my vision started to get blurry. I gave one more hard push, and I felt his grip was slipping. I knew that I needed to capitalize so I pushed as hard as I could and pulled my neck out. It had been a close call, but now I was on top and I would make him pay for it.

I punched him in the side of the head several times. He pulled me close and tied up my arms, but I lifted him in the air and slammed him down against the hard floor with a thud. I stood up straight and unleashed a barrage of punches to his face. He pulled at my ankles and I thought I might fall down, but I regained my balance and continued punching wildly. I knew that I had to make the most of my time on top because he was so dangerous on his feet, so I smashed my elbows and forearms into his face.

When I passed to side control, I tried to punch his face but he smashed his bony elbow against the side of my head. I was on top, but I was taking more damage than he was, so I lifted my body up and started grinding my forearm into his face. I slammed my knee into his ribs with full force. The crowd started chanting, "Peru! Peru! Peru!"

I was breathing hard as the round ended. I had been in a dominant position the entire period, but it had sapped a lot of my energy.

The referee called us to the center and the second round began. Again, he low kicked my left leg. Despite all of the training I had done with Agulha, I turned my body away and it smacked against the soft thigh muscle. It hit me with so much force that I slipped and fell to the ground. The crowd cheered and my Peruvian rival pounced on me with full force.

As he came forward, I ducked and grabbed his legs, but he turned and pulled his leg out, leaving me vulnerable as I knelt on the ground. I stood up, but he hit me with a jab on the chin.

His next punch narrowly missed my face. In desperation, I tried to shoot into his legs again, but he just stuffed my head down and backed away. He kicked his leg high in the air toward my head, but I stepped back and he missed.

I was struggling on my feet, gasping for air. All he needed was one stiff punch to drop me. I started to panic. I was in over my head. I had worked with Agulha, but I still had so much to learn before I could stand confidently with a top-notch striker like Vallejo.

I came in with a jab then a right, which he blocked. As I threw the second punch, I dropped my head and shot into his legs. It was the exact combo Agulha and I had drilled hundreds of times.

I charged through him and pinned him against the cage. He went to his knees and I spun around to his back. I snaked my arm around his exposed neck. Just then he turned his body and I slipped off of him.

He immediately took advantage of the situation and climbed on top of me into full mount—the worst position in all of MMA. He began raining punches down on my face.

I flipped my hips over and scooted out backwards until he fell off me. I grabbed onto his ankle but he kicked away.

I was on my knees again and he turned around, standing in front of me. The flurry had drained a lot of my energy and I was slow to stand up. I dreaded getting back on my feet to face his strikes but I pressed my hands against the floor and started to rise to my feet.

Vallejo pulled his leg back and kicked his shin directly at my face. I saw it coming in slow motion, and raised one arm up in defense. His shin smacked against my forearm, making a loud sound.

I was stunned from the kick, but I knew I had to press forward, as Ivan had always instructed me. I charged towards him, driven by momentum and adrenaline, but something didn't feel right. As I pressed forward, I crashed into the referee. When the action stopped, I held the ref's leg in the air like an idiot.

What had happened? Did he think that I had been knocked out with that kick? No way! I blocked it! I threw my arms up to protest the stoppage. I looked to my corner. No one was speaking English and I felt lost and confused. The referee brought us to the middle and raised my hand in victory.

What? Why? I was so confused.

The rules stipulated that you weren't allowed to kick your opponent in the face while they are on the ground. Because I was coming up from my knees and my hand was still on the ground, Vallejo's last kick had been ruled illegal.

Much like Hamill's reaction to his disqualification victory against Jon Jones, I didn't want to win that way. I would rather go the distance to determine the true winner. I felt that I had been winning the fight, but that gave me little consolation.

The ring girls came out and we snapped a photo, but I wasn't smiling. On the way back to the locker room, I walked behind Vallejo. I ran up to him and shook his hand.

"*Lo siento*," I said. "I didn't want to win in that manner." He was friendly and shook my hand in congratulations. We were both warriors and he understood.

Immediately following my match, Fuerte fought and defeated his opponent by decision. In the main event, Pinedo faced Humberto Bandenay. It was a bloodbath of a fight and both fighters showed heart. In the end the decision went to Bandenay. We were all upset with the decision and thought that Pinedo had deserved the win.

After the event, I went to a bar with Claudio and Calero, my only two English-speaking friends. Ben was still in California. I bought the first round of beers and we all clinked glasses in the middle.

"Rollie, I am proud of you," said Claudio.

"Yes, Rollie you are a champion," echoed Calero in heavily accented English.

"Thanks guys, but I don't really want to talk about it. I hate the way it ended."

"But you won. Think about Agulha or Pinedo, they lost tonight."

"Yeah, I guess you're right. I just don't want to talk to it." I took a big slug of cold beer.

"This is the first beer I've had since coming to Peru," I said. I counted the months out loud. "One. Two Three. Four. I have been in Peru four months, it feels like so much longer."

"This is the first beer I've had since I turned eighteen," said Claudio, who was now of legal drinking age in Peru.

"I'm embarrassed that Jon Jones saw me fight like that tonight."

"Don't worry, Jones actually left the stadium before your fight. He was getting attacked by so many people for autographs that he didn't even see your fight."

"Great."

ROUND
THREE

" *If I draw up the balance sheet of the hours in my life that have truly counted, surely I find only those that no wealth could have procured me. True riches cannot be bought... It is not money that can procure for us that new vision of the world won through hardship—those trees, flowers, women, those treasures made fresh by the dew and color of life which the dawn restores to us.*

ANTOINE DE SAINT-EXUPÉRY, *WIND, SAND AND STARS*

CHAPTER
22

The following week, my college friend Jordan arrived to Peru. When I met him at the airport, he had two bags and a large backpack that looked equipped to climb Kilimanjaro. Back at my apartment, Jordan started unpacking his bags. He had packed more than I had brought when I moved to Peru. I pulled out my computer and started planning our trip.

"Don't we need to buy bus tickets and hotels?" Jordan asked.

"No, we can figure that out when we get there."

"How many pairs of pants should I bring?" he asked.

"I don't know."

"How many are you bringing?"

"One."

"For two weeks?"

"We can do laundry, maybe. I just have a small backpack."

Jordan laid his shoes across the floor. He had two pairs of running sneakers, a pair of sandals, and a set of hiking boots.

"Are you kidding me? What are these?"

"Water shoes."

"What for?"

"For when we go to the Amazon."

"You're joking, right? I don't even think you can swim in the Amazon."

"Really? Oh well. What about sandals? I heard that you should wear them in the hostel showers."

"I don't know. I'm just bringing one pair of shoes."

I studied the map and began planning a route down the coast. Paracas, Huacachina, Nazca, Arequipa, Puno, Cuzco. I wasn't sure if it was possible in six days. We would have to hustle.

"What's in that bag?" I asked.

"That's my med kit." He opened it and showed me.

"What are all of those?"

"Pills for different things. Imodium for diarrhea, Pepto for stomach-aches, and Zantac for antacid. Tylenol, Dayquil, altitude sickness pills. Oh, and these are malaria pills. You got those, right?"

"No."

"Well you need them for when we go to the Amazon. Don't worry, I have extras. Did you get your vaccines?"

"No."

"You're supposed to get them in advance."

"Really?"

"Yeah. Yellow fever, Hepatitis and Tetanus. I read that they check your paperwork at the airport."

"Well, let's hope they forget to ask me."

In the morning, I packed my bag and woke Jordan.

"Let's go."

I put my backpack by the door and sat down. His belongings were scattered across my living room floor and he slowly packed them into his massive green backpack. When it was almost full, he started filling the side pockets.

"Is that a flashlight?"

"Yeah, for when we go camping."

"We're going camping?"

"Yeah, in the jungle. Did you talk to Mike at all?"

"A little."

"Oh shoot, I didn't pack my hiking boots. I don't know if I'll have room."

"Just leave them, you won't need them."

"No, I got them just for this trip."

He unpacked some clothes and jammed them in, lashing the top down with a series of grey nylon straps.

"It's been over an hour since you woke up, let's go."

"Okay, let me do a final check."

"No, we're leaving."

"Okay, okay. Fine."

We got to the bus station and bought tickets to Paracas. We drove south along the beach. It was an unusual landscape where desert, mountain, and ocean met in one place. We passed many towns with flimsy wooden shacks built into the side of the hills.

At the bus station in Paracas I walked over to the counter and asked the lady if she could recommend a hostel.

"We have one right here," she said, pointing to the building behind the station. "It is just a five minute walk to the waterfront."

"Okay, great. And where do we catch the boat to the Ballestas?"

"The van comes here at seven in the morning."

After getting settled in the room, Jordan and I walked to the ocean. Seafood restaurants lined the brick promenade and men stood outside offering menus as we passed.

"Best seafood in Paracas. Two free pisco sours for you."

"*Mariscos. Ceviche. Pescado.* Two pisco sours, free."

We chose a restaurant and sat down. Because it was a Monday night in the winter, the town was fairly empty. Two mangy dogs wrestled on the walkway in front of our table. I dug around my plate of calamari, scallops, and fried fish.

We ordered Chilcanos, a Peruvian cocktail made with pisco, lime and ginger ale. It was a cool night and I looked down the beach. To the south, the shoreline curved outward into a peninsula where something caught my eye.

"Look at that fire down at the end."

Jordan turned around and noted the huge bonfire that burned in the distance. We decided to investigate after dinner.

When we finished our food, we set out like moths to a streetlamp, attracted by the allure of flames. We reached the end of the promenade and continued down an unlit street. Two stray dogs trotted alongside us, nipping each other in the neck.

We followed the road along the peninsula and it got darker as the glow of the restaurants faded behind us. The beach was blocked by a string of vacant homes.

When an opening appeared, we cut through a narrow alley to the beach. It was quiet except for the waves breaking on the shore.

"Where is it?" I looked back and forth.

"That fire was huge, it couldn't have just disappeared."

"I think it was further out."

"No, the end of the peninsula is right there."

We began to walk towards a cluster of trees back in the direction of town. My feet sank into the sand with each step and we stumbled over mounds of dead plant matter with the moonlight as our only guide.

We peered through the trees, but still saw no fire, so we continued until we came upon a beach resort and hopped over a small railing. The pool reflected the lights of the hotel.

On the other side, a high chain-linked fence blocked us from returning to the beach. We scaled it and jumped down onto the soft sand and continued through the dark. Ahead of us lay a small beach shack. *Three Little Birds* by Bob Marley bellowed from inside.

A blur of motion leapt from the base of the shack. Sand flew in the air, followed by a yelp and then barking. Before we knew it, two large dogs darted towards us. One of them looked like a husky with shorter hair, and the other one was a bit smaller and black as the night. They charged at us, snarling and snapping their jaws.

"Let's run," said Jordan.

"No, that's the worst thing to do, they'll chase us."

They stopped right in front of us. I fixed my eyes on the bigger dog. He was crouched with his front legs bent and his butt in the air. He snarled and bared his teeth. The fur on the back of his neck stood up straight like a mohawk. That concerned me the most.

I took a step back and then another. I thought maybe we could back away slowly, like in the cartoons, but the dogs followed us with each step.

"I don't know what we're supposed to do," I said between spastic breaths. We stepped back again. The dogs followed and barked louder than before.

"I think we should run," Jordan said.

"They'll chase us."

"*GRRRR!*"

"What, then?"

Just then, two men came out of the shack and whistled. The dogs turned their heads and trotted back. The guys on the porch laughed and yelled something in Spanish that I didn't understand.

"*Gracias!*" I yelled back. "Let's get the fuck out of here."

In the morning a van pulled up and took us to a small dock where we boarded a motorboat with about thirty other people. As the boat lurched away, we heard a deep laugh from the seat behind us. I turned around to see an old American man and his wife. He talked nonstop and laughed at his own jokes.

The tour guide at the helm spoke up. "To your left you will see the Candelabra." Everyone pointed their cameras over the side of the boat. The sandy mountain face reached the water's edge. A six-hundred-foot candelabra was carved into the stone. The guide explained that no one knew when it was made.

"Why can't they carbon date it?" asked the old American man.

"Because it's made of stone."

When the boat pulled out into the open ocean, our guide pointed to groups of sea lions playing in the surf. The old man started ranting to no one in particular.

"They must follow the Humboldt Current. It comes up from Antarctica and brings cold ocean waters. It's the opposite of the Gulf Stream. The cold water here is the reason they have penguins. In fact, they're even called Humboldt penguins. They have them in the Galapagos too. We went there last year. You should really go. It's fantastic."

The motorboat sliced through the ocean currents as the craggy islands appeared on the horizon. Large pelicans swooped down over our boat as we turned along the shoreline. Birds of all different species huddled together on the rocky slope.

We circled around before pushing on to the next island in the archipelago. Our guide pointed out a penguin on the rocks, among a cluster of pelicans and terns. Two fat sea lions waded in the shallow water.

As we came to a third island, the old man spoke up, "Do they ever harvest the guano? I've read that it can be very profitable."

"Yes," the guide replied. "They harvest it every seven years so they don't disturb the natural habitat of the birds. They have a group of workers who come for the whole summer."

"What do they use it for?" I asked.

Before our guide could answer, the old man answered. "It's a very good fertilizer. It's a huge industry worldwide."

"Exactly," said our guide.

"So crews come out here to shovel bird shit?" I said.

"Yes."

We turned back toward the shore.

"How were the islands formed? Were they volcanic?" I asked.

Again, the old man answered before the guide could. "Yes, this is a very heavy seismic region where the two plates," he thought for a second before turning to the guide, "Was it the collision of the Nazca Plate with the South American Plate?"

I was embarrassed for him.

"Yes, that is correct," the guide said. "The Nazca Plate is pushing into the South American Plate. That is what causes the earthquakes in the region." He looked at the old man as if to say, "*Satisfied?*"

Back on shore, we booked a tour of the nearby nature reserve. The driver was the same guide from the boat.

Once in the reserve, there was nothing but desert in every direction. The road ahead disappeared into a cluster of sandy mountains. We pulled to the side of the dusty road and got out. The guide pointed to a pile of scallop shells in a neat little mound.

"How do you think these shells got here?" he asked.

"Did this used to be part of the ocean?" Jordan asked.

"No, but that's a good guess. Actually many fisherman take this route and their trucks are loaded with scallops. They eat them and throw the shells over the side of the truck."

"Fascinating," I said.

"And this road here that we are driving on," he took a screwdriver out of his pocket and scraped a line in the road. The scrape he made was white as snow where it had been dusty brown before. "It is made from salt. There is a salt refinery over those hills where they extract salt from the seawater. They used it to build the road."

"Did we really pay for this?" whispered Jordan.

We drove over the mountain ridge and pulled off the road to another empty stretch of desert. The guide took out a paintbrush and started dusting the sand away, revealing crustaceous fossils below. He handed the paintbrush over and let us uncover our own.

"I was expecting more of a nature reserve," said Jordan, "you know, with wildlife and all."

"Yeah, the name is a bit misleading."

We stopped at a scenic overlook and followed a path to a sandstone platform bordered by a fence. On the other side, a cliff dropped off hundreds of feet to the ocean below.

Jordan turned back to the guide, "So why exactly is this a reserve?"

"It is protected by the government as a nature reserve."

"Yeah, but why?"

"Because it has beautiful scenery and views and—"

"But is there any wildlife here?"

"There are birds that make their home in these cliffs."

"But, well, does it need to be...?" His voice trailed off and he never asked the question.

We got back in the bus and drove down a hill to a large bay full of boats. For lunch, we pulled into a small fishing village.

The bay was dotted with wooden boats. The flaking paint belied years of weathering but gave them a certain charm. Nearby, workers unloaded buckets of fish.

Hundreds of pelicans sat confidently on the boats moored in the harbor, and several of them stalked in front of our table. They bobbed their elongated beaks up and down like saxophone players keeping a rhythm.

I ordered a fish called corvina and Jordan ordered a plate of scallops. A plump young woman appeared in the doorway of the restaurant wearing a light blue shirt and white apron. The pelicans all flocked to her. They pecked at each other and belched deep throaty sounds.

She held her hand closed above the squawking bird and opened her palm, revealing a chunk of fish. When she tossed it in the air, the largest of them flapped its wings and snatched it.

We paid our bill and stood up to watch. She held a small fish in her hand and dangled it above the birds. She looked at us and winked. She tossed it up, causing a ruckus as they fought over it.

Our tour guide was nowhere in sight so we walked along the beach. There was dead seal in the sand, decomposing and covered in flies. Further along we came across a dead sea lion, bigger and huskier than the seal, but also more decomposed. We saw a dead dolphin with white bones that stood out against that rotting brown flesh. Finally, we spied a large sea lion that was so decomposed that only a gelatinous pile of off-white blubber remained.

"Does this count as wildlife viewing for you?" I asked Jordan.

"It may be wild but it's certainly not life," he replied. Neither of us laughed.

Feeling queasy, we retraced our steps back to the restaurant. The pelicans were still gathered around the girl with the fish. She motioned us to come over. Without exchanging any words she handed me a piece of fish. I threw it in the air and they snatched it up.

CHAPTER
23

That night, we arrived in Ica by bus and caught a cab to our hostel in Huacachina, a desert oasis famous for dune buggy rides and sandboarding.

We woke up early the next morning and decided to explore the oasis. The town was empty, but around the corner the street opened up to a large pond. A cluster of paddleboats was strung along a buoy in the middle. Palm trees bordered the beach and a smooth stone promenade traced the perimeter.

It was truly an oasis like you see in the movies. The small town was bordered in every direction by skyscraping sand dunes. We were in a valley of sand.

We went back to the hostel and packed our bags so that we could catch the first bus out of town after our morning activities. We hoped to arrive early enough for an aerial tour of the Nazca Lines.

"The dune buggy tour is cancelled," the man told me flatly.

"What? Why? We already paid for it."

"There are not enough people going. Only the two of you signed up."

"Are you kidding me? We paid for it already."

"Well, we don't do the tour with only two people."

"Then you shouldn't have sold us the trip."

"I cannot control this."

"Give me my money back," I shouted.

"You will have to wait."

The last shred of patience had left my face and I started to open my mouth. He almost shrunk away and flinched. He reached into his pocket and peeled off some bills.

We found another tour down the street and boarded the dune buggy minutes later. It had three rows of vinyl benches behind the driver and a steel roll cage made of red pipes. Jordan and I sat in the back row and a young Peruvian couple sat in front of us. The seats had barely any padding to conceal the metal support bars.

The driver was an overweight Peruvian man who didn't speak any English. He started the engine and we lurched down the street. After circling the town we picked up a trail through the sand and left the oasis behind. We slowly climbed the dune until we went over a crest and left the town behind.

Sand dunes stretched as far as I could see in every direction. Before we got a chance to enjoy the scenery, there was a loud roar and my head snapped back over the bench. Jordan clutched the seat in front of him as his hair was blown back. We approached a small dune and the driver pressed the gas further. We hit the bottom with a jolt and exploded to the top, showing no signs of slowing down. When the front wheels went over the crest, the earth dropped from underneath us and my stomach flew up past my lungs.

I was still screaming when we landed with a thud on the downward grade. Instead of slowing down, we hit the ground with even more velocity. We shot down the other side of the dune and the seatbelt held me in for dear life.

When the slope leveled out, we executed a hairpin turn, and skidded through the sand. Even with my seatbelt, I felt like I was going to fly out of the vehicle.

After a few more terrifying stunts, we climbed up the steepest and tallest dune around. We parked at the top and the driver fetched the sandboards out of the back. They were like plywood snowboards.

He explained that this was the first of three hills we were going to visit. He instructed us to lay flat on our stomachs for this first hill. Sand flew in my face the whole way down. Jordan followed and met me at the bottom.

The driver signaled us to walk across the small valley to another dune. This next hill was slightly smaller but steeper. The driver lit a cigarette and waved his hand, as if to say, "Do whatever you want."

I strapped my feet into the bindings, leaned over the edge, and shot down the steep slope. It was over in just a few seconds. Jordan caught his front edge on a rough patch of sand and went tumbling down the sandy slope. At the bottom, he stood up and threw his arms in the air triumphantly. The front of his shirt was covered in sand and he shook it off like a wet dog.

We got back in the buggy and rode to the next slope. It was the most gradual slope of the three, but also the longest. I strapped in and rode down. When I got to the bottom, I sat down in the sand until the others came down.

It had been a lot of fun but now I was tired. The driver pulled the buggy down and lit another cigarette. The others trickled in and soon we were ready to go back.

He took us on another gut-wrenching ride through the dunes, racing over razor-edged spines and screaming like banshees each time he surprised us with a violent turn. I couldn't understand how we didn't flip over.

We climbed up one long hill and stopped at the top. The driver got out, lit another cigarette, and suggested we make one last run. The terrain formed a large bowl that was not only the longest, but also the steepest hill. I was dizzy just looking down.

I leaned forward and barreled straight down. It was going great until I hit a patch of rough sand and lost my balance. I tumbled several times before getting back to my feet and continuing with my momentum down the hill. I caught another edge and tumbled all the way to the bottom, flayed out across the sand. I groaned at the aches that filled my body.

We ran back and caught a cab to the bus station in Ica and were able to catch a one o'clock bus to Nazca. We hadn't showered and were still covered in a fine layer of sand. There was sand in every one of my pockets and in my socks and shoes.

After a two-hour bus ride we arrived in Nazca. Everywhere we looked there were agencies advertising flights over the Nazca Lines. We were immediately surrounded by people holding pamphlets about flight packages. After shopping around, we got the best deal from a guy who spoke with a British accent.

"Where are you from?" I asked.

"I am Peruvian," he explained, "but I studied in England for four years."

"You sound like a native speaker."

"Thanks man," he looked at me. "And are you a fighter?"

"Yeah, how did you know?" I asked.

"Those ears gave it away, man."

"Where do you train?"

"In Lima with Ivan Iberico."

"Oh yeah, The Pitbull. That guy is a legend."

He gave us a ride to the airport where we met the pilots. We followed them to a four-seat propeller plane that sat on the runway. We climbed into the back two seats and the pilots sat up front. The pilot's window was open. He turned around with a smile, "Ready?"

"*Vamos!*"

He reached out and closed the window. The whir of the propellers slowly increased and we raced down the runway. We lifted off and passed over plots of farmland. The whole landscape was flat and dusty, but in the distance, mountains seemed to rise from nowhere.

We banked to the left, turning almost perpendicular to the ground. I pressed my face against the glass window and stared at the terrain below.

The copilot turned around, "We are coming to first figure, *la ballena*, the whale." The pilot turned the plane so we again faced the ground and could see better. The outline of a whale with its mouth open was carved into the desert sand about the size of a football field.

The airplane continued to bank and we passed over another geometric figure. "Those are the triangles." Three triangular points jutted out like barbs. The plane leveled out again and we approached another geometric figure, the trapezoids.

"Next comes *el mono*, the monkey." We approached a geoglyph of a monkey with a spiral tail. I had seen this one before, as it was featured on Peruvian currency.

The next figure was a dog. Then came the outline of a tree, branches and all. Then two outstretched hands with fingers extended. We crossed over a road and our guide pointed out the shape of a parrot in the desert sand.

We banked and did almost a full U-turn and I saw the ground pass by through the window. I clenched the armrest tightly as we rumbled over choppy air.

The hummingbird's sharply delineated wings were made of parallel lines that resembled feathers. The spider had a large torso with pincers up front and eight narrow legs of parallel lines. The condor had the intricate geometric lines for wings.

"We will see the astronaut next."

"Did the ancient people here travel to space?" Jordan asked.

"Ha ha, no."

"So these were built by aliens, right?" I asked.

"Some people—well, some people think that."

The guide pointed to a dusty mountain face and we saw a humanoid outline. The figure had skinny arms and legs, and a disproportionately large head with two circular bug-eyes.

"That definitely looks like an alien."

CHAPTER
24

T he bus to Arequipa left at 10:00 p.m. and we had three hours to kill. We found a hostel that would let us take a shower for just ten soles. After washing all the sand away, we found a bar and downed a few pisco sours.

It was a ten-hour bus ride to Arequipa, and we arrived at eight in the morning. We debated staying to visit Arequipa but decided we didn't have the time. We rushed through the terminal and caught another six-hour bus ride to Puno.

We cut through steep mountain passes until Puno rose towards us from the shore of Lake Titicaca. We disembarked into the small bus station. I hadn't the faintest idea what there was to do in Puno. On the sidewalk outside we found a man with a bicycle rickshaw and I asked him where we should go.

"El puerto," he said.

For just four soles, he pedaled us down the road to the base of a long wharf that stretched out into the lake. As we walked out, a man with a green vest approached us.

"Do you want to make tour of floating islands?"

The old man from the boat in Paracas had ranted about the floating islands. They were made of reeds and anchored to the bottom of the lake. The natives still lived in huts there.

"Can we spend the night?" I asked.

"Yes, I can find a family for you to stay with for twenty soles each. I was born there and know some families."

An hour later, we loaded our bags onto a small aluminum motor-boat with a plump native woman and took off for the islands. She was dressed in a thick wool overcoat and a long red skirt. We navigated a small channel through the reeds as the sun was beginning to set. When we emerged on the open lake, the floating islands appeared on the horizon.

After arriving at the island, she tied the boat to a wooden post and we stepped cautiously onto the reed-covered ground. She showed us to our room, which was a small reed hut with two beds. Each bed was covered in a layer of colorful blankets stacked about a foot thick. The walls were so thin that sunlight came through the gaps. I could see my breath in the cold air. It was starting to get dark also.

It suddenly occurred to us: we were trapped on a small island with no amenities. When we arrived, we had asked about bathroom and she pointed out behind the huts. We followed a path made by wooden planks through the wet soggy reeds to an outhouse. There was no handle to flush and no toilet paper.

"What do we do if...?" Jordan asked.

"No clue."

"You should ask them."

"My Spanish isn't good enough."

The falling temperature was the most pressing problem. There was a small hut across from us that had some local crafts for sale. We went inside and found an old lady who was missing most of her teeth. An infant clung tightly to her side. I bought a lime-green woolen hat em-broidered with blue llamas. But the store was small and she couldn't find another hat. The only one left for Jordan had long earflaps and a cartoonish bear face on the front with a black button for a nose and two large eyes. And there were two bear ears on top. Faced with no other choice, he bought it.

Before we left the shore, we had bought a bottle of pisco. I poured it into a cup with peach juice and handed it to Jordan. My hands shook from the cold and I realized that I could see my breath even inside our hut. I wore a pair of sweatpants under my jeans as well as four layers of shirts. Our new hats helped too.

"This is a goddamn adventure!" I tried to elevate the mood.

"I think most people would hate this," Jordan said, "but this is amazing."

"Yeah, most people want to be sitting on a beach in Mexico sipping Mai Tais, but they never get an experience like this."

"Amen."

The woman who brought us to the island appeared and asked if we wanted dinner. We waited in the kitchen until she entered and laid two plates in front of us. There was an entire fish on each plate, scales and all.

"What type of fish is this?" I asked.

"*Trucha.*" Trout.

When we finished our meal, we said goodbye and went back to our hut. The temperature had dropped further and we started taking slugs directly from the bottle.

With the remainder of the pisco, we climbed to the top of the wooden watchtower that stood next to our hut. We passed the night telling stories and looking at the stars. It was amazing how many stars were visible to the naked eye on this clear winter night. When the bottle was empty, we retired down to the cabin. As we were getting ready for bed, the light bulb went out.

Jordan pulled out his flashlight triumphantly. "You said I wouldn't need this, but look!" he said as he hung it from the rafter with small nylon cord. I admitted that he was right.

We both wore three layers of clothes and slept under the mountain of blankets in our ridiculous hats. In the morning, our host explained that the boat would come for us in the afternoon.

"Is it possible to make a tour of the islands?" I asked.

"We have a rowboat you could take."

She showed us the old wooden rowboat. The paint was peeling off, and the oarlocks on each side were made of tattered rope. Jordan and I tried rowing, but it was hard keeping a rhythm with both oars at the same time.

"Put more into the left side!" Jordan said. "We're drifting."

Jordan and I took turns rowing until we reached another small island. We hopped off and walked around for a few minutes, but the inhabitants did not look welcoming so we struggled back to our island.

An old man who had been lingering around offered to take us on a tour and we accepted. He looked to be almost fifty years old but handled the heavy oars with relative ease. He wore dirty brown slacks and a tan sweater. He kept a steady pace and we passed several other islands. I asked him where we were going, but I couldn't understand his Spanish because of his strong local accent.

He pointed to an island on the horizon. "*Escuela.*" There were two schoolhouses with open doors. We stood outside and peeked in cautiously, not wanting to interrupt the students. There were about a dozen young children running around the room. The teacher motioned us to enter with the wave of her hand.

The kids stopped their screaming and looked up at us. The teacher explained that the students were aged four to eight. She instructed them to line up in front of us. The girls all wore bright yellow sweaters and blue dresses that reached the floor. The boys wore black slacks with white collared shirts and light blue vests.

The teacher held her hands up and addressed the kids. Suddenly they began to sing *Twinkle Twinkle Little Star*, but it was quickly apparent that none of them actually knew English. They all sang to a different rhythm.

"Trikre trikre yitter shar. Hauwy under ere yuar." They missed just about every word. One of the boys on the end gave up and started looking down at his feet. When they finished, we roared with applause.

The teacher looked pleased with our response. She raised her hands again and counted to three in Spanish. This time they sang *Row Row Row Your Boat.* We joined in singing. "Merrily merrily merrily merrily."

When they were done, they wasted no time in singing, "My yonnie ise o'r t'ocen." We sang along and I tried to emphasize the B in Bonnie. As we prepared to leave, the children encircled us in a group hug and we took a photo together.

We walked to the other schoolhouse, which buzzed like a hornet's nest. Kids zipped past in every direction. The teacher, a young man, was trying to keep up with them. When he noticed us, he walked over and introduced himself. While he was talking, two young boys circled around us. One child held a large pair of scissors and snipped them in the direction of the other boy. He chased the other boy around in a circle several times, each time snipping the scissors just inches from the other boy's face. I tapped the teacher and pointed at the boys. "Stop," he said gently and then turned back to us and continued to talk. The boys continued their game.

Jordan noticed too, and we both watched the two boys play their dangerous game. I motioned to the teacher one more time, but he still didn't seem interested, so I went over and grabbed the boy on the shoulder. *"Por favor no hagas eso."* I reached down and grabbed the scissors from his hand and handed them to the teacher, who was still talking.

Back in the boat, we pulled up to a small clearing among the reeds where three men were building a new boat. They were weaving reeds to form a sheath around the pontoon. The inside was made from two-liter soda bottles gathered together inside a clear plastic sleeve and the whole pontoon was about the size of a Banana Boat. They covered it with reeds just to make it look authentic. I bet those tourists riding around snapping photos had no idea.

Our bus arrived to Cuzco at one in the morning and we found a hostel near the Plaza de Armas. In the morning I showed Jordan around the main square, where a group of young girls performed a traditional dance and twirled their colorful dresses in unison.

A Peruvian friend had suggested I go to a place called the Temple of the Moon, so Jordan unfolded the travel-sized tourist map we had been given at the hostel. It had numbers and letters marking different sights within the city, but we couldn't find the temple anywhere, so I asked a guy on the sidewalk.

"*Templo de la Luna?*" he laughed and pointed, "Go four blocks in that direction, then ask someone else."

We did as told and stopped another guy. He looked confused, he pointed up the hill, "More higher." The narrow cobblestone street began to steepen. The thin mountain air made it difficult to breathe and we stopped for a minute. An old man hobbled up the hill towards us. He walked slowly but sturdily, supported by his slender wooden staff. I asked him how many more blocks to the temple.

"Blocks? It's still a kilometer, or more," he said in raspy Spanish. "This direction, I go too."

We looked up at the mountain ahead of us and realized that this would be much harder than anticipated. Still, we marched on, leaving the old man behind.

"*Despacio,*" he whispered. "Slow."

We came to a fork and didn't know which way to go, so we took a right. As we coasted along, the old man yelled from behind and pointed down the other path before walking that way himself.

We hurried back and followed him. He may have been old, but he was steady on his feet and he continued climbing slowly. We stopped to view the city below and then jogged to catch up with him. We took deep breaths but still panted like dogs.

"*Tranquilo.*" Calm.

He introduced himself as Benigno and I asked him what he did for a living.

"I'm very old. I don't do very much."

"Well, what did you do?"

"I worked in a church," he explained. He spoke in a gentle whisper that made it difficult to understand him.

We climbed higher, leaving the city below. The trail opened up to a highland meadow bordered by a stone wall. We came across a field of crops, which Benigno explained was quinoa. He pointed to the stone wall, "*Muro Inca.*" Then he pointed to the trail, "*Camino Inca.*"

We climbed higher and came across a large boulder that was split by a series of grassy pathways. We began to walk through, but the old man called for us to continue down the trail.

Further up the hill, we approached another large rock formation that jutted out of the earth like a breaching whale. "Temple of the Moon," the old man said. "Inca place of sacrifice." We drew closer and scaled the rocky steps up the left side. A small cave led down into the heart of the structure.

Jordan and I descended into the dark cavern. The walls were smooth and there was a mysterious source of light ahead of us. After passing into another small chamber, we noticed a hole in the ceiling about a foot in diameter that allowed sunlight to shine through onto a flat surface that looked like an altar.

The bus we had taken from Puno had shown the film Apocalypto, which depicts the Mayan ritual of human sacrifice. I knew that was a different civilization from a different continent, but nonetheless, chills ran up my spine. Was this a place of human sacrifice?

"Let's get out of here," I said.

The old man waited for us to emerge and took us around to the other side of the temple.

"Did the Incas sacrifice people here?" I asked.

"No, only plants and animals."

The old man pointed to another set of stairs that led to the top and said he would wait for us. I couldn't believe how far we had climbed already. From the top, we viewed the city far below.

We passed a middle-aged man with his young son and he addressed us. "This is a very special place," he said in accented English. "The Temple of the Moon was set up as a lunar calendar—like a sun dial but for the moon."

He brought us to a waist-high rock. "This is where the moon rays hit and refract across the Temple." He held a small wooden rod in his hands and placed it on the top vertically, like the headpiece from *Raiders of the Lost Ark*. "They had ceremonies up here during the full moon and—well, you see, I am anthropologist so I have studied these things."

He glanced towards the sky.

"Tomorrow night there will be a full moon ceremony up here. The moon will be in a perfect position," he said. "Are you guys free?"

"I have to go to Machu Picchu tomorrow," said Jordan. "I already bought my train ticket."

"Well, I have nothing to do," I said. I had already been to Machu Picchu and decided against paying the costly admission.

"Well, you are welcome to join us then. Have you ever heard of San Pedro?"

"No."

"It's similar to peyote. It comes from a cactus and the Incas took it during sacred ceremonies. The truth is that you don't get the real experience of the full moon without San Pedro."

145

He had my attention.

"We will also be going to the Temple of the Wind," he pointed to a nearby mountain peak. "It's called Wayra."

The last word rolled off his tongue with mythic zeal.

"I'm definitely coming," I said.

"Okay great, my name is Jalil." We shook hands and exchanged phone numbers.

"And you are welcome to come if your plans change," he said to Jordan.

I looked over and the old man was patiently waiting for us. Jalil was still talking, but I interrupted him. "We have to meet our friend down there, but I have your number."

We regrouped with the old man and walked to the end of the Temple. He stopped purposefully.

"I am going to continue up higher," he pointed to an adjacent peak, "if you want to come."

Jordan and I looked at each other questioningly. We were still adjusting to the altitude and it had been a difficult hike already.

"There is a *fuente natural* at the top. From the Incas. But you need money for entrance."

"A natural fountain," I told Jordan. "That sounds interesting."

We followed Benigno through the alpine meadow. There were horses roaming the countryside and locals with blankets spread out selling crafts. We left the path and started hiking up the meadow. About halfway up, we stopped to catch our breath. The old man pointed to a boulder and told us to have a seat. I tried offering it to him, but he insisted. He took out a plastic bag containing two oranges. He peeled one and handed the other to us.

"No, no, no. It is yours," I insisted.

"Take it please," he said gently.

"Are you sure?"

"Yes."

We had been hiking together up steep grade for over an hour at high altitude. He had packed two oranges and was now sharing them with two kids he didn't even know. I was deeply humbled by his generosity.

Jordan and I had not had anything to drink since our morning coffee and the orange was revitalizing. When we finished, we thanked him again and continued up the meadow. We hiked over a crest and came to a paved road, which led through a small village.

We followed Benigno about a mile down the road before coming to a welcome center. The woman at the window pointed to a chart on the glass and said it would cost us each seventy soles to enter. Jordan and I stepped aside to count our money and found that we didn't have enough. I noticed on the chart there was a student rate of forty soles.

"Him and I, we are students," I lied.

"That is only for Peruvians. You pay seventy soles each."

It was free for the old man because he was a local, but they wanted one hundred and forty soles for both of us to enter. That was an absurd amount of money for Peru. Our hostel in Cuzco had cost twenty soles a night. Our eight-hour bus ride from Puno had cost twenty soles. I asked again if we could get the student rate since we didn't have enough to enter.

"No!" she said firmly. "I cannot. They will sanction me."

I started to lose my temper.

"But we walked all the way from the Plaza de Armas." I pointed to the old man. "With him."

"I can't do anything. They sanction me," she too was losing her composure and the tension escalated. She pointed to a brochure, which showed several different archeological sites.

"You can see all of these things."

"I don't want to make a tour, I only want to see this fountain."

"But you have to pay for it all."

"GOOD! We are not able to enter. We came here for nothing. Thanks!" I began to walk away. Upon hearing this, the old man came to the window and started pleading with her.

"*Por favor, Señora,*" he said. His face was painted with genuine sadness. "Please let them enter with me. They have come a long way. *Por favor.*"

She appeared genuinely moved by his plea. He could have continued ahead and left us behind, but he stuck with us. Again, I was humbled. She looked at him and then looked at the sign. "Let me call my manager."

She returned with a sour look on her face. "He said that you still have to pay seventy. There is nothing I can do." Benigno looked distraught, but this was final.

"Good, we don't want to enter anymore," I said. "Let's go, Jordan." I was mad at her, and her stupid fucking fountain. I said goodbye to the old man and started to walk away. He grabbed my arm and walked me back to the counter.

"*Por favor Señora,* just this one time."

"I cannot."

"I promise I will take them there and back," he added.

She bit her lip and furrowed her brow. Her face showed her inner-conflict. Finally she pulled out a ticket and drew a big X on it with a black marker.

"Okay, eighty soles in total. You can only go there and back, *no más.* But don't tell anyone. They sanction me because my boss told me no."

We thanked her profusely and climbed up the trail until we came to a stone structure on the side of the path. It was built from large, neatly positioned stones and looked like a fortress wall. A small stream of water shot out of a hole at the bottom of the structure.

"Bath of the Inca," the old man said. "Guards stand at the top, there and there."

The path continued, but the old man sat down to rest.

"Wait," Jordan said, "is this the Inca fountain he was talking about?"

"No, it can't be."

I asked the old man in Spanish.

"*Sí.*"

148

"Great," I rolled my eyes.

"Well, you know what they say, it's about the journey not the destination," Jordan added with a laugh.

We walked back down the trail and waved to the woman who had let us in. Jordan and I were dreading the walk back down the mountain.

"Come with me," said Benigno.

We followed the road around a bend and boarded a small bus. As it sped down the curvy mountain road, Benigno reached into his pocket and handed the conductor some coins.

"No, no, no," I said reaching into my pocket.

He shook his head and waved his hand, ignoring my protests. We passed the rest of the ride in silence until we arrived back to the city and Benigno leapt from his seat.

"We get down here," he said as the door opened.

He hadn't explained much—or rather, I hadn't understood much—so we didn't know where we were going, but we followed him. We pushed through crowded streets until we reached a plaza with a large cathedral.

"Santo Domingo," he said with pride. I remembered hearing the words earlier when he mentioned that he had worked in a church.

"Jordan, I think he's a priest at this church," I suddenly realized out loud. "Do you think we should tell him you're Jewish? I wonder if they'll even let you inside."

"Well, hopefully I don't burst into flames."

Once inside, he led us into a small room that was constructed from massive stone blocks.

"This is an ancient Incan room."

When the Spaniards first arrived in Cuzco, this was the most sacred Incan temple, *Coricancha*, the Temple of the Sun. The Spaniards proceeded to strip the gold from its walls, and eventually built this church right on top of it.

The Incas were forced to renounce their pagan beliefs and convert to Christianity, or else suffer the Spanish brutality. As a lifelong cynic, the hypocrisy of such actions had often clouded my view of the church. But today was different. It was hard for me to reconcile these views with the generosity that Benigno had shown us, two complete strangers. His simple kindness left me in awe.

As we walked through the courtyard we passed a tour group and the guide spoke in English about their collection of Incan relics.

"I may not be able to understand a word of what Benigno says, but I wouldn't trade our tour for anything," said Jordan.

We walked out onto the balcony and Benigno pointed to an empty nook. He explained that the Incas used a large golden disc to reflect the sun into a beam during the summer solstice.

It may be easy to dismiss the Incan cosmology as mere fairytales, but even Benigno seemed to regard them with a certain respect. The sun was one of their most holy of deities, and why shouldn't it be? The sun rises every single day and brings with it warmth. It brings life and growth and harvests. The moon carries the tides and guides us through the night. What more could you ask from a divine being?

When we arrived back to the main entrance, Benigno paused. It felt like years had passed in the few short hours that we had known him. Jordan and I promised that if we were ever back in Cuzco we would come see him. We said goodbye five or six times before we actually left.

We walked to the Plaza de Armas and sat down for dinner, still spellbound by the magic of the day. "I am... just... that was... I can't believe," I began to say. "I'm speechless. Today was like a religious experience."

"I thought he was going to try to convert us at the end," said Jordan. "I probably would have let him baptize me." He paused for a moment before continuing. "Don't repeat that, if my mom ever heard me say that she would kill me."

CHAPTER
26

That night we went out to a club called Mythology. Jalil called to confirm that I was coming to the Temple of the Moon the following night. "Of course," I said.

"And Jordan?" he asked.

I turned to him.

"Well, I don't know. I already bought my train ticket."

"Okay, well I'm going," I said.

"Wait, yeah I'll come," said Jordan.

"You sure?"

"Yeah."

I stayed out until four in the morning dancing with a beautiful Peruvian girl. The next day, Jordan and I lay in our room with agonizing hangovers. Jalil called us in the morning and said to eat a big breakfast because we weren't supposed to eat for the rest of the day. We bought some bread from a street vendor but I didn't have an appetite. Back at the hostel I tried to nap but I just shifted in bed uncomfortably for hours. The minutes ticked away in the dark cave of a room, each of us trying to find some peace but ultimately falling short. Hours passed without either of us speaking. Around six o'clock we abandoned trying to sleep altogether.

Jordan shot up suddenly. "We should get ready."

"Relax Jordan, we still have four hours."

"Yeah, but—"

"We'll be fine."

"What do we need to bring?"

"He just said a few water bottles. And to dress warmly."

"Should we buy the water bottles now?"

"No, we will get them on the way."

"Okay. I just wanna be ready."

"We are ready, Jordan."

Twenty minutes later he shot up again.

"Wait, do we need to bring anything else?"

"Like I said Jordan, just warm clothes and water."

"Wasn't there something else?"

"No, I don't think so."

"I'm gonna bring my flashlight."

"That's probably a good idea."

We each fidgeted and tried to pass the time. He stood up and walked to the bathroom. He stopped at the doorway with his hand resting against the frame and turned his head back towards me.

"We should, um..." he began.

"Yes?"

"Well, uh, I don't know. Nevermind."

He had an empty gaze in his eyes and I knew that I had to hold it together for the both of us.

"This is, I think, the craziest thing we've done so far on this trip," he said.

"I think so too."

"I mean, we are going off to meet a guy that we don't even know, to go into the mountains at night to..." he paused.

My mind picked up where he left off. What were we doing? This was a bad idea in just about any way you looked at it. We didn't know anything about this guy. He could be a serial killer. Maybe he regularly lures naïve and unsuspecting tourists up to the temple to harvest their organs. We were in a far corner of a distant country. If we disappeared, it would be days before anyone noticed.

He was a small man and we were both athletes, so if we did get in trouble, we could probably run. He had been with his son when we met him, so that was a good sign. He was friendly and did seem fairly educated. But don't you always hear that serial killers are always charming and intelligent? He could be sitting at home sharpening his knife at this very instant, laughing maniacally at our foolishness.

Maybe he was part of an ancient society that still performed Incan rituals. Maybe the old man had been wrong and they actually did practice human sacrifice. Maybe they needed fresh victims every full moon. Maybe we would reach the top and be greeted by a group of torch-carrying men in brown cloaks.

"Wait, what else do we need to bring?"

"Jordan! If you say that one more time, I'm going to come over there and kick your ass."

"Okay, okay. I just want to be prepared."

"We are."

"Should we, uh, bring a knife or something for protection just in case?" He had clearly been following the same line of thought over the past hour.

"I thought about that too," I said. "But I don't think it's smart to bring a weapon while taking a hallucinogenic we've never done before. We have no idea what this will be like."

"Okay."

We sat in silence for the next hour. I was simultaneously anxious and excited. Under no circumstances was this a good idea. But before I had time to twist myself up any further, it was time to go. We gathered our things and set out into the night.

We met Jalil in the Plaza de Armas and he jumped out to shake our hands excitedly. He wore a tan baseball cap and a navy blue sweater. His other friends had backed out, he explained, so it would just be the three of us.

"How did you learn to speak English so well?" I asked.

"I lived in San Francisco for a few years in the early seventies," he said.

He talked a mile a minute and I sometimes wondered how he found space to breathe. His mind was like a typewriter and you could almost hear the clickety-clack of the keys followed by a *ding* as a new thought occurred to him and he pecked furiously away at the keys until his words were stamped colorfully across the night air.

"I also lived in Manhattan."

"What part?" I asked.

"Alphabet City."

"I used to live there too!" I shouted. "At Tenth and A."

"Ah, right near Tompkins Square Park."

"Exactly!"

"In those days Alphabet City was a tough area, but it was also bohemian and there were a lot of artists and musicians."

Jalil was Chilean by birth, came from Egyptian ancestry, but had grown up in Cuzco. He had also lived in Australia and Mexico at different times of his life. Jalil explained that he was a musician and played just about every instrument, but mostly the guitar. He still played in a band here in Cuzco a few times a week.

We walked up the long cobblestone street away from the Plaza and Jalil talked continuously. His hands whirled as he spoke, and when he got excited, he eschewed punctuation until his words mashed together and he couldn't even keep up with his own pace and his voice exploded with a pop. We entered into a small plaza and Jalil led us to the front of a church.

"This is the Plaza San Blas, one of the oldest churches in Cuzco. See that tower right there?" He pointed to a rectangular spire that narrowed in steps until it reached a point with a metal cross at the top.

"See how the tower is made of brown stones but about halfway up they change color?"

"Oh yeah, I see it," said Jordan.

"Well, I was here one night a long time ago with a girl. We were parked in my car right here facing the church. It was a stormy night and lightning struck the tower and it fell down in front of us."

"Wait a second," I said. "You're saying that you were here at the exact moment that it happened?"

"Yes, we were parked right there. They rebuilt it afterwards, but the stones weren't exactly the same and that's why they're a different color halfway up the tower."

"And you saw this happen?" I repeated.

"Yes," he said.

He led us out of the plaza and we returned to the path. As we left the city behind, the road narrowed to a small footpath. It was a cloudy night and the moon was not even visible. Several times, we ran into locals on the dark path and Jalil stopped to converse with them. He seemed to know everybody.

"Did you see that?" said Jordan.

"What?" I asked.

"That black cat that just crossed our path. It's over there in the shadows now."

"You're kidding me. Talk about a cliché." Just then it stalked carefully out onto the path in front of us, its tail sliding up and down. It approached slowly, brushing its body against Jordan's leg.

The cat followed us up the trail, weaving in and out of our feet as we stepped. In the darkness, Jalil managed to find a narrow path that split off through a cluster of bushes. We inched our way up the slope with Jalil's constant banter as a comforting background noise.

We reached a grassy path that was lined with tall eucalyptus trees, the same one that Benigno had called *Camino Inca*.

"You know, in ancient times, this path went from the southern tip of South America all the way up to Alaska. All of the different tribes along the way maintained it."

The trees fell away as we approached the top of the path. The city lights below twinkled like a reflection of the cosmos above.

The clouds had cleared and the night sky was now illuminated by moonlight.

"Look at that," Jordan pointed to the sky. "I thought you said it was a full moon tonight."

The moon was three-quarters full. Jalil put his hands on his hips and tipped his head sideways. "Humph," he furrowed his brow. "I was positive that it was supposed to be full tonight."

He shrugged and we continued up the trail.

"This is called the Temple of the Monkeys," Jalil explained. "Because you come here to leave your monkey behind before you go to the Temple of the Moon." We walked into the cluster of rocks that Benigno had shown us the day before. A labyrinth of grassy pathways cut through the enormous boulders.

"Um, you do what?" Jordan asked.

"You leave your monkey body behind. You leave the world of flesh because you are about to enter into a different realm."

We followed Jalil through the rocks, pushing deeper into the night. He showed us a smooth bench carved into the rock face.

"This was built as a lunarium. If you lay here like this," he stretched his body across the bench, "you have a perfect view of the moon."

My teeth began to chatter and a chill fell over me.

"I think we're ready," said Jalil. "Let's find a quiet place where we won't be disturbed. Sometimes park rangers come through and you can get in trouble if you're here at night."

We walked out the back of the temple and Jalil led us down a small ravine that was lined with a soft bed of undergrowth. There was a wall of earth on one side and the other was blocked by thick shrubbery.

We sat facing each other with our legs crossed. Jalil explained that the San Pedro came from cactuses that he himself had grown at his house in the Sacred Valley. He handed each of us a folded piece of paper containing coarse brown powder. It tasted awful but we washed it down with water.

Jalil gazed behind me.

"Oh look, a dog," he said.

"What?"

"There's a dog behind you," he said.

I spun around and came face to face with a small dog with tan fur and a stubby nose. It stood just a few feet behind me with its tongue hanging out of its mouth.

Jordan and I were startled, but Jalil remained unfazed. As soon as we broke eye contact, it trotted around us and occasionally poked its snout into our circle.

Suddenly it started snarling and growling off into the darkness. "Grrrr," it rose slowly like thunder in the hills. He bared his teeth into the night and began to bark.

"What is he barking at?" I spat the sentence out as one long word. "Is there something out there?"

"Oh, it's probably nothing," said Jalil with the wave of his hand. But the barking continued.

"Are you sure? Are there any dangerous animals in these hills? Like pumas maybe?"

"No, we are fine," he said, reaching out and patting the dog on the lower back. "You're a good boy, aren't you Mr. Dog?" The dog turned and looked back for a second and then resumed its tirade. "Mr. Dog is a good boy."

"Señor Perro," I said.

"Señor Perro," Jalil echoed with a chuckle. After a long pause, he suggested that we return to the temple. Jordan and I agreed, eager to get away from whatever lurked in the darkness. We climbed out of the ravine and noticed that Señor Perro was following us.

"See?" said Jalil, "He's here to protect us tonight. You're our good luck charm, aren't you Señor Perro?"

We marched once again through the stone walls of the temple and Jalil showed us several more places to view the moon. We turned a dark corner and looked up to see Señor Perro standing on top of a large boulder. The moonlight illuminated him against the starry sky. His chest puffed out and he looked down at us.

"See? He's still watching over us. Our little protector."

Jalil said we were ready to go to the Temple of the Moon and we started back towards the trail.

"Later tonight, I will show you some of the hieroglyphics they carved in the rocks."

"Are modern people able to translate them?" I asked.

"No. They haven't been able to…" he hesitated and looked straight at us. "The thing is, they weren't written by anyone from this planet, but—well, you will understand by the end of the night."

When we reached the Temple of the Moon, we descended into the cavern we had visited the previous day. I used my feet to feel each stone before lowering myself to the next step.

"Shine that light up ahead," I called to Jordan. He did so and illuminated the cavernous chamber.

Jalil placed his open palm on the cave wall. "See how smooth this stone is? It's almost like polished glass." I ran my hand along the surface and noticed that it was smooth like a granite countertop.

"It's impossible to replicate the process with modern technology. They would have to heat the entire cave to an extremely high temperature. Modern scientists are able to do it a laboratory, but no one knows how they did it here."

He led us into the next chamber. Moonbeams pierced through the hole in the ceiling onto the platform. Jordan and I sat on the altar, an audience to his one-man show. He would say things like, "Have you ever seen in multiple dimensions at the same time?"

And then answer his own question, "No, of course not. You haven't experienced San Pedro yet."

He spoke of things like "gnomes marching out of the walls," as if describing his breakfast. He explained that each mountain had a guardian spirit, called the Apu, which lived inside of it. He insisted that he once spoke to the Apu of this mountain and it had allowed him to communicate telepathically with his son. There was a fresh rose lying on the altar.

"Sometimes people leave offerings of flowers or even food," he explained. "That's why I brought this." He placed a slender canvas case onto the altar and opened it to reveal a wooden flute. "I will leave a musical offering."

He picked up the instrument and put it to his lips. The smooth melody filled the cavern. I followed the soft rhythm up each crescendo and then fell back down the other side. A sense of certainty washed over me, as if convinced beyond reason of some inexplicable truth that floated in the air.

When the music stopped, Jalil led us around to the other side of the temple and we climbed to the top. He pointed out, as he had the day before, that this whole structure was built as a lunar calendar.

I enjoyed the sound of his voice and its steady cadence anchored me to the earth. I began to notice that the rocks looked different. Not so much *different*, actually, but more similar. I sat down on a rock face and noticed a small crack that ran vertically down the middle of it. It was the crack that gave this rock its beauty. The crack gave it something that those museum pieces of polished stones would never have. I ran my fingers along the rough surface and felt each contour in detail.

I looked up at the almost-full moon. There were so many things I had never noticed before. Each crater and mountain appeared clearly delineated to me for the first time. The white light pierced into my eyes.

"We are going to go to Wayra now," said Jalil.

◇

"Try not to use the flashlight now that we're out in the open," Jalil advised. "We don't want the park rangers to find us."

Guided by the moonlight, we followed a dirt path higher into the mountains and descended a small sandy hill. Jordan shouted and I looked up. At the bottom of the hill stood a ghost-white horse that seemed to glow in the moonlight. It was looking away from us but slowly turned its head towards our approach.

We crossed through the valley floor and passed several more horses. When we reached the other side, we followed a path up the mountain. Soon, we left the path altogether and cut through brambles of thorns and cactuses. Whoever walked in front had the task of identifying thorn bushes and either navigating around them or pushing the branches aside as the other two passed.

"Smell that?" Jalil stopped and inhaled through his nose.

"Yeah, it's kind of minty," Jordan said.

"Exactly. That's the menthol you smell."

"Menthol?"

"Yes, this tree right here," he plucked two leaves and held them in the palm of his hand, "is a baby eucalyptus tree, which is where menthol comes from."

He crushed the leaves in his palm and held them under my nose, flooding my nostrils with the harsh fragrance.

"That's amazing," said Jordan.

"You like that Jordan? Here, let me give you something." He snapped off a small branch and handed it to Jordan. "Hold onto this."

We pushed through the brambles until we arrived at a dead end and had to retrace our steps down the hill to find another passable route.

Jordan clutched the eucalyptus branch at his side like it was his firstborn child. He gazed steadily ahead and climbed with vigor. We came to a boulder that we couldn't circumvent. I reached up and grabbed a crack in the rock and pushed my foot against a small ledge, pulling myself to the top. Jordan followed behind me. As Jalil came up, I offered him my hand.

"No thanks. I may be old, but I'm like a mountain goat," he hoisted himself up effortlessly.

We climbed over a final ridge and then it appeared before us: Wayra, the Temple of the Wind. We followed Jalil into the mouth of the mountain. It opened up into a large chamber where moonlight penetrated from various angles. A gaping hole in the ceiling afforded a view of the stars above, and three passageways led out towards different sides of the mountain.

I walked quietly around the temple, examining every crevice. There was a hole in the floor about as wide as I was tall. It dropped down as far as I could see into the darkness. I traced my hand along the wall in silence.

"The Temple of Wayra has incredible healing powers," Jalil said. "I often come here with people who are suffering. You wouldn't believe some of the things we have accomplished. One time I brought a young girl up here. She suffered for years from a pain in her throat. She had been to all types of doctors and they couldn't cure her. When we came up here, she sat right there on that rock."

He stretched across the smooth boulder that was angled like a reclining chair.

"You won't believe this, but the spirit of a medieval knight rode out of that wall on a horse. He took out his sword and stabbed her in the throat."

He jumped up excitedly.

"After that, she never had the pain again. We learned that in a previous life, that same knight had stabbed her in the throat, and she was still carrying around that injury in this life. But the knight undid the damage. And every single person in our group saw it happen."

I walked through an archway that opened to the outside world and started climbing the boulders.

"Be careful Rollie," Jordan yelled.

"Oh he's just fine. We're all fine. Jordan, let's follow him." They climbed up the rocky arch behind me.

Jordan still carried the eucalyptus branch at his side. When I reached over to pluck a leaf off, he pulled it away quickly.

"I can't even get a leaf?" I asked.

"Fine. You can have one." He carefully selected one and handed it to me.

"Thank you, Jordan."

I walked around the brim of what had been the hole in the ceiling inside the temple. I raced along the sandy ridge, bounding from boulder to boulder.

We came to a natural amphitheater among the boulders. "This is called the Theater of Therapy. I've seen many people cured here. You wouldn't believe..." I jumped from one boulder to another and stopped listening as I breathed in the cool air.

When he finished his story, Jalil suggested that we lay above the temple to view the moon and stars. We found a flat area on the ridge and lay on our backs to look up at the sky. Jalil and I had agreed earlier that our favorite Pink Floyd album was *Animals* and now I took my cellphone out and began to play it.

"You gotta be crazy..." The words echoed and I fell into the sky. "You gotta have a real need..." My eyes jumped from one star to the next. "You gotta sleep on your toes..." I selected one and concentrated my focus. "...and when you're on the street..." I squinted my eyes and gazed into its light. "You got to be able..." It opened up in a slow fiery explosion. "...to pick out the easy meat." The entire universe collapsed into me. "...with your eyes closed." It engulfed me.

I was a part of it and it was a part of me. We were all made of the same matter and we would always be part of the same system. If I didn't exist, that star wouldn't exist and vice versa. There was no dividing the universe into component parts.

Magnificent colorful shapes burst out of the star like neon signs in the night. With a small puff of energy, a cartoonish polygon emerged and floated towards me until it popped and fizzled out in the air. A Kool-Aid blue spiral whirled through the night sky, pulsating with electricity. I was spinning in the infinite space that projected outward.

I sat up and started across the top of the temple. When the others stood up, we began to climb back down in silence. Back in the cavern, we sat down.

"WAYRA!" I shouted and it echoed off the walls.

There was a pile of ashes at the edge of the cavern and Jalil explained that someone must have camped here. I was mad that other people had been here. I just wanted to seal this place away in time so that no one else could ever visit. No one would ever see it the way I was at that moment and that was a tragedy.

We slid down sandy slopes, trying to avoid the cactuses and thorn bushes. When we reached the base, we crossed a small brook to a clearing where three horses stood.

Jalil led us to a large boulder that rose out of the ground. "This is called the Serpent's Head," he explained as we walked around it. The stone was round except for an alcove just big enough for me to walk into. "Take a few steps back," he instructed and we followed him. From a distance it looked like a snake's head rising out from the ground with its mouth open.

There were steps carved into the back that elevated like auditorium seating. We climbed up and Jalil got down on his knees. "Here are the hieroglyphics that I was telling you about." He ran his finger along the flat surface in front of him. There were rudimentary figures carved in the rock face. Time and weather had worn them down so they were barely recognizable.

I looked around and noticed Jordan was not standing with us. I pointed the flashlight and saw that he was walking towards the horses, still clutching the eucalyptus branch by his side. He extended his hand towards a muscular brown horse and began to pet its sleek fur. Jordan hadn't said much in the previous hour and we had left him alone.

It was after four in the morning when we finally left the field and started our descent back to the real world. We passed the Temple of the Moon and the Temple of the Monkeys, and then started walking back down to Cuzco. I felt a combination of satisfaction and remorse, like when the last firework explodes in the night sky.

"We never saw Señor Perro again!" It felt like I had lost an old friend and this realization dragged me down further.

When we reached the city, Jalil invited us to get a cup of coffee and we sat down at a small café just off the Plaza de Armas.

Jalil taught us about the various types of coffee beans from Peru. He seemed to know everything there was to know about coffee. He taught us about the different wine regions of South America. He had once worked as a sommelier. He even knew about MMA. He knew about Ivan and Ben. It seemed he could talk intelligently about any subject.

When he finally ran out of steam, there was a long pause as we looked across the table. We stood up and walked out.

"If you ever come back to Cuzco, please give me a call and we will do it again! You can even stay with me."

As we walked back to our hostel, the sun began to appear on the horizon. I collapsed in bed. Jordan had to leave in an hour to catch his train to Machu Picchu. He set an alarm and I lay down to sleep.

I have a vague memory of Jordan waking up and packing his bag. He mumbled something to me but I didn't hear him.

At seven in the morning, I shot up and started frantically packing my bags. I had slept less than two hours. I had been planning on catching a bus back to Lima, but now I wasn't sure if I had the mental fortitude to brave the twenty-five hour ride.

I looked on the nightstand. Jordan had left me a small twig from his eucalyptus branch. His thoughtful gesture was not lost on me as I stuffed it in my backpack and walked out the door.

I still had a quarter of a pouch of San Pedro left over from the night before. I opened the package and poured it into my mouth. I was already in this deep, why not go all the way? I went outside and hailed a cab.

"*El aeropuerto,*" I said.

I sat in the back of the cab in a daze, watching the crumbling brick buildings pass by. At this hour, the entire city was covered in a grey pall. Without the benefit of sleep, the world around me was cold and emotionless and the buildings seemed to be etched with geometric precision.

I stepped onto the airport curb not sure what to expect. I waited in line at the LAN Airlines ticket counter and asked about a flight to Lima, but they were booked solid. I tried StarPeru and Avianca, but they were completely full.

I waited at the Peruvian Airlines counter. My temples swelled in waves of clarity followed by pangs of despair. What was I doing? I couldn't tell if the San Pedro was kicking in or if the lack of sleep was driving me crazy.

The woman at the counter said there was a flight available in two hours. I bought a ticket and passed through security to the terminal.

The terminal was a madhouse and I was a transient madman. There were no seats available and hordes of travelers milled about aimlessly. I collapsed against the wall and pulled my knees to my chest.

I was unshaven and disheveled and had barely slept, but I smiled. I was among the Olympian gods. I had stolen the sacred fire and now it burned in my mortal soul.

I saw my whole life stretched out before me, like a series of connected dots. It occurred to me that a small disruption in the chain of events might have rippled into a larger change that could have taken this moment out of the realm of possible futures. I thought about losing that match at NCAAs my senior year. Without that pain I had experienced, I would never be here today, living my personal adventure. I thanked fate for its bountiful treachery.

CHAPTER

27

The city of Iquitos is so deep in the Peruvian Amazon that you can't reach it by car because no roads go there. I met Jordan at the airport along with our college friends Harrison, Mike and two of their friends: Adam and Ethan.

From the Iquitos airport, we took three separate mototaxis to our hostel. A mototaxi is a motorcycle-driven rickshaw with two seats and a small canopy. We passed huts and shanties with corrugated tin roofs and shabby walls. Children ran through the streets, barefoot and shirtless. They played among heaps of garbage and chickens bobbed through the streets.

We checked into our hostel and went out to a local bar. In the morning, I was covered with a layer of sticky sweat. Our jungle expedition leader, Andres, met us on the sidewalk. He brought a large van with a metal roof rack and lashed our bags down one at a time.

Andres introduced us to his partner, Wilder, who was coming along. Unlike Andres, Wilder spoke no English. He was barely five feet tall and had a small frame but smiled immensely. Both Andres and Wilder had both grown up in villages deep in the Amazon jungle.

"Are we gonna see some anacondas?" asked Adam.

Andres turned around from the front seat. "Maybe."

"No way," said Adam, "how big do they get?"

"The largest one I ever saw was fifty feet."

"Uh, are you sure about that?" said Adam.

"Yes, it was many years ago."

"I think that would be a world record or something."

"When they grow over thirty feet they become magical."

After an hour and a half, we reached Nauta, a small but bustling port town with dusty streets. Every storefront opened into the street and their wares spilled out to the sidewalk.

We pulled up to the banks of the Amazon, where a string of narrow wooden boats were docked. We left Wilder to unload our bags and Andres brought us to the market. Whole chickens were laid across the counters and butchered animals hung from metal hooks. One countertop was piled with some bizarre meat.

"Look! It's monkey meat," shouted Adam excitedly.

The small creatures were skinned, leaving only muscle and sinewy tendons. You could make out each individual finger and toe. The fat and unkempt man behind the counter noticed our curiosity and cracked a sadistic grin. He grabbed one of the small carcasses by the torso and jiggled it up and down until the limbs flapped like a dancing marionette. Andres approached from behind us.

"I see you found the howler monkeys," he said apologetically.

"I can't believe people eat this," I said.

"Yeah, some people in the jungle do."

"Have you ever eaten it?" I asked.

"Yes, when I was a child. My grandfather used to cook it. I didn't know any better. But when I grew up, I never ate it again. I don't think it's right."

Andres led us back to the shore. Our boat was thirty feet long with a thatched canopy. Wilder untied the boat and we pushed off.

It was a sunny day, but the cool breeze passed through the open air. I climbed out onto the front and spent the next few hours in the sun, watching the jungle drift past. Occasionally Andres pointed out fields of yucca plants, one of the chief crops of the region. After several hours, we reached a river junction and Andres got our attention.

"Dolphins," he pointed. Two humps appeared on the surface of the water a hundred feet away.

"Do people eat the dolphins?" Jordan asked.

"No. The dolphin is a sacred animal with mystical powers," he said. "You can even swim with them."

"I'm confused," said Mike, "how can swim when there are piranhas in the water?"

"Piranhas only eat dead fish."

"What if you're bleeding?" Mike asked.

"Do you have any cuts?" said Andres.

"No, but—"

"Then you'll be fine," he said. "Just make sure you don't pee in the water," he added. "There is a small fish that will swim up the stream and get stuck in..."

We all cringed.

"I dare one of you to pee in the water and test it out!" said Adam as he cannonballed into the river. When he emerged he started swimming in the direction of the dolphins. "You guys coming in?" he taunted. We all followed in the direction of the dolphins.

"I just felt a warm patch of water!" Adam shouted. "Which one of you just peed? Everybody check yourself for the peehole fish!"

The closer we got to the dolphins the further they away they swam so we climbed back aboard the boat and continued down the river.

We rounded a bend and came upon two wooden huts raised up on stilts with thatched roofs. When we pulled up, we were greeted by three small children in bare feet and muddy clothes. A young girl waded through the water and held a spear in her hand. She thrust it down, and when she pulled it back up, a small fish flopped at the end. She dropped it in a green plastic bucket and continued wading through the mud.

Andres emerged from a hut with a ten-foot snake draped over his shoulders. "They caught this anaconda last week."

Andres put the snake around Ethan's shoulders and he posed for a picture. Just then, the snake expelled several gobs of white paste that dripped down the front of his shirt. Andres' eyes widened. "Well, he just pooped on you."

While Ethan washed his clothes in the river, the rest of us laughed until we couldn't breathe anymore. Andres led us up the rickety wooden stairs into the hut. He introduced us to a large woman who had fewer teeth than fingers. Two old men sat at a wooden table. Chickens clucked around the house and two large pails overflowed with unrefrigerated dead fish.

Andres walked over to the old men, who grinned, revealing an equally concerning lack of teeth. One man handed him a clear glass bottle with a cork in the top and a brown liquid inside.

"Want to try some aguardiente?" he asked us.

"What's that?"

"Fire water."

It was jungle moonshine. He poured some into a small glass and each one of us took swig and gasped for air.

After another hour of navigating the twists and turns of tributaries, we pulled up to a cluster of trees that rose up out of the shallow water. A platform of wooden planks stretched across the trunks. We had arrived at our campsite.

We spent the next half-hour assembling our tent amidst a swarm of mosquitoes. They were as big as hummingbirds and ubiquitous as the air around us. I would slap my arm and kill two or three at once. We had stockpiled a small arsenal of bug spray back in Iquitos, and now we virtually bathed in it.

Wilder had retrieved a wooden canoe from the local villagers, and we all got aboard once the tent was set up. We paddled to a small clearing as darkness fell. Wilder began building a fire to cook dinner, and we set off into the woods with Andres. He carried the machete and hacked his way through the vines and underbrush. The thick jungle would have been impassable without a machete.

The jungle was alive with the sounds of coooo's and eeeek's and huffffaw's that echoed through the night air. We followed close at Andres' heels as we pushed further into the darkness. The jungle came alive in my imagination. Every tree root became a poisonous snake, every bush a stalking predator.

We came upon a small marsh, and at the edge of the water lay a four-foot snake. It's yellow underbelly stood out against the dark mud.

"Don't worry, it's dead," said Andres as he used the machete to flip over.

"Is it poisonous?" I asked.

"Yes, it's the second most poisonous snake in the jungle."

"So if it bit you, it would kill you?"

"Only if you didn't get to a hospital in two hours," he said.

We were at least twice that distance from anything that resembled a hospital.

After dinner we set out in the flimsy wooden canoe again. There were nine of us onboard and the water level was dangerously close to the edge. "Now we're going to catch a caiman," Andres said with a hearty chuckle. "A small alligator."

It annoyed me that he was feeding us lines that other tourists probably gobbled up. As he paddled, he instructed us to point our flashlights towards the shore and look for a pair of red eyes shining back.

Andres pointed his flashlight ahead and told everyone to quiet down. "I see one," he whispered. He lay down on his stomach over the front of the canoe. We drifted silently towards a bed of reeds at the edge of the river. He suddenly thrust his weight forward and reached down. I heard a splash, and then silence as he lay still. He sat up and pulled his arm up, revealing a three-foot caiman that he held firmly by the back of the neck. I was shocked.

The next morning we left for another jungle trek. We pulled the boat into a narrow stream and set off into the woods.

Andres cut a branch off of a small tree and held it up. This tree was used as protection against snakes, he explained. Each tribe had a *curandero*, or a shamanic medicine man, who performed a ceremony when the child was small and in which they would be beaten with this sapling limb and the magic from the branch would protect the child from poisonous snakes. I grabbed the branch and whacked Harrison.

"Now you are protected."

Andres stopped in front of a large tree with roots like a shark's fins. Andres stopped and sliced a root with his machete and a light trickle of sap oozed out.

"Do not touch," said Andres, "it is very poisonous. In the jungle we use it for poison darts. Even a few drops of it could kill you. But the *curanderos* also use it as medicine. If you take just a small drop and mix it in with water and a few other plants and drink it, it kills all of the parasites in your system. For days you have diarrhea and vomit and become very sick. But after, it cleans your system. I do it every year."

Earlier, we had been impressed when Andres drank a cupful of water he scooped right out of the river. He must have an amazing immune system, we had remarked. Now Harrison laughed, "Some kind of immune system, my ass. These guys just poison themselves every year."

There was a skinny tree that sat alone in a clearing and Andres called our attention over to its trunk. "Fire ants," he said. Large red ants climbed up and down its stalk. "We use them for spice in some of our dishes. And also for sexual improvement."

"Excuse me?" said Harrison.

"If you let the fire ant bite your skin and leave it there, without scratching it for twenty-four hours, after a few days it makes you—you know—stronger in bed."

"Have you done this before?" Harrison asked.

"Once," he replied, "but it was with a bullet ant." He crunched his face in grim remembrance.

In everything Andres told us, he highlighted the importance of the *curandero* in Amazonian society. These shamans had come into vogue as people came to Iquitos from all over the word to take ayahuasca and participate in the shamanic ritual. Ayahuasca comes from a mixture of vines in the jungle, which produce deep spiritual visions. Many people have hallucinations of multi-dimensional odysseys or conversations with otherworldly beings.

"I take ayahuasca every six months," Andres explained. "It's like medicine for us. It restarts your life."

Andres explained the various food sources of the jungle and I got the impression that you could drop him in the jungle with nothing but a pocketknife and he could survive indefinitely. Adam asked if they ever ate bugs.

"Yes, you want to try one?" Andres challenged him.

Adam seemed pretty enthused by the idea and Andres led us over to a tree with small coconuts on the ground. Wilder split one open with the machete and pulled out a small white grub. He handed to it Adam, who looked at the two guides to make sure it was safe before putting it in his mouth. He bit down once and swallowed it.

"Crunchy and slimy," he said.

Wilder hacked his way through a thicket and cut a U-shaped section from a thick vine. "This is the water vine," Andres explained. "If you need fresh water, you can drink out of this." Wilder tipped it back and water trickled out of the end. Each one of us took a long sip from the branch.

As we walked away, Andres called for us to stop. "We are going to cut some palm leaves down and sit in a circle now. The water we just drank will make us hallucinate for the next three hours."

My jaw dropped. No way. Is that legal? Do they even have laws against that here? This is insane.

"Ha ha!" he laughed deeply. "I'm joking."

Back on the boat, Wilder navigated towards a large tree that grew out of the water. As we pulled up, Wilder jumped out and began climbing. Andres explained that he had seen a sloth in the tree.

He climbed forty feet and all we could see was leaves shaking as

Wilder chased it down the tree. When the three-toed sloth appeared in front of us, Andres pulled it off of the branch and let each of us hold it.

Wilder had cut some saplings to use as fishing poles for piranhas. As we set out in the boat, he tied fishing lines and hooks on each. It had been a long day and I was exhausted already. We navigated down a series of tributaries and approached a marshy strip of reeds that blocked our route.

We backed the boat up and gathered momentum to plow through a narrow opening. When we crashed into the reeds, we continued ten feet before getting stuck. Wilder leaned over the front of the boat and started hacking away at the reeds with the machete. He hacked large patches loose and tossed them aside. Andres used a wooden oar to push the floating plants away from the sides as the motor strained to push us through.

As they worked to free us from the entanglement, we sat around helplessly. A half hour passed and we had made little progress. We started to wonder why we didn't just give up and try to back out instead. We were only a tenth of the way through the reeds, but Andres felt confident we could make it through. After another half hour, we had only moved ten feet further into the marshy cluster. We had, in a way, passed the point of no return. The route had closed off behind us after passing through and the boat was not very powerful in reverse.

When another hour passed and we had made little progress, we started to lose faith in our guides. They had both been confident at first, but now their faces belied a more wary expression. When they needed a break, we jumped in and took turns with the machete and the oar. The sun was starting to sink lower in the sky, and the orange hue of dusk warned us of the coming night.

The mosquitoes were eating us alive as we debated our options. Ethan had been running around like a madman, trying to use any implement he could find. Now, he was insisting that our guides were wrong and we shouldn't push forward, but we should go backward instead. He spoke promptly and with certainty. He ran around shouting commands and defying the guides.

"Ethan, let's trust Andres and not work against him," I said.

"What? No, they got us in this mess."

"Take it easy, man," I said. "We will survive."

"ARE YOU KIDDING ME, ROLLIE? YOU HAVE JUST BEEN SITTING THERE WHILE I HAVE BEEN TRYING TO GET US FREE. YOU ARE NOT HELPING IN ANY WAY. SOME OF US ARE TRYING TO HELP. MAYBE YOU CAN TOO!"

I had only recently gotten to know him, and in my experience, he was a rather quiet guy. But the stress of our predicament had hit him the hardest and now he snapped. After his tirade he hung his head in embarrassment.

"Okay, captain," I said. "Hand me the oar."

We toiled away and made a major break in the reeds, but we still had another thirty feet until we reached the open lake. Now, to our detriment, the sun was setting. The color had vanished from the sky-line leaving only a dismal gray in its absence and our pace became even more frantic.

We were stranded in a swamp, hours away from any civilization. None of our cellphones worked, and even if they did, who would we call? There were no boats in the area. There were no people in the area. Maybe one of the local villagers would pass us in a canoe eventually, but what could they do? We could be trapped here for days. The idea of sleeping on the boat would be hell on earth. The mosquitoes alone would devour us alive.

It became clear that we were not going to make it through before nightfall, and we grew desperate. Jeff retrieved a long coil of orange nylon cord from his bag. "Could this help?" he asked, but Andres was indifferent. He was starting to show the strains of stress. He was, after all, the man we had trusted to guide us safely through the jungle.

We tied a small log onto the end of the rope and threw it toward a tree on the other side of the reeds. If we could only wrap the cord around the tree, we could maybe pull ourselves free. We each gave it a try but no one could reach the tree. We were stranded.

"Could one of us swim to the tree?" Jordan suggested and we laughed. The murky water was full of tangled roots and god knows what types of animals. Piranhas, caimans, and snakes. I shuddered at the prospect of even entering the water.

"Seriously, I'll do it," Jordan continued.

Surprisingly, Andres nodded his head. At this point, we were so screwed that no plan was too stupid.

"You really don't have to do this, Jordan," I reassured him.

"Well, someone has to."

After conferring with Andres, he stripped down and grabbed the rope. He stood on the edge of the boat and plunged in the muddy water. I think he started to swim before he even hit the water and I am positive that he never swam so fast in his entire life. When he reached the tree, he climbed up and tied the rope around the thickest limb.

Three of us grabbed the rope and pulled. Wilder gunned the motor and Ethan pushed with the paddle. We heaved and the boat lurched forward. Once we got moving, we cut through the rest of the swamp and into the open water. Jordan had saved us.

Andres began to turn the boat around.

"Can't we just camp on the shore here?" I asked.

"No, we need to go back," Andres replied.

Night had fallen, leaving us in complete darkness. We all started to panic. Instead of heading back through the reeds this time, we turned towards the forest. The water level was so high that the trees were submerged in water. The forest was thick, but Andres thought that he had seen an opening large enough for us to pass. It was déjà vu. We begged him to change course but he was insistent. Each of us held a flashlight so that we could find our way through the trees.

After ricocheting off one tree like a pinball, we slammed into another and became wedged between them. Andres asked us to push against the tree trunks. The sound of the hull scraping against the tree branches filled the otherwise quiet night. We pushed through, but the submerged forest became thicker and we all moved to the front of the boat to push off new trees as they emerged. When a flashlight was pointed on the tree I was pushing against, I saw it was covered in ants and pulled my hands back quickly, but not before a stabbing pain shot up from my wrist. Another tree was covered with brittle spikes that made it impossible to touch.

We reached a clearing and the only thing blocking us from the open river was a tangle of thick branches. Wilder gunned the motor and slammed headlong into them. As we broke through, the sound of snapping branches filled the night and we ducked as wooden shrapnel flew in every direction.

Back on the river, we used our flashlights to assess the damage. We tossed the branches over the side of the boat. Suddenly I heard a scream. When I came over Ethan pointed his flashlight at a spider about the size of a padlock. Before we could do anything, it disappeared under our supplies. With that knowledge, none of us could sit peacefully.

Wilder started the motor and we left the disastrous day in our wake. The thick clouds obscured the moonlight and the darkness became an unmistakable obstacle. Andres sat up front with a flashlight shouting directions to Wilder, who steered from the back. Andres instructed us to turn off our flashlights so that he could see better. We turned sharply down another narrowing branch of the river. We were still worried about the massive spider creeping underneath us and were using our flashlights to search for it.

Just then Andres yelled back to Wilder and there was a loud crashing sound. We slammed into a low hanging tree that draped over the river. We fell out of our seats as the boat bounced back and limbs snapped around us.

"I TOLD YOU TO TURN THOSE FLASHLIGHT OFF!" Andres yelled. It had been an emotional day, and finally he too had snapped. We eventually made it back, but each of us had trouble sleeping after the excitement of the day.

The next morning we went piranha fishing, but only Harrison caught one small piranha. Even after chumming the water with bloody fish guts, there was no feeding frenzy.

Andres bought a large fish off of some villagers. We stopped at a clearing with a thatched hut on stilts. Andres went inside and began cooking the fish with the native woman who lived there. When the fish was ready, we sat around the large wooden table covered in palm leaves. He plopped the large fish on top and invited us to dig in. I noticed several ants crawling on the palm leaves, a sight which would have disgusted me just days ago, but I didn't care anymore and devoured the fish savagely.

As we waited outside afterwards, Andres brought out a small wooden bowl of a milky substance made from the yucca plant and we each took a sip. It was sour and I didn't like the taste.

"This is a traditional drink in the Amazon. The old woman in the village chews the yucca plant and then spits it into a large bowl. They let it sit and then—"

"Wait, what?" I said.

"They chew it and it ferments," he repeated.

"That's terrible."

"No, no!" he said. "It's okay. Only the women chew it, because they have the right enzymes in their saliva. Men aren't allowed to chew it."

Finally, I too snapped.

ROUND FOUR

" *There's a profound need that psychology has never adequately studied—the need to experience an ecstatic state of consciousness. An experience that shatters the ordinary walls of reality and lifts a person to another plane and entirely another level of feeling. Some people seek that experience in religion and in the promise of union with God. Others seek it in sex or in passionate love affairs. Some seek it in drugs or in military battle or in music or in creative work or in an athletic performance that seems to break the bounds of the possible.*

NATHANIEL BRANDEN, *MY YEARS WITH AYN RAND*

CHAPTER

28

T hat tour of Peru had been my first real break from training
since coming to Peru. When I returned to the gym, though,
things felt different.

Rumors were circulating that Martin was losing interest in funding
the gym. Just looking around, I could tell that the whole setup was a
money pit. Ivan offered classes during the day to paying members,
but there were definitely not enough students to fund a facility of its
size, not to mention our extensive support staff. The gym couldn't
stand on its own feet without Martin's patronage. They used to call
him a "sponsor," but in reality, he just threw money at the gym.

Over the next few weeks, we began to see these rumors come to
fruition. The first to go was our chef, Jordan. He had been living in
the back of the gym and now he packed his things and hit the road.
We were all sad to see him go, as he was always good for a wisecrack
or a deviant comment.

The next one to leave was Agulha. This upset me because he had
helped me so much. They couldn't afford to keep him around so he
returned to Brazil.

The worst blow came when we stopped receiving our stipends.
Many rising MMA fighters have to work day jobs to support their careers, but we were in a unique position where Martin paid us monthly salaries. This allowed us to focus on training full-time.

Because I still had savings from my finance career, I was in a better
position than the other guys. The cost of living in Peru was low and
I had been living modestly anyway. My rent was 150 dollars a month

and it cost about two dollars to get a haircut. But now, everyone had to adjust their lifestyles.

Next, Hector stopped coming in. Hector ran much of our training during the week when Ivan was busy organizing Inka FC. Now, we were on our own for many of the practices.

Hector began focusing more on his own gym and his own fighters. His small gym in Breña was called Team Perros Sarnosos, or Team Mangy Dogs.

When Ivan opened the Pitbull gym, he took many of Hector's top fighters and brought them over. They had left their day jobs so that they could fight full-time for Pitbull and receive a salary. However, right before I arrived in Peru, Ivan cut some of these fighters from the roster. After they left Pitbull, they went back to training with Hector.

It was a sensitive subject that sometimes tested allegiances. All of my teammates were still friends with the Perros Sarnosos fighters, but there was a slight undercurrent of bitterness. Now that Hector was no longer on the staff at Pitbull, this chasm seemed to open wider.

One day, Ben approached me with some news. "I think Ivan wants you to fight Zury," he said.

"Really? I'd rather not. I mean, we're friends."

"Yeah, I agree. It's kind of messed up. But who knows? It isn't official or anything."

While it wasn't a matchup that I wanted because of my friendship, on paper it was a good fight for me. Zury was the former Inka FC champion and I was confident that I could beat him. Ivan was trying to find another fight for me, but was having a hard time.

I knew that Ivan wanted me to fight Zury, despite my protests. Since they had cut him from the team, Zury sometimes badmouthed Ivan and the Pitbull gym. Now, Ivan wanted me to beat his old pupil. Before I had a chance to give it more thought, a fight poster depicting the two of us appeared online and it was official.

Around the same time I was preparing for this, Ben received some news. For months, he had been speaking with several large MMA organizations around the world. With a record of 14-0-1, he had become a top prospect. He had spoken with Russia's largest promotion, M-1 Global, and had exchanged e-mails with Joe Silva, the matchmaker for the UFC. But in the end, he signed with Bellator.

Ben signing with Bellator was the biggest news in the Peruvian MMA community in a long time. Bellator was the second largest MMA organization in the United States. Over the years, the UFC had bought out most of the competition to secure a stranglehold on the market, and Bellator was one of the last holdouts. Recently, Bellator had been snatching up some of the top talent and had made major gains in market share.

I was confused at first when he began talking to these organizations. "Won't Ivan be upset that you won't be able to fight in Inka anymore?"

"Nah, he wants me to fight in the big leagues. It's good for Peruvian MMA and the gym."

"And you'll still live in Peru?"

"Yeah, they'll fly me up for each fight."

People from all corners of Peru came to congratulate him. It didn't matter that he was American by birth; he was their adopted son. He had been in Peru for four years and was quick to explain that he was going to be there for life. Having known Ben for a long time, I was glad to see him happy. He was among his people and he had found a home.

On August 18th, Ben further cemented himself as a Peruvian when he married Fiorella. They didn't do a big wedding, but instead had a small party at our apartment. That night, he invited all of our MMA friends over to celebrate.

Ben warned me, "I just wanted to let you know that I invited Zury. I don't think he will come, but I just wanted to make sure you're cool with it. I also invited Hector and all of the guys from their gym."

"Yeah, it doesn't matter to me at all," I said.

The day of his wedding, none of the guys from Team Perros Sarnosos showed up. I felt guilty, like I was the one who had caused the rift.

CHAPTER
29

My visa had expired so I had to leave the country and come back. Ben was going to Arequipa for some Luchas Nobles work so I decided to join him and then cross the border to Chile from there.

I was in the middle of training and I wanted to make the trip as quickly as possible so we set out on the sixteen-hour bus ride to Arequipa.

In Arequipa, Ben went up to the mountains to distribute blankets to the impoverished people. I met up with one of Ben's old friends, Scott, to watch the World Cup. Scott was a tall British man in his thirties who had been in Peru for four years but barely spoke any Spanish.

"Who are you rooting for?" I asked.

"I'd like to see Americans win actually."

"Why?"

"Because England already got eliminated. And you bloody Americans always bitch about *soccer*," he made the air quotes with his fingers. "You have no appreciation for it, but you should. And I think it would help the sport's popularity in your country. The rest of the world loves football and you guys watch that American football rubbish. Why is that even called football anyway? They don't even use their feet now, do they?"

One soccer player slid into another and he fell to the ground clutching his leg.

"See? That's what I hate about *football*," I said. "That guy barely even got hit and he is laying on the ground bitching. He's an adult, he should take it like a man."

"But football isn't a contact sport. It's not MMA. It's not wrestling. These guys out there are, on some level, performing. It's more like... a ballet."

"You're trying to make the case that soccer is a cool sport by comparing it to ballet?"

"Mate, have you ever been to a real ballet? They're talented."

"Actually, I went to a show at Lincoln Center in New York once. And you know what? I was actually surprised how impressive the whole thing was."

"You were so quick to make fun of me and you liked it too. It's typical that the two guys from London and New York can both appreciate ballet. I bet none of these other wankers could appreciate such an art form."

He had a way of making ballet sound manly in his deep British accent. As we talked, my phone buzzed with a notification. I was using the dating app Tinder as a way to meet girls. I began to show him how the application worked.

"Man, dating was so much harder in my day," he griped. "I remember when you used to have to call a girl on the house phone and speak with her mum before you could talk to her."

I had matched with an English girl named Ashley and we began chatting in the app. She was going out with her friends later and invited me to join.

"See?" Scott said. "You guys have it so easy."

That night, I met Ashley at a bar called Mono Blanco. There was a foosball table in the middle of the crowded room and large wooden beams ran across the ceiling. Every other person had a cigarette in their hand.

Ashley had dirty blonde hair and a light complexion. We ordered two mojitos and began to talk, but it was too crowded so we climbed up the stairs to the mezzanine where we could be alone.

Ashley was spending the summer in Arequipa volunteering for a charity. She still had one more year of university to finish in England, where she studied French and Spanish. Her Spanish was much better than mine. She had even lived in Spain and France for brief periods.

"I've always wanted to live in Paris ever since reading Hemingway," I said. "But I would live anywhere in the world really."

"Paris is amazing," she said.

"Have you lived anywhere else?" I asked.

"Well, I grew up in Uganda."

"Excuse me?"

"Uganda. My father is a doctor and he was doing missionary work there."

She moved back to England when she got a scholarship to a boarding school to play the flute and the piano. She also studied many different types of dancing, from ballroom to salsa. She took a salsa class twice a week in Arequipa.

"Is there anything you don't do?"

"Well, I couldn't fight like you do."

"I could teach you," I said, gently nudging her in the arm.

"I think I'll stick with dancing."

"Well, I am possibly the world's worst dancer."

"Maybe I can teach you," she said with a smile.

She took out her purse and removed a bottle of nail polish. "Do you mind if I paint my nails?"

"Ha no I don't mind."

"Well, I haven't had a chance to the past few days and I need it badly."

"Whatever you say." I was trying to be playful, but it seemed like a bad sign. Was I boring her?

Her friends soon joined us on the mezzanine and I chatted with them. When Ashley finished with her nails, she took out her cellphone and read a message.

"I've got to say hi to one of my friends downstairs actually."

"Okay."

"He's my salsa dancing partner. He's just stopping in for a minute."

"Interesting."

"He is such a nice guy. A lot of the guys in my dance classes have been creepy, but he is just a friend. I'll be right back."

"Okay."

She walked downstairs and I continued talking with her two friends. When she returned, she introduced Eddie, her salsa partner. He was a tall goofy-looking Peruvian who smiled ear to ear. He shook my hand vigorously.

Eddie talked nonstop and was friendly to everyone. He leaned around me to talk to Ashley. It was almost impossible to get a word in. He was smiling and laughing the whole time. Occasionally he would pat me on the back. "You're the man. You must be really tough. You train with the Pitbull? He is famous here in Peru."

"Yeah, I know."

I got up and excused myself to get another drink, and when I returned Eddie had stolen my seat beside Ashley on the couch.

I chatted with her friends, but I kept her in the corner of my eye. Soon, we all walked over to a dance club. Down on the dance floor the music blasted and I lost Ashley in the crowd. Her friends started dancing in a group, but I stayed on the outside.

When I found Ashley, she was dancing with some of her friends in a circle. I grabbed her and we danced lightly for a minute.

"You told me you would teach me some moves," I said.

"Well okay, you have to follow the rhythm, like this." She put her hands on my hips and moved them. "You know, actually, I don't know the guy's part. Maybe Eddie could teach you." She reached over and grabbed Eddie's arm before I had a chance to resist. "You should show Rollie how to dance." He gave me a few pointers, then we separated and I found Ashley again.

"I'm going to the bar in the other room," I said. "You want a drink?"

"No, but I'll come with you."

She grabbed my hand and dragged me through the crowd. We sat down at the bar and talked. We talked about our dreams.

"You have such a cool story," she said.

"I feel like I've discovered this secret," I told her. "And now that I know it, I can't go back. I don't want to move back to America anytime soon."

"I want to live everywhere too."

I looked into her eyes as she spoke and she looked back into mine. She stood close to me and I put my hands on her hips. We swayed back and forth to the music. Sitting on the barstool, I pulled her between my knees. When the conversation slowed, I gently kissed her.

Moments later Eddie walked over and approached Ashley. "Come back to the dance floor."

"No, I am comfortable here," she replied.

He motioned for her to speak privately and pulled her down the bar. A stern look flushed across her face. After several minutes, Eddie charged out of the room and she returned to my side.

"Wow," she said with a heavy sigh.

"What happened?" I already knew the answer.

"He just confessed that he had feelings for me. He said that I've been sending him signals, that I was flirting with him and leading him on. That couldn't have been farther from the truth. He said that I shouldn't be with you. He said that you are a bad person. He really doesn't like you."

"I knew it. He was too overly friendly from the beginning."

"Really? I never notice these things."

Her friends had gone to a club called Déjà Vu and we went to meet them. We danced on the second floor in the open air. It was late and I had to travel to the Chilean border in the morning so I finally had to say goodbye.

In the morning, I caught an eight o'clock bus to Tacna and arrived seven hours later. From there, I caught a shuttle over the border to Arica, Chile. It was a one-hour ride on the small bus and we had to disembark at customs. As soon as I arrived in Chile, I got off the bus and boarded the next one back to Peru. I stayed in Chile less than twenty minutes, but I had gotten my passport stamped and a fresh new visa.

I arrived back in Arequipa at five in the morning. It was still dark when I arrived at the hostel and I slept for a few hours.

I invited Ashley to get lunch and watch soccer ("football"). She had a few hours before her class started, but agreed to meet me.

"But I have class right after so I have to prepare some things too," she said. As we sat at the counter, she made vocabulary flash cards for her students.

"What does that word mean?" I pointed to *travieso*.

"Naughty or mischievous."

"*Yo soy muy travieso*," I said and she giggled.

We went to a nearby restaurant for lunch. At the end of the meal she was late for her class. We said a hasty goodbye and she ran out.

CHAPTER
30

Three weeks before my fight with Zury, I hurt my back in practice and couldn't move without excruciating pain. I stayed in bed the whole next day and went to a chiropractor. He showed me a plastic model of a spine and bent it into an S shape. "This is your back," he told me. I stayed in bed for several days without moving much and I went to the chiropractor every night. It was starting to get better after a few days and I was eager to get back on the mat to prepare for my fight.

Ben left for practice one night and I was alone with Fiorella's cousin Mariana who was babysitting Ghaela. I was dieting so I ate only an avocado for dinner. I put the empty plastic bag in the trashcan and pushed it down with my hand.

"Oww!" I pricked my finger on something sharp. I pulled my hand up to have a look. My finger was covered in blood and there was a deep gash on the second joint of my left index finger. I stared for a moment before realizing the severity. A piece of broken glass in the bin had sliced my finger open.

"Ahhhh!" I screamed from the kitchen. Mariana rushed to see what was wrong and I held up my bloody hand. I ran to the sink and washed it the blood away. When I pulled it from the water, it gushed again. Mariana ran to the pharmacy to buy gauze.

I applied pressure with a napkin until she returned. When the bleeding slowed, I looked inside the wound. My white sinewy tendon was visible to the naked eye. The glass had sliced my finger open like a surgeon.

I debated all night if I should get stitches. The next day I went to the gym to see what my teammates thought. They were split on the matter. Fuerte thought I needed stitches.

"Come with me," he said. "I know a guy by my house that will do it for cheap."

"How much?"

"*Cincuenta soles, no más.*"

"Fifty soles? No way."

"*En serio.*"

"No, gracias," I told him.

There was no way I was going to get stitches from a guy who charged less than twenty dollars.

"Is it a doctor?" I asked.

"*Es mi carnicero.*"

"What is *carnicero?*"

"*El que vende carne.*" The guy who sells meat. A butcher. That was the kind of neighborhood Fuerte came from—he would get stitches from his local butcher.

I never did go to the doctor and I didn't practice for the second week in a row. I couldn't do anything but run. I couldn't punch at all. I couldn't grapple because I couldn't grab anything. I couldn't even close my hand into a fist because my finger had swollen up. Pinedo was fighting in Argentina and Ivan had gone to coach him, so we were on our own.

A week passed and the cut was still gaping. It was right on the joint. In hindsight, I probably should have just gotten stiches. Instead, I bought a bottle of Super Glue. Back at my apartment, I applied the glue to the wound and pressed it closed. By some miracle, I managed to seal it without gluing my fingers together.

There was only one week until my fight and I hadn't trained for two weeks. I still couldn't close my fist, so I passed the third week without training. When Ivan returned from Argentina, he started to grow concerned that I hadn't been training. He had a lot of pride at stake.

"You don't have to fight," he assured me. "You can back out."

"I'm fine."

"This is a serious fight, you know," he said.

"I'm fine," I kept saying.

He didn't know the secret of Flu-Like Symptoms.

CHAPTER

31

T he morning of the weigh-in we went to a sauna called *Los Delfines* in Breña. It is the only sauna open early in the morning so Ivan and Hector often brought their fighters there.

I stripped down and planted myself on the dry wooden bench. Minutes later, Zury strode in with a big smile and slapped me five.

"How much weight you have to lose?" he asked.

"Just a few kilos," I tried to sound cool and casual.

"Did Ivan tell you? We can weigh in right here at the sauna."

"Yeah, that's fine."

He bounded around the sauna and talked the entire time. Claudio sat on the other end and rolled his eyes. The cut on my finger was still fresh so I kept it hidden from him.

"*Quiero comer parrilla!*" Zury said over and over again. "I want to eat barbecue!"

He talked and talked until I couldn't stand it anymore. I left the sauna and went to the steam room. It wasn't just because I was fighting him, but he was genuinely annoying me.

Still, we were sort of friends. We were always pleasant when we saw each other. I still had mixed feelings about fighting him. During a fight, you have to have some measure of hatred for your opponent. You are going into the cage with the sole purpose of inflicting damage. It was a strange position to put yourself in mentally: hammering bony elbows down on the bloody face of a friend who was writhing in agony. For this reason, people who train together typically don't fight each other.

But one of things I'd always loved about martial arts was the sportsmanship and mutual respect. I'd seen so many fights where two guys beat the crap out of each other, and afterwards they hug. You can see it in their eyes—genuine brotherly love and respect. It doesn't matter how much shit they talked before the fight; they embrace like old friends afterwards.

There is something special about an MMA fight, a unique moment in time that you share with your opponent. You are locked in a cage and battling against each other. There is a literal cage that separates the two of you from the rest of the world. When it's over, you have shared a moment together: the highs, the lows, and everything between. When all the emotions come crashing down, you remain a warrior in the presence of another warrior. I have respect for anyone who will enter that cage, win or lose.

I stayed in the sauna as Zury sat outside chatting with Hector. After my last sauna session, I was down to weight. I was dead but I tried to look alive in front of Zury. I sat on the lounge chairs and waited for him to lose the rest of the weight. Ivan had left to run some errands and I sent him a message. He said he would be there in twenty minutes, but I asked if we could just weigh in when we were both ready.

"Okay, but do not gift Zury even a single gram," he replied.

When Zury came out of the sauna we both stepped on the scale. Hector came over to watch. I was on weight. When Zury stepped on the scale, he was 0.2 kilos overweight. Hector looked up at me. "That's fine right?" Zury looking at me and his eyes pleaded me to let him off the hook.

Ivan had specifically told me not to give him a gram, and now he was 200 grams over. That was almost a half-pound. He was being weasely and lazy. He was so pitiful as he stood there begging.

I gave it to him, not because I pitied him, but because it was so pathetic that he even needed it. I was losing much more weight, but he was the one who couldn't get it done. For the first time, I looked at him in disgust.

CHAPTER

32

T he next day, I stood inside the cage and looked across at Zury. We both bounced in place as they announced our names. It was a serious moment, but I smiled. I looked at him and he smiled back.

I had been worried about my finger beforehand but now I didn't even think of it. As Ivan taped my hands, he told me he would tape that finger up tight so it didn't move.

"No, leave it normal," I told him.

"*El Loco*," he said with a laugh. He had recently started calling me that. It made me proud that, among a group of South American cage fighters, they considered me the crazy one. After making weight the day before, I said I didn't need an IV. "*Loco!*" Ivan shouted and ordered me to take one.

I still couldn't close my fist and my injured finger stuck out from the rest. During a fight, adrenaline generally masks the pain. I hoped the fight would end quickly, but I prepared myself for the worst.

The bell rang and we approached the center. I assumed that Hector had spent weeks preparing his takedown defense to counter my wrestling. They knew exactly what I was going to do: shoot a takedown. But I knew that they knew, so I decided to do the opposite.

We touched gloves and I immediately shot forward and slammed him in the face with a jab. I had the element of surprise because he was thinking about defending his legs. He started to back up and circle away. I stepped forward and put all of my weight into an overhand right. It connected hard on his cheek and a startled look crossed his face.

He had backed up further and now I shot into his legs. He sprawled—as he had probably trained hundreds of times—but instead of landing on top of me, he slumped over the side. Feeling his imbalance, I backed out and he fell to the ground. I locked my arms around his head and arm. He attempted to pull me into his guard, but I held tight.

I had practiced this position many times with Ivan. I leaned over and released the pressure. He took the bait and pulled his arm out of my hold. I then relocked my hands around his throat in a guillotine choke. I passed my knee through his guard and squeezed.

I felt a faint tap on my lower ribs. I couldn't believe it at first, but then I felt it again and the ref jumped in and stopped the fight. He had tapped out in just 42 seconds.

Ivan came in the cage and lifted me in the air. He looked so happy. He had been genuinely worried and now his fears were allayed.

Zury still lay on the ground clutching his ribs and a few people gathered around him. I went over to shake his hand and he shook it with a dramatic grimace of pain. There was no stretcher on hand, so three of the volunteers came in carrying a folding table to carry him out. I hoped that my mother wasn't watching.

Claudio fought in the main event against David Cubas. It was Claudio's toughest test yet. Cubas and Ivan used to wrestle together on the Peruvian national team. They both began fighting MMA around the same time. When their wrestling coaches found out, they were told to choose one or the other.

Ivan chose MMA and Cubas chose wrestling. But he continued to fight in underground shows under an assumed identity so the coaches wouldn't find out. He wore a mask and fought under the name Mister X, a nickname that stuck with him to this day. With a 14-3 record, he was undeniably one of the best active fighters in Peru.

That was an integral part of Ivan's philosophy: never back away from a tough fight. Most trainers would protect their fighter by waiting for easier opponents. Ivan, on the other hand, wanted to test us against the best.

I sat cageside and screamed for my teammate. Claudio tried to keep his distance but Cubas would pin him against the cage and throw knees into his ribs. Cubas controlled the pace and Claudio never got his offense going. It was Claudio's first loss in MMA.

After the event, I went to eat with Claudio at La Lucha. I wanted to celebrate my victory, but I knew he was suffering. I knew his pain all too well. My mind flashed to my NCAA loss, and it pained me to watch him cope.

Several days later, we all met back at the Pitbull Center. Ivan made sure everyone was in attendance for the important day: belt promotions. Under the luta livre system, Ivan was a black belt and he was tasked with assigning belt levels to his students. In the previous promotion ceremony, I had been promoted from white belt to blue belt. The order was white, orange, blue, purple, brown, black. There are subdivisions within each belt class in the form of bands of white tape, or stripes. After three stripes, you reach the next color belt.

Ivan gave stripes to several other students, then called me forward and awarded me three stripes on my blue belt. The stripes didn't mean as much to me as the speech he gave.

He recited the tale about how I cut my finger. He explained that he had given me the choice to not fight, but that I did anyway. He told them how I had left everything behind in New York and abandoned my career to come fight in Peru. He looked across the room slowly at all the other students lined up against the wall.

"Every one of you could learn a lot from him about mentality. He is a true warrior."

CHAPTER

33

shley had come to Lima a few days before my fight. I took her to Parque Kennedy and Larcomar. I kissed her on the railing looking out over the Pacific Ocean. I took her to get a sandwich in Miraflores, but I couldn't eat because I had to lose weight for my fight.

"Nothing at all?" she said.

"No, I still have four kilos to lose."

"WHAT? You're already so skinny."

"When you get back, I'll be much fatter," I said. "Trust me."

She was leaving for a weeklong bus tour of Peru, so she wouldn't be able to see my fight.

I took her to Barranco and showed her my neighborhood. We rented bikes and rode along the beach. I showed her the stinky fish market at the end of the beach and the long pier. Together, we searched for the small boat, *Mis Tres Amores*.

"I love that story," she said. "It's so cute."

"Well we can ride to the top of that hill there, if you want." I pointed up to the giant cross that looked out over Lima.

"Sure," she said. I liked that she was adventurous.

We rode to the top of the hill and sat on a bench overlooking the city and the ocean. I put my arm around her and she leaned onto my shoulder.

"I don't want to leave this place ever," I said.

She looked up at me. "Me neither."

After my fight, she returned to Lima.

"You're right, you do look totally different."

"Are you calling me fat?" I said.

"No, you're still very fit, but much healthier looking."

We spent the next twenty-four hours lying in bed watching movies.

"I'm so proud of you," she said. "But I wish I could've seen the fight."

"Do you think you'd actually be able to watch me fight?"

"Why wouldn't I?"

"Because it's violent and bloody."

"I'd be fine."

"What if I got hurt?"

"I just want to watch you beat people up."

That night, she fell asleep in my arms. There was much that remained unsaid, but she was going home to England. I wasn't sure if we would ever see each other again, but I knew that I wanted her in my life.

By coincidence, we were both flying out of the Lima airport on the same day, so in the morning we shared a cab. I was going to Michigan to watch Ben fight in his Bellator debut. We waited in line at the airport, but she had to run to catch her plane.

"It's gate A22, come find me," she said as I checked in. By the time I made it through security, her plane had already boarded and I missed her so we never got a proper goodbye.

When I landed in Detroit, I was picked up by Jorge, a Peruvian who lived nearby. Whenever Jorge came to Lima, he trained with Team Pitbull. It was a lucky coincidence that he lived so close to where Ben was fighting.

Jorge let me stay at his house and his son even called me *primo*, or cousin. I met his parents and cousins and they all asked me questions about Peru. They took me in like a member of their extended family.

Ben was facing Shamir "Bam Bam" Garcia, who was also making his Bellator debut. Shamir was a local Michigan fighter with a professional record of 6-0.

When Ben arrived he still had a lot of weight to lose. Ben fought at 185 pounds, which was shocking to anyone who knew him in college when he weighed 300 pounds. Even now, he sometimes approached 230 pounds between fights. Every time he fought at 185, he had to lose forty pounds.

It was Ivan's first time in the United States and he stuck out like a sore thumb. Whenever Jorge, Ben, and I started speaking in English, Ivan would tell us to shut up and we switched back to Spanish.

The lobby of the Sheraton was alive with MMA fighters. We passed Randy "The Natural" Couture, one of my all-time favorite fighters. Randy was the former UFC Heavyweight and Light Heavyweight world champion. It is hard to overstate Randy's accomplishments and his impact on bringing the sport of MMA to the level it is today. His career lasted until the astonishing age of forty-seven. He had fought in a record fifteen title fights, securing him a permanent spot in the UFC pantheon. His son, Ryan Couture, was fighting in the Bellator event the following day.

We stopped him in the lobby and Ivan was giddy with excitement. Randy was humble and took the time to speak with us and wished Ben luck.

Ben spent the entire day in the sauna until he was down to weight. His face looked hollow and he had trouble moving. He walked slowly and each step looked painful. Ben had brought an IV bag and the needle but we had been unable to find a nurse to administer it. We asked Jorge if he knew any nurses and he made a few calls, but was unable to find one.

"It's okay, my dad can do it," Ben assured me.

"But he isn't a doctor," I countered.

"He's a chiropractor though and knows a lot of medical stuff." Ben's dad had actually delivered all of his children himself in their own home.

"You sure?" I asked. "I bet we can look up a nurse in the phonebook."

"It'll be fine," he said.

The weigh-ins were held in a conference room at the back of the

Sheraton. I walked Ben down and we sat with him. He struggled to sit up straight and shifted uncomfortably as we waited. At 185 pounds, he was a shadow of his former self and it scared me. Ben's dad was up in the hotel room getting the IV set up and I went upstairs to check on him.

I found him sitting on the bed tinkering with the bag. He had taken the ironing board out of the closet and rigged a clothes hanger to the top.

"That will hold the IV bag," he said.

I walked over to the standing lamp in the corner of the room, unscrewed the top, and pulled the lampshade off. "This might be better," I suggested.

"Yes, good idea."

He held the needle and tube in his hand, turning them over and studying them from every possible angle. His mind was busy rehearsing the logistics of the procedure. We had to figure out how to attach the tube to the bag. There was a soft area at the bottom of the bag where we inserted the end of the tube.

"You've never done this?" I asked.

"No," he seemed lost in thought. "It's more complicated than I thought."

The needle had a thin plastic catheter inside. After you stuck the metal needle in, you pulled it out, leaving only the catheter inside the vein. That way, the flexible plastic doesn't do any damage as it shifts around.

A wave of panic flushed over me, but I tried to keep it together. He was the one who actually had to put the needle in. "I bet there are instructional videos online," I suggested as I loaded some videos on the laptop before leaving to check on Ben. When I returned, he was still watching the videos.

"How's it going?"

"I'm starting to figure this out," he said, "but we need a tourniquet."

"What about my belt?" I suggested.

"No, I think it would be better if we had something elastic."

I searched around the room.

"I have an idea," he said. He dug through his bag and pulled out a pair of underwear with an elastic waistband.

"But, uh, how...?"

"Can you ask the front desk and for a pair of scissors?"

I ran down to the lobby and returned with the scissors. Ben's dad cut the fabric off the underwear, leaving only the elastic band.

"This will have to do."

I went down to check on Ben. I massaged his shoulders, "Almost there buddy."

They called him up to the stage where the Bellator president, Scott Coker, presided over the weigh-in. Ben and his opponent Shamir each stepped on the scale as people in the conference room snapped pictures. After he came down from the stage, I handed him a Gatorade and we rushed back to the hotel room where he lay down in the bed.

"I need this IV. Is it ready yet? I feel awful and need it." Ben was so dehydrated that he couldn't function until he got the solution in his veins. His dad put the final touches on the apparatus.

"Now, I want to lay out some rules," his dad began. "If at any point, I feel that this is going wrong, I will take the needle out and we will forget the whole thing."

My mind started to race. Something could go wrong? I felt the room constrict around me. I walked out in the hallway and slumped against the wall. In a few minutes, Ben's brother Charles came out to sit with me.

"You can't take it either?" I asked.

"Yeah man, bunch of amateurs in there."

We waited in the hall for five minutes before heading back inside. We walked into the middle of an argument. Ben's dad had missed the vein on his first attempt.

"Just try it again, dad," Ben pleaded.

"No, it's not safe and there is only one needle left. We need a professional to do this."

"Please, dad."

"No, this was a bad idea."

Ben's brother Charles was arguing with both of them and then stormed out of the room. Ben continued drinking Gatorades and ate from the large tray of pasta that Jorge's mother had prepared. Jorge started to make phone calls looking for a nurse.

Suddenly Charles burst through the door, "I found one!" He looked like he had sprinted to the room. "I was at the hotel bar and Randy Couture was sitting a few seats down. I bought him a beer and we started talking. I told him about the situation and he said that he had a nurse in the hotel to do his son's IV. He gave me her number."

After all we had been through, it seemed like an act of God. Charles called the number and spoke to her. "She said after she is done with Ryan Couture, she would come here."

Just a few minutes later, Jorge's phone rang. It was one of the girls he had called before who was an EMT. She had gotten his message and was just a few minutes away.

Charles got back on the phone and told Couture's nurse that we didn't need her anymore. We had gone from having no options to having too many. When Jorge's friend arrived, she had to stick the needle in Ben's arm three times before she hit the vein. Ben's veins were like garden hoses usually.

"When you are this dehydrated, your veins shrink," she explained.

The next day, we drove to the Compuware Arena with Ben. He sat in the locker room and bowed his head. He had fought fifteen professional fights and now it was his time to show the world how far he had come. He was representing Peru, he was representing Team Pitbull, and he was fighting for all of us.

When Ben entered the arena, the crowd cheered. Ben had both a

Peruvian flag and an American flag draped over his shoulders. He made his way to the center of the arena and we took our position cageside.

Both fighters came out cautious and threw probing jabs from a distance. They were both undefeated and debuting in Bellator, so there was a lot at stake. Ben opened with a flurry of punches and clinched Shamir's neck. As Ben punched him in the ribs, Shamir threw his knee forward. His knee hit Ben right in the groin, an illegal move in MMA even though fighters wore cups. There was a loud popping sound and Ben waved his hand and the referee stopped the action. He shifted his cup around and said something to the ref, who walked over to us.

"Hey corner, the cup broke. I gotta get him a new cup," he barked. "Guys, you got another cup?"

I looked at Ivan and Jorge, who both looked confused.

Suddenly Jorge's eyes lit up, "I think, wait, yeah." He jumped off the platform to grab his backpack. He dug through the side pocket and miraculously pulled out a cup.

He handed it over the cage to Ben, who was still adjusting himself. The ref waved his hand, "Come here, open this cage," signaling one of us to enter. I was the closest to the cage door, so I walked through.

Ben was wearing MMA gloves so he couldn't change it himself. I stood there for a moment before realizing what I had to do.

"You want me to...?"

He was fumbling with the string that secured his shorts around his waist. I helped untie them and ripped the Velcro open. There were cameras pointed at us over the edge of the cage and I looked around. The ref stood beside us, and the three of us formed a closed triangle.

I looked down and noticed that Ben wasn't wearing any under-wear. *Goddamnit, Ben.* He held his shorts open while I reached in and pulled the shattered cup out. It was broken into three pieces.

The crowd started booing at the delay. I placed the new cup into his jock strap. I opened my mouth to say, "You owe me for this," but stopped. This was the most important fight of his life and there was

no time for jokes. We could laugh about this later. I tied his shorts
back up and left the cage.

When the action resumed, they began to open up and attack. As
Shamir was backing up, Ben came in with a right and caught Shamir
with his hands down. Shamir took another step back and Ben grabbed
his far knee. Shamir stumbled and Ben pounced on a front headlock.
He threw some knees to Shamir's body. They wound up chest to chest
again and then they broke free.

They circled and traded punches. Shamir came in for a left hook
and Ben dropped his level. He shot into Shamir's legs and swept him
to the side, planting him on the mat. Ben passed into his half-guard
and dropped elbows down on his face. Shamir stood up against the
cage and they finished the round on their feet without either fighter
taking much damage.

Only Ivan was allowed in the cage to talk to Ben between rounds.
Ben sat on the small wooden stool as Ivan shouted commands to
him. The second round began and Shamir landed a few hard jabs to
Ben's face. He threw a high left kick that hit Ben in the face. Ben's
momentum from the first round seemed to be waning and his mouth
was bleeding. Shamir became more aggressive and launched a flurry
of attacks as Ben stepped backwards. Shamir threw a low right kick
to the body, which Ben caught and grabbed Shamir's legs, taking him
to the ground. For the first time, from half-guard, Ben began landing
blows to Shamir's face. He pinned him against the cage and Shamir's
face started bleeding. Ben passed into side control and continued
to grind his elbow into Shamir's face for the remainder of the round.

In the third round both fighters were sweaty and their pace began
to slow. Ben took him down again smothered him with his weight.
With one minute left, Ben passed his guard into side control. Ben
dropped elbows on his already bloody face and threw his knees into
Shamir's ribs. The bell rang.

The ref raised Ben's hand in the air. He had won his Bellator debut
by unanimous decision.

CHAPTER
34

On my return from Michigan, I stopped in New York where I met Bellini, Brian, and Clinton for a drink. I wasn't sure how they would react—I hadn't done a good job of keeping in touch.

"I've watched all of your fights!" Bellini said. "Are they gonna let you fight for the title soon?"

"Maybe."

"If you let me know," said Bellini, "I will fly down to see it."

"Seriously?"

"Yes, I'll be there in a heartbeat."

"No way."

"Yes, I have some vacation time coming up."

It was satisfying hearing this from my old coworker.

"Are you happy with what you're doing?" Clinton asked me.

"Yes," I replied.

"Good, that is all that matters. Don't listen to anyone say anything else."

As the night gathered steam, we went out with a large crew of traders from different banks. Everyone had been following my story and they asked me different questions about my new life. We posed for pictures with fists raised. It felt like I had never left.

"How are the girls treating you down there?" Bellini asked.

"They're good," I said. "But I found one I really like."

"A Peruvian?"

"No, but it's kind of embarrassing," I said. "She's British."

"What's wrong with that?"

"Well, she just moved back to England."

"Wow, that's tough. Think you will make it work?"

"I don't know, but I think I'm gonna try."

True to my statement, I talked to Ashley nonstop the whole time I was back in the States.

"I was so sad that we never got to say goodbye at the airport," she said.

"Me too."

It had been fun seeing everyone in New York, but it was time to return home to Peru. I messaged Ashley from the airport.

"I still have an hour of layover."

"Fun times," she replied. "I'm making vocabulary flash cards."

"That sounds like fun too."

"Funner than you," she teased.

"*More fun," I corrected her. We were both sticklers for grammar and it was something we debated endlessly.

"Yeah, I thought that didn't sound right," she agreed.

"Maybe you should make grammar flash cards too," I teased her.

"But it's a one syllable adjective so you should technically put -er on the end."

"Is that the rule?" I asked.

She didn't miss a beat.

"Two syllable adjectives ending in –y change to –ier at the end. Some two syllable adjectives add –er. Some two syllable adjectives and any more than two always put 'more' before the adjective. But obviously there are always irregulars."

Then she caught herself: "I'm such a dork."

"I like that you know that," I said. "I'm stupider than you I guess."

I knew at that moment that I was in love with her.

When I arrived back in Peru, I was effectively homeless. Ben had moved out of the apartment. He now lived with Fiorella's two sisters and their two sons. I had planned to look for a new apartment, but in the meantime I decided to live at the Pitbull Center.

I got a cab from the airport and arrived at one in the morning. I was too tired to even unpack my bags. I found a free bed with old sheets crumbled up on top. The twin mattress was stained and dirty, but I didn't care. I spread the sheet out and fell asleep in my new home. It wasn't a Manhattan apartment, but it suited my needs.

I had a fight scheduled in just a few weeks against a Peruvian Greco-Roman wrestler named Sidney Guzman, who had competed at the 2004 Olympics in Athens. I began training again, but my finger still hadn't healed. I couldn't bend it all the way into a fist, and even when wearing heavy boxing gloves, it hurt to punch. Instead, I focused on grappling and would kick the heavy bag in the corner of the room when everyone else was boxing. I continued trying to work around my injury, but it was taking a toll on me. It had been a month and a half since I had cut it and it hadn't healed.

Everyone offered different theories about my finger. Some thought it was scar tissue that blocked my movement. Some thought I had damaged, or even cut, the tendon. Maybe it was still inflamed. Maybe pieces of glass remained inside. Was Super Glue a bad idea? Probably.

I expressed my frustration to Ivan. "You don't have to fight," he told me. "It is no problem." It felt like déjà vu. I looked into his eyes and saw he was sincere. I went back and forth in my mind for a few days before I finally told him that I wouldn't be fighting.

"Not this time, sorry Ivan."

"No problem," he reiterated.

I went to see a doctor—a joint specialist—and he took a look at my finger and told me that I had damaged some of the flesh around the tendon. From the Spanish I understood, he was telling me that I had irritated the casing through which the tendon ran. He told me to give it time, that it would take three or four months to heal. Ice it and stretch it every day, he told me.

I followed his instructions religiously, but in the weeks that followed my finger began getting worse. I grew discouraged and completely gave up trying to punch. At first, I would shadow box and work on my kicks, but that became too depressing after a while. I began to train grappling more. It hurt when I locked my hands or grasped an opponent's wrist, but I was able to work around it for the most part. I taught classes in wrestling and worked with the other fighters on their takedowns.

Fuerte asked me to do a lesson one day and we got on the mat between practices. He wanted to learn takedowns like former UFC champion Frankie Edgar, who had transitioned his wrestling style to MMA at the highest level. We watched Edgar's videos and broke down his takedowns. We reviewed every detail and tried to mimic his sense of timing. He did a cutback, which we drilled over and over. I taught Fuerte a series of six different takedowns, each with various finishes. We began drilling them every day after practice.

When we wrestled in practice, I would intentionally let him get to positions we were working on. Each time, he found his way to finish the takedown. His wrestling was improving in leaps and bounds. He learned quickly and I was proud that I could repay him for the infinite ways he had helped me.

In addition to wrestling, I wanted to work some submissions with him. I began scouring videos online for new moves and came across a submission called the Twister, which was made famous by a Los Angeles-based jiu-jitsu black belt named Eddie Bravo.

In 2003 Eddie Bravo had come out of relative obscurity to knock off the one of the all-time greats, Royler Gracie, at the jiu-jitsu world championships. I watched his videos online and deconstructed his techniques. Fuerte and I drilled the Twister hundreds of times. We drilled it every day and figured out unorthodox setups. It was similar to a wrestling position that I knew, so it blended well into my style. I practiced every variation and soon I began using it to submit people in practice. Some days I would successfully hit it two or three times in one practice, even though all my partners knew it was coming. While my boxing abilities atrophied, I found other ways to improve.

It was hard to believe that Fuerte had just started training martial arts two years earlier. He was not only a natural athlete, but also an incredibly hard worker. He had a certain toughness that you just can't teach. He gritted his teeth and never complained. It was rare that he was sidelined with an injury and he never made excuses.

Representatives from the UFC had recently done a tour through South America to scout new talent. They were trying to expand their reach into the Latin American markets and wanted homegrown talent. Ivan took us all to meet with one of their representatives one day. Unfortunately, simply living in Peru was not enough to be considered Latin American, so I was out of contention. They were looking for fighters to fill the Latin American edition of their reality show, The Ultimate Fighter (TUF).

I was thrilled when I heard that Fuerte had been selected. This was great for Peru and Team Pitbull, but it meant that my teammate and friend would be leaving. The UFC had selected him for a special program where they would sponsor him to train at American Top Team in Coconut Creek, Florida. It was one of the top MMA gyms in the United States and consistently produced and trained fighters in the upper echelons of the major promotions.

It was the opportunity of a lifetime for Fuerte, who had all the tools to succeed at the top level. His work ethic and talent would surely shine though in his new training camp. For someone who had never traveled outside of the country, this was a huge opportunity.

Fuerte's last day of training was a special day at the gym. Ivan made sure everyone was there. All the other guys had mischievous grins on their faces, but I didn't know what to expect. We were fulfilling a Pitbull tradition of saying goodbye to a fighter.

"*Guantes!*" Ivan called out. "Boxing gloves!"

There were twenty-three of us in the room that day. As a goodbye present to Fuerte, he was going to do one minute of sparring with each person in the gym.

He started off with some of the younger fighters, each of them eager to prove their value against the seasoned professional who was heading off to the UFC. Fuerte was clearly trying to pace himself as he handled them easily. Pinedo stepped in against him and they stood on their feet trading hard blows to the face. Fuerte was starting to tire, and the opponents continued. Claudio came in and took him down and beat on his ribs. By this time, Fuerte had slowed down and was breathing hard.

Ivan sent me in next, but I couldn't box so we just wrestled. I took Fuerte down in five seconds and Ivan told me to let him go and I stood back up. He slowly lifted one knee, then the other, like he was trying to hoist a grand piano on his back. I took him down another three times before I held him down and let him catch his breath. Fuerte was drowning in sweat and I felt bad for him. He had been fending off attackers for almost twenty minutes.

Kike opened with a hard jab and a pop-pop-pop of combinations. Fuerte was struggling to stay standing as Kike beat on him mercilessly. Fuerte just covered his face as he received a savage pounding.

Ivan was the last to go with him. Someone had to lift Fuerte to his feet. Everyone chanted and shouted encouragement. *"Vamos Fuerte!" "Ultimo minuto!"* He slumped over and put his hands on his knees. Ivan was one of the meanest guys to spar with; he never gave you an inch. But this day, Ivan showed a rare flash of mercy and toyed with Fuerte. He pressed forward but only faked attacks and circled. Each time he faked a jab, Fuerte stiffened up as if expecting the worst, but it never came. We were all proud at the heart Fuerte had shown.

CHAPTER
36

Ashley and I had defied the extreme distance and continued talking. We talked every day and it became a ritual I couldn't do without. I had never fallen for a girl so quickly.

"I have to get to bed soon," she would say, "so we can't talk that long tonight." Two hours later we would struggle to get off the phone.

I told her about how I thought that she wasn't into me when we first met because she was painting her nails at the bar in Arequipa.

"Really? I never would have thought of that. I just had to paint my nails, so I did."

That was the kind of girl Ashley was: no bullshit. She did what she wanted and said what was on her mind. She didn't let me get away with anything either. When I complained about my finger for weeks, she made me promise I would go to another doctor the following day.

One afternoon after practice, Kike came over to my apartment. He and his girlfriend had been fighting. The three of us had gone to a Halloween party together a few weeks before. I had dressed as Captain America and Kike dressed as a construction worker. He held a small stop sign and pretended to direct traffic. When his girlfriend started talking to a guy in the corner of the party, Kike lost it. He charged and slammed the stop sign down over the guy's head, causing a scene. Security was called.

"I don't know," he explained, "I am loco."

There was something about fighters. Maybe it was the thing drove us into the cage in the first place. We were loco.

Kike thought I was loco for being with Ashley.

"You barely even know this girl," he said. "How many times have you even been with her?"

He was right that I had barely spent any time with her. But it didn't matter—I just knew that she was the one for me.

"That is not important," I replied. "We're in love." Even though I hadn't told Ashley I loved her yet, it was only a matter of time.

"No way, huevón," he said, shaking his head. "All of the other girls here in Peru, and you want one in England?"

Being an American in Peru was like being a rockstar sometimes. They even have a slang word for girls that like gringos: bricheras. Everyone in Lima knew which bars were full of them. Again, Kike had a point. I was missing out on a lot of opportunities, but I didn't care. I didn't want to be with anyone else.

Almost right away Ashley and I realized that we both wanted to live in some distant country and that our lives could still line up. She wanted to teach English to children. Like Ben, her desire to help others inspired me. Soon, we began planning our life together.

"But won't you get sick of me?" she said.

"Never," I replied.

"Good, me neither. I can't wait to be with you every day."

Kike had fallen asleep on my couch and I began texting Ashley. We discussed all of the improbable places we could live together.

"I'd happily come to Lima," she said, "but do you want to move away from there?"

"I don't want to, but going somewhere else with you would be fun. I'm really open to whatever works for you."

I had told her before that I would move wherever she could find a job teaching.

"I hate this pressure though. You can't base your life on my decision!" she replied.

"Yeah, I can. I can do whatever I want."

She was messaging me from England, which was five hours ahead, so it was getting late.

"I'm still wide awake," she said. "You're getting me super excited.

But can you really imagine spending every day with me?" she asked.

"I'd be really happy."

"I want the exact same, but sometimes I can't believe my luck. You're everything I look for in a guy."

"I think we're perfect," I said. "I am usually so much less sappy, but you make me crazy."

Maybe some of Kike's loco had rubbed off on me.

"I love it when you say stuff like that."

I fixated on the second word she had said. Love.

When Kike woke up and left, I called Ashley.

"I love you," I said into the screen.

"Wait, what?" she said with a gasp. "I just—I wasn't expecting that."

There was a long pause.

"I just..."

"It's okay, babe," I interrupted. "I am going to go now. Goodnight."

And I hung up the phone.

CHAPTER

37

That night, Ivan invited me to go to a cockfight. It seemed like a good distraction so I caught a cab to El Rosedal. When I arrived, the fights had already started and I could hear the fans screaming. El Rosedal is not an arena or a stadium, but a pit. The floors are dirty brushed cement, varnished over the years with layers of beer and spit. At a table in the front, you can order anticuchos, or cow hearts, that come on skewers.

I found a seat with Ivan and his friends near the top row of benches. In El Rosedal there are no bad seats. The stands are steep enough that, even in the back row, we were practically on top of the action.

A new fight began and two trainers each cradled their roosters in their arms. One was black and white with a bright red coxcomb and the other was mostly brown with speckled white feathers. The trainers met in the center, each one held his rooster like a quarterback handing off a football. They thrust them to the center until they pecked at each other. The trainers pulled them back and pushed them forward again, until they became more aggressive. One trained swatted the palm of his hand across his rooster's head. The pit was lined with a green cement floor and surrounded by a waist-high yellow brick wall.

"I want to put a bet on this," I told Ivan's friend.

"Which one?" he asked.

"Hm," I faced the birds, "The one that is white and black."

"How much?"

"Fifty soles."

He shouted to a man four rows ahead when then confirmed my bet with a thumbs-up. The two roosters met in the center and attacked each other immediately, thrusting their beaks forward at difficult angles, each trying to counter attack with more force.

Ivan explained the rules to me. There was one eight-minute round and the winner was the bird that killed or maimed the other. They had sharp plastic barbs fastened to the back of their talons.

"What if neither dies?" I asked.

"*Empate*," he said. Tie.

The roosters flapped their wings forcefully and you could hear them cut through the air in swift intervals. The rooster I had bet on seemed to be winning but I couldn't tell. The other rooster turned around and started to run away. My rooster chased him but then gave up and stood in the middle of the ring with his chest puffed out.

"What happens if they don't want to fight anymore?" I asked. But before he could reply, the trainers below answered my question. They both climbed into the ring and lifted up their birds. They brought them to the center and thrust them toward each other. This time, my rooster was on the receiving end of the violence and started backing away. As suddenly as it began, my rooster was on the ground and the other bird lashed out. My bird keeled over and lay sprawled across the green surface, limp and twitching.

Before the next fight, Ivan and I bet ten soles against each other. He let me pick the bird, even though they all looked the same to me. When my bird stood triumphantly over its dead rival, Ivan handed me ten soles. We bet on every fight after that. With beginner's luck, I won the first five bets.

Sometimes, one bird would crouch to the ground and bow its head passively like a dog rolling over on its stomach in submission. The other rooster would peck at it several times and then stand indifferently over its rival. A man would get on the microphone and start counting. "Uno. Dos. Tres..." Ivan explained that they had thirty seconds to get up or the fight was over.

The roosters were bred specifically to be aggressive and this passivity was a shameful behavior that reflected poorly on the trainer and the breeder. I could see how cockfighting fit Ivan's personality perfectly.

Ivan was recognized by numerous people who passed and each of them stopped to pay respects. There was squawking and shouting and it smelled of cigarette smoke and sawdust.

Ivan's friend had a rooster coming up next. He brought it over to the stands where we sat and began fastening the white plastic barb to its talons with thick white tape. I bet fifty soles on his bird, but unfortunately, it ran away the whole time and was eventually counted out by the judge.

Ivan and I continued betting the whole night. During one of the final fights of the night, my bird was winning, and suddenly his rooster sprang into action and came from behind for a win.

"*Un gallo herido es el más peligroso,*" he said with a wink. An injured rooster is the most dangerous. I nodded my head in agreement. Flu-Like Symptoms.

When I returned home that night I read a message from Ashley.

"So now I really can't sleep. I'm so sorry. You must be so disappointed. I've already said to you how I can't believe a guy like you even talks to a girl like me. So you telling me you love me came as such a shock. I guess I need to have a bit more confidence in myself."

I wrote back to her.

"I love you, I am more sure of it than I've ever been and I want nothing more than to be with you. I really don't care what you say, because that doesn't change how I feel. I wouldn't be talking about moving around the world for you if I didn't care about you a lot."

We tried to carry on like nothing had happened, but I was hurt and confused. Didn't she love me back? I didn't know how to react. Over the next few days, when she wrote to me, I would reply with "Yeah" or "Sure" or "Okay." I didn't know what else to say.

"I hate this," she said. "Please don't give up on what we have just because I didn't say I love you back. Just know that when I do say it, I'll truly mean it."

I respected the fact that she didn't say it just to appease me. I valued her honesty, but I felt backed into a corner. I felt like an injured rooster and one day I lashed out.

"I thought we were communicating on the same level, but I guess not. It's really been an uphill battle for us given the distance and I'm just not sure if this is worth the fight."

We already had so much stacked against us, and now, I wasn't sure if it was a battle that we could win. I stewed in bitterness for days and eventually stopped talking to her completely. Maybe Kike was right. Maybe I had rushed into this.

Days passed without speaking, but I only grew more and more miserable. I loved this girl, what was I doing running away from her? I sent her a message.

"I give up, I can't be without you. I'm yours if you want me. If not I understand too. I want you to be happy and I am sorry I caused all this drama. What I have with you is too good to let go."

"You're a dick for leaving me hanging for that long. I thought you'd given up on me," she said.

We made up and went back to normal. I couldn't imagine my life without Ashley. A week later, she called and whispered, "I love you." I couldn't have been happier.

CHAPTER
38

I had finally moved out of the gym and was living with an American expat friend in the upscale neighborhood of Miraflores. For the first time since I came to Peru, I was starting to explore the bars and clubs.

It had been several months since I had hurt my finger and I still couldn't make a fist. When I woke up in the morning, it was completely rigid for the first hour of the day and I couldn't bend it at all. I would slowly work it closed until the flexibility increased throughout the day. Sometimes it would get locked in a bent position and I would have to use my other hand to snap it open with a pop as I winced in pain. I went to another clinic in Miraflores, but the doctor looked confused and just told me to ice it and take anti-inflammatories. He seemed to be telling me, "Just deal with it." But I was having trouble dealing with it. I brooded and became more frustrated. I started going out drinking more frequently with my new American friends.

I felt like I was serving no purpose in Peru and it ate away at me. I had come down to Peru to do one thing—to fight—and now I couldn't even do that.

When I had visited Peru for the first time, over a year earlier, I had gotten very sick and didn't sleep well for days. Fiorella's cousin had taken me to a pharmacy and bought me a packet of sleeping pills called Clonazepam. They put me right to sleep and I felt better the following morning. Now, as I grew anxious about my life, I began taking Clonazepam to go to sleep and I found that it helped tremendously. For the first time in a while, I was waking up every morning feeling completely refreshed and ready to train hard.

There was an MMA event a month away, but again, I had to tell Ivan that I couldn't compete.

"What about grappling?" he asked.

"Sure, why not?" I said.

I began training for the submission bout, but my anxiety over my finger increased. I looked up Clonazepam on the internet and learned that it was an anti-anxiety drug that went by the brand name Klonopin in the United States. One morning, I decided to take a pill before practice. I had been tightly wound and needed to loosen up. That day at practice I was in a state of flow, as sports psychologists like to describe it. I was hitting submissions on everyone and my timing was perfect. With Clonazepam, I blocked out all distractions. There was no more idle chatter in my brain, no second-guessing myself.

I began to take it every morning after that, as well as at night to sleep. I noticed other benefits too. I was a much more pleasant person to be around. Now, I would have the patience to listen to a friend's problems and commiserate.

When I ran out of pills, I went to the pharmacy again. I didn't notice this at the time, but they gave me 2-milligram pills instead of the 0.5-milligram pills I had been taking. These pills zonked me out right away, and I start to lose my memory around this time period. One of the effects of a higher dosage is short-term memory loss, but at the time, I didn't notice any of this. I didn't notice much of anything. I became like a zombie. Some days, I must have taken three or four pills. I popped them like candy, without giving it a second thought. In my mind, I was self-medicating. In college, pills were everywhere. It was common for people to take uppers like Adderall before a big exam. Whenever someone had surgery, they were usually prescribed an excess of painkillers like Percocet, Vicodin, or Oxycontin. As an athlete, my friends were often had injured, and we were awash in these pills. It just seemed normal to me.

Ivan had found me an opponent named Pablo de Noriega, who was a jiu-jitsu black belt. Pablo was also the head coach of a local gym called Academia Sniper. He had been the referee at the luta livre tournament that I had won when I first arrived in Peru.

Pablo had challenged me months ago at a different event, but had backed out at the last minute as the date approached. Now he was challenging me again.

"You're going to kill him," Claudio said.

I was confused, "Isn't he a black belt?"

"Yeah, but he never competes."

The problem with belt designations is that they are subjective achievements, and some people, like Pablo, rarely competed to justify theirs. Pablo had much more to lose from this bout than I did. I was a blue belt who had been practicing submissions for less than a year, whereas he was a black belt and the head coach of a gym. If I beat him, it would damage his reputation and his black belt would mean less.

I decided to seize on this dynamic and play some psychological games. I usually didn't like to talk trash before a competition, but something implored me to try to push his buttons. In the pre-fight interview, I made sure to point out the fact that he was a black belt but it didn't matter to me. "*Voy a ganar.*" I am going to win, I said as I stared into the camera.

I explained that I knew he was a black belt, but I was preparing for his techniques. "*Lo voy a finalizar.*" I will submit him. It was more aggressive than I had acted in other interviews, but that was part of my strategy. I even added Pablo as a friend on Facebook so that he could see my further taunts. I wrote a post disparaging his black belt and saying that I was going to submit him regardless.

I continued taking a high dose of the Clonazepam and I was feeling better than ever. I felt like I was bulletproof. I had nothing to lose and I was having fun taunting my opponent.

When they tried to do a pre-fight interview with Pablo, they couldn't get in touch with him. Ivan told me that there was a chance he was going to back out again.

"*Concha su madre!*" I yelled. I had been excited for a chance to prove my skills against a top competitor. I asked around and many people confirmed these rumors from friends who trained with Pablo. Some said that the owner of his gym wouldn't let him compete. Others said he was mad that Inka FC had promoted it as luta livre versus jiu-jitsu (ignoring my years of wrestling). Others contended that he was simply a spineless coward. I tended to agree with the latter.

"*Maricón!*" I said as I stalked around the gym. "*Voy a matar ese huevón!*" I cursed and cursed, but it didn't help.

"Calm down," said Claudio. "We all knew this might happen from the beginning."

"I will destroy him."

By now, I was taking a massive dose of Clonazepam every day, but I still had fits of rage. I vacillated between periods of narcotic detachment and lunatic indignation.

The next morning, I ran out of pills. It was just eight days before I was scheduled to fight. I went to a pharmacy in Miraflores and asked for more, but the lady said I needed a prescription. Previously, nobody had asked for a prescription. I tried three more stores, but got the same answer.

The next morning, I tried two different pharmacies and was denied. When I went to a third and asked about the pills, the woman behind the counter began to shout at me, "I TOLD YOU YESTERDAY! YOU NEED A PRESCRIPTION!" I was embarrassed and darted out of the store then shuffled down the street nervously.

For the first time in my life, I felt like a drug addict. I felt dirty and vile, like I should duck down an alley and sleep behind a dumpster. I was forcefully snapped back to reality. You always hear about how addiction sneaks up on people, but to live it was a different thing. I was glad I caught my problem before it spiraled out of control.

That night, I had one of the most vivid and gruesome dreams of my life:

> I met two friends at a bus station somewhere up in the grassy mountains. We were waiting for a bus tour around the country. Soon, the driver arrived and we boarded, but it was a party bus and we started to drink.
>
> One of my friends was a boisterous redhead who was insisting that we drink hard even though I didn't want to. He ordered shots of tequila and I was repulsed. I realized that I despised him, even though he was my best friend.
>
> We arrived at a large castle and entered its walls. I noticed that the stone walls were adored with gems and I realized we were in an Incan palace.
>
> The next thing I remember, we were standing on the coast of Lima near my apartment. We were under a highway overpass, and there were people milling about.
>
> Suddenly, on the other side of the overpass, a human body fell from the sky and landed on the sidewalk with a splatter of blood. I was shocked and horrified. It had been someone who was parachuting. Soon, more people began to fall out of the sky as their parachutes failed and collapsed. People were splattering on the sidewalk at a rapid rate and it became a torrential downpour of blood and bodies. A pool of blood accumulated on the street. I began to realize that maybe I was dreaming and I wanted to get out of it, but I couldn't.
>
> The worst part was that my redhead friend started laughing manically at the scene. "Stupid fucking people who go parachuting," he said. "They deserve it." It bothered me a lot and I realized again how much I despised him. All of the other people started yelling at him and he just taunted them back. Then I woke up.

Later that day, I got news from Ivan: Pablo had officially backed out of the fight. My friend Scott was visiting from Arequipa and was staying on my couch. That night, I was fuming with rage as we sat at the bar. I bemoaned the situation until long after he was sick of hearing me.

I drank heavily and it wasn't until three in the morning when I got home and went to bed. I lay in bed but was unable to sleep. My mind turned over with anger and unease. I watched the sun's light creep through the window shade in my room.

Later in the morning, I gave up and got out of bed. I went on Facebook and began typing an announcement in Spanish. By this time, I had a fairly large following in the Peruvian MMA scene.

> People, I have bad news. My opponent for the match on the 10th of December does not want to fight, and because of this it's canceled. I was excited to fight and I am bothered by this news. It's just that in martial arts we are warriors. My coach Ivan Iberico has taught me the mentality that we always advance and never have fear...there aren't big opponents or small opponents, only fights. I am proud to train with a warrior like him. I would never want to train in another academy where the coach doesn't put importance on these mentalities. Advance!

It was an unrestrained jab at Pablo and his academy. Not long after, Pablo himself commented on the post.

> My esteemed, we can fight whenever you want. I also awaited and still await this fight with much eagerness. It's just that the organizers have changed the date on me various times.
>
> It's simply a matter changing the event so that the fight is impartial. Unfortunately this is not so clear because the organizers are in your corner.
>
> It will not happen brother, I say from experience.

I wanted to punch a wall. What a liar! The event had always been December 10th and had never once changed. If he had a problem with the event organizers, why did he accept the fight in the first place? I wanted to physically hurt him.

If he thought that Inka FC judges would be unfair, I was fine facing him under a different promotion, but it was clear that he simply didn't want to compete. I replied to his comment and called his bluff, "We can fight in another event then."

Peruvian MMA fans began commenting on the unfolding drama. It seemed like everyone was watching. I was an outsider calling out the local black belt and implying that he was a fraud. But I was also worried that I had overstepped my bounds and disrespected the wrong person. Then Ivan stepped in with a knockout punch:

> Hi Pablo, I want to first clarify that I have nothing against you. Quite the contrary, I like you. Each time we see each other, we greet each other and everything is cool and respectful. But what you posted above is very serious. You are saying that I have changed the date of the event. I am the organizer, and I initially put December 10th and that date has remained firm up until this moment. Next, you are basically saying that I manipulate the results of my events and that is the most serious accusation because you are putting doubts on the credibility of an organization that has been working for years on the growth and development of MMA in Peru. It's clear that you don't want to fight Rollie for whatever reason, but using my job as an excuse not to fight, that is serious. I believe respect breeds respect. You should have expressed all of your doubts before confirming that you were going to fight. It is already advertised on social media, and just yesterday, December 2nd, you said you would not fight.
>
> I know why you do not want to fight and I will not mention it so that this does not escalate any further, but you should be

honest with your heart and principles as a martial artist, with your WORD. On the other hand, Rollie fights in any event, without regard to the referee or judges or time!

You know why Pablo? Because we like to compete no matter the results, the idea is to compete and measure yourself. For the years I've known you, I've always told you not to trade your spirit of competition for a belt. As I always say, you set an example. Remember, in combat sports people train to be champions and must fight anyone.

In Peru some people fight once, three times at most, and choose their opponents carefully and then consider themselves great champions! Others do not even compete in fights except in the gym and they also consider themselves champions. Fine, they can do that, but they should not say that they are champions because roosters are always in the arena without much ceremony!

Insecurity is often times present with these small champions, and it is worse if they become instructors or coaches, but I know that is not your case.

I hope that you do not lose that competitive spirit you had. Greetings and congratulations on your success, Pablo. And congratulations on your black belt in jiu-jitsu.

CHAPTER
39

n all of the excitement, I felt like a jack-in-the-box, wound-up and ready to explode. It had been fun attacking Pablo so publicly, but now I began to worry. Did I make myself look like an asshole? I was an outsider, and Pablo was respected in the local martial arts community. Martial arts were supposed to be about respect, especially to elders. I worried I had tarnished my reputation.

I began pacing my apartment like a caged tiger. Something wasn't right. I needed to go for a run. I put my running shoes on, went downstairs, and ran along the ocean. The palm trees and ocean views normally calmed my nerves, but today was different: my mind was clouded and filled with dread. Part of me felt guilty. I had attacked Pablo's livelihood, his gym, and his reputation in the community. But he deserved it, didn't he? Still, I felt an overwhelming sense of apprehension.

I clenched my teeth and ran harder, but the feeling grew worse. Out of nowhere, I suddenly had a premonition that I was going to die. I remembered my horrific dream from the other night and suddenly it took on a new meaning. I was running near the exact spot where the bodies had fallen from the sky in my dream. I was sure that death waited for me around each corner. I clenched my teeth and ran faster, but I couldn't shake the sense of doom.

That night, Pinedo had a fight at El Rosedal and we went to watch. People I didn't even know approached me to ask about my beef with Pablo. I was the talk of the crowd. Everyone I saw made a disparaging remark about Pablo's manhood. I saw him sitting in the stands on the far side of the pit but I tried not to look at him.

Ivan informed me that he had found me a replacement match. I would be competing against Tano Fernandez, the same guy I had beaten in the finals of my first luta livre tournament.

Pinedo won his fight with an armbar submission, and it was three in the morning when I got home. I went to bed, but my mind continued racing and I couldn't sleep. I lay awake as the sun appeared through the edges of my window. This was the second night in a row of sleeplessness. I was exhausted, but each time I closed my eyes, my mind opened. I couldn't figure out why I was so anxious.

The next morning Kike brought me to practice and we got stuck in a traffic jam. My head began to throb and I got a burning sensation at the base of my skull. I began to panic and breathe heavily. The traffic gave me insatiable anxiety and my head felt like it was going to explode. "Calm yourself," Kike repeated.

When we arrived at practice, I grappled with Claudio and Pinedo. I was dead tired because I hadn't slept in two nights. Again, the physical exercise did nothing to ease my sense of dread.

Eventually, I gave up and told Ivan that I was going for a run, but I actually just walked and tried to clear my mind. I felt like I was going to vomit.

When I arrived back to my apartment, and I lay in bed and tried to sleep, but head was still throbbing. I got up to make a sandwich but couldn't eat it. I hadn't eaten anything in over twenty-four hours and I had no appetite. I couldn't sleep and I paced back and forth in my room. I couldn't sit still. Kike called and asked if I wanted to go for a run. He came over and we ran along the ocean. I tried to hide my deteriorating mental state.

When we returned to my apartment, I realized I had locked my keys inside. "Fuck, fuck, fuck, fuck," I began repeating and pacing the sidewalk clenching my temples and screaming uncontrollably. "Calm yourself, imbécil," Kike said with a concerned look. "How did you ever work on Wall Street?"

"I don't know."

"You are a gringo loco."

Eventually, we found my roommate and picked up the keys. I went to the supermarket and wandered the aisles. I couldn't even remember why I had come. The next thing I knew, I was standing in line and someone tapped me to inform me there was a free register.

That night, I took a Tylenol PM and tried to go to bed early. I hadn't eaten all day and I tried to force down a piece of bread but I couldn't eat.

I drifted in and out of a tormented sleep.

2:00 AM: I jump out of bed. I am drenched in sweat and I begin pacing around my room. My neck and back muscles are twitching and convulsing in agony.

3:30 AM: I try to lie down again but am experiencing waking nightmares. When I close my eyes I see dragons and demons and snakes and ghosts. They snarl and lunge at me and explode in bursts of flames. I am freefalling through oblivion.

5:00 AM: What is happening? I am losing my mind. I should be put in a padded room with a straitjacket. My mind is like a Jackson Pollack painting.

5:30 AM: I must have taken too much Clonazepam and overloaded my circuits. I've heard stories about people who just blew a fuse one day and were never the same again. I'm a fucking idiot. Why did I do that? Why? Why? Why? They're going to commit you to an institution.

6:00 AM: I am going to be such a burden on my parents. They are going to be so upset. I ruined my life. People will say, "And then one day, he just went crazy..." I might have to—no, don't say that. But I might. I see no other way out.

6:30 AM: I haven't slept in three whole days. I need to talk to Ben. I call him but get no response. I need to get to practice. I begin walking. The world outside looks different. I want reality back. It was so neat and clean. Now it is warped and cruel.

7:00 AM: I send a message to my friend Thomas in the United States saying it's an emergency. It. Really. Is. An. Emergency.

7:30 AM: I am walking to practice when he calls me. I begin crying. "Dude, I need help. I need help. I need help. I fucked up. I've lost it." I explained the situation. "I don't know what to do. I think I need to come home. I need to be institutionalized or something. I just don't know what to do." He listens and offers some comforting words, but he is arriving to work and has to leave.

8:15 AM: I arrive at the gym but no one is there. I lay in one of the bunk beds and try to control my spastic breathing. My heart is thumping loudly in my chest.

8:45 AM: Ben arrives and I ask to talk privately. We walk behind the building. I am embarrassed so I don't tell him the full extent. I tell him that I am having muscle spasms and headaches. I tell him that I accidentally took too many sleeping pills.

9:00 AM: He takes me to the emergency room. In the cab I keep repeating, "I fucked up." He is confused, and doesn't understand my panic. He tells me to calm down and rubs my neck. I am experiencing hot and cold flashes. One minute I am shivering the other minute I am sweating. We stop at a gas station where he buys me a cold bottle of Gatorade and holds it on the back of my neck.

9:15 AM: He checks me into the emergency room. At this point, I am having trouble formulating words. I keep jumping up out of my seat and running to the bathroom even though I don't have to go. "Calm down," he says over and over again. "Just breathe and try to relax." I pace around the waiting area.

10:00 AM: I see a doctor and tell her about the Clonazepam. She does some blood work and gives me something "like ibuprofen" intravenously. It is extremely difficult for me to sit still with an IV in my arm. I repeat myself over and over. My voice is shaky and I want to jump out of my skin. Ben sits with me and tries to comfort me.

11:30 AM: I am waiting for the blood results. They leave the needle in my arm even though the bag has finished. The clear tube begins to fill with blood. I can't look at it. Ben has to leave to pick up Ghaela from school.

12:30 PM: My tests come back without anything wrong. They tell me there is nothing else they can do. I catch a cab to meet Ben at Larcomar. I roll the window down and hang my head out. I feel dizzy and disoriented. I can't be stuck in here. I need to get out. He takes Ghaela to play in an arcade. The bright lights and loud noises are too much for me to handle and I have to wait outside. Whatever IV they gave me calmed me down slightly and I am a functional human being again.

1:00 PM: Ben comes back to my apartment. Scott is still staying with me. Ben entertains us with his old college trick of ripping a full phonebook in half.

2:00 PM: Ben has to leave. I haven't told Scott or my roommate Josh about my problem so I try to hold it together in front of them.

4:00 PM: Thomas sends me a message with a link about benzodiazepine withdrawal. Benzos are a class of drugs that include Xanax, Valium, and Klonopin. I am not able to read and process words fully, but I get the gist of it. The symptoms match exactly what I am experiencing. This knowledge should be comforting, but it does little to alleviate my symptoms. "You're a warrior, man, if anyone can beat this thing, you can!" he tries to sound cheerful.

8:00 PM: Josh is making dinner and my madness begins to return with tidal waves of pain and confusion. It feels like there is a flaming golf ball at the base of my skull. Every few minutes it explodes like a cherry bomb in my brain. I wince and cry out in agony. I tell my friends that I am having migraines as I pace in a figure eight around the apartment. The pain is so unbearable that I occasionally claw at the back of my head.

9:00 PM: Sensory overload. Any loud noises or bright lights send me off a cliff. I need to get away. Away from this world of pain and confusion.

9:30 PM: I've been bad at communicating with Ashley during all of this. I am worried she will leave me if she learns what I did. She calls and we talk, but I am clenching my temples. I tell her that I am having migraines and I am having trouble speaking. I tell her that I had been taking sleeping pills, but since I stopped I haven't slept well. It's a partial truth that eases my conscience a little. "Aw poor baby," she says. "I wish I was there to take care of you." But I am actually glad she is not here to see me like this. "I love you, Rollie," she whispers gently. Her voice is so pure and sweet that it seems to contrast with my infernal reality. "I love you too." I rush to get off the phone as quickly as possible.

10:00 PM: I try to go to bed early. My mind is turning over like a washing machine, and each revolution brings me back to the same line of thought. Why did I do this? I am such an idiot. I fucked my brain up. I hope this goes away. If this doesn't go away, I will have to kill myself. I wish I were anywhere but here and now. I wish I wasn't me. It hurts too much. Can't things go back to normal? Why did this happen to me? Of course they did, I deserve this. This is karma. Now I am going to have to back out of my new fight. I am in no condition to get in the ring. I haven't slept in days. I haven't even eaten anything. I will be weak and sleep deprived. I should cancel the fight. No, I can't. I just bitched out Pablo for doing the same. Fuck, I am such an asshole. Why did I do this?

11:00 PM: Repeat.

1:00 AM: I hear a sound out in my living room. I jump up and hide in my closet. There is a man with a knife out there, I am sure of it. I can see it in my mind. The door is locked, you idiot. It doesn't matter. They're here to get you. Locked doors don't stop them. Ahhhh. I hear a scream in the distance. I am rubbing my temples. They are coming for me. Delirium. Paranoia. Confusion.

2:00 AM: No sleep. I walk back and forth in my small room. I get dressed and walk to the 24-hour grocery store. It's Friday night and people are roaming the streets in herds. Drunken men shout to girls who walk by. I would give anything to be able to lead a normal life like them right now. I buy a Gatorade and walk home.

2:30 AM: I try to read about the effects of withdrawal. On multiple websites I read the words, "More dangerous than heroin withdrawal." I read about people losing their jobs and marriages breaking up. People are checked into asylums. The acute symptoms usually only last a few days, but they can linger for four to eight weeks and in some cases even longer. Under no circumstances are you supposed to stop cold turkey. It can cause seizures. It can kill you. That's what is happening to me—I am dying. Death would almost be a welcome relief at this point, but the idea itself terrifies me. I want to die, but I don't want to put my family through that. I think of how terrible it would be for them to learn of my death and tears begin to pour down my face. I see the image of them standing around my grave. It's clear as a photo.

3:00 AM: I am back in bed and my head feels like it's in a vice being cranked tighter by a power lifter. I am more tired than I have ever been in my entire life. My body wants to sleep so badly. I get very close to sleep, but can never actually get there. My eyelids droop and muscles begin to slack and I feel myself falling asleep. Just when I am 99% there, some detonator fires deep in my cranium. Every muscle in my body twitches at once and I sit up with a violent convulsion and gasp for air. Every time I get near sleep, I swear that I stop breathing. Maybe I have sleep apnea and my brain has stopped regulating my breathing. Or I'm having an aneurysm. That would explain the pain. I want to sleep so badly, but I'm positive that if I fall asleep, I will never wake up again. I'm on balancing on the brink of nonexistence.

3:30 AM: It all makes sense: the bad dream, the sense of doom, the bad karma. I has all come down to this. I am going to die here tonight.

3:45 AM: I take out my journal and scribble a note. "If I don't make it, I just want you all to know that I love you. Mom, Dad, Sara, Kenny, and Ashley." I leave it open on my dresser so they will find it easier. I want to write a last will and testament, but have exhausted all of my energy in writing just those few words. Should I leave my door open so they will find my body quicker? I don't want to be decomposing for days before they find me.

4:00 AM: My heart is pounding out of my chest. I can hear my heartbeat and see my chest pounding irregularly. I can't breathe. Maybe I'm having a heart attack. That's one more way I could die.

4:15 AM: I am no longer a coherent human being, but a bag of flesh with a sputtering motor inside. I can't take this anymore. I've reached the end of my rope. I walk into the other room and wake up Scott. He is startled. Between hysteric breaths of air, I tell him the disjointed story. He has suspected there was something wrong. I curl up in fetal position on the cold tile floor and begin crying uncontrol- lably. I am screaming. "I don't know what to do! I don't know what to do! Help me!" He searches for an emergency room. Luckily there is one just two blocks away. "Do you know where that is, mate?" he asks. "Yes," I reply. "Okay, good luck," he says and goes back to bed. "Wait, one more thing," I say. "Can you look up how to say 'with- drawal' in Spanish?"

4:30 AM: I arrive at the clinic. The receptionist tells me to calm down and speak slowly. I am trying my best to speak Spanish, but she doesn't understand me. There are two other people in the lobby. They look at me like I'm an alien with slimy tentacles. She admits me into the hospital and they put me in a bed.

4:45 AM: Not one person in the emergency room speaks English. A nurse comes over and asks me what's wrong. I scream to her. "You have to help me! Help me!" I tell her that I took too many pills and explain the withdrawal symptoms. "*Síndrome de abstinencia!*" I shout at her. She goes to speak with a doctor. "Don't leave me! Help!

Help!" I grab her arm, but she pulls away.

4:50 AM: I go to the bathroom and start pacing the halls. A security guard comes and tells me to get back in bed.

4:55 AM: I scream again and the nurse comes over. "What's wrong?" she asks. "I am going to die and I can't be alone," I say. She replies, "Can I say a *rezo* for you?" I ask her what that means and she clasps her hands together in prayer. "*Sí,*" I reply. She places the palm of her hand on my head and begins reciting a prayer. "I ask the Holy Father to protect..." I am shaking and twitching in my bed. "Please help him..." Oh my god, she is reading me my last rites. She must know that I'm going to die.

5:00 AM: The doctor comes over and asks the nurse what is wrong with me. "He partied too much tonight," she replies. "No, no, no. I didn't!" I try to explain myself, but they can't understand me. He gives me an IV. I think it contains the same drug they gave me at the other emergency room. The nurse comes back and gives me a shot of Diazepam in the ass. Diazepam! Beautiful lovely Diazepam! Valium! A benzodiazepine! I think they are just trying to shut me the fuck up.

5:05 AM: I continue groaning loudly. At this point, all the nurses start to ignore my cries for help. I can't even seem to articulate what I need anyway. I just want it all to end.

5:10 AM: I roll over on my side and pull my legs to my chest. I am cold and I pull the blanket on top of me. If my heart stops beating, at least I am already in the hospital. My cries begin to sputter out in the cold clinic.

5:15 AM: I fall asleep.

CHAPTER

40

wo days later, I stood on the platform at the prefight press conference facing my opponent, Tano Fernandez. After they took photos of our staredown we stepped off the platform together. I thanked him for taking this fight on short notice. He weighed almost twenty pounds more than me, but I didn't even care.

Two days before, I had faced my own death. Of all the things I cared about, winning this match was not one of them. In fact, I didn't even want to be here. I wished I could have backed out, but I had just publically embarrassed Pablo for doing the same thing. I had trapped myself in a awful situation because of my own arrogance. My world was upside down, but I tried to steel myself against the coming challenge.

In the time since I had last competed against Tano in the luta livre tournament, he had graduated from a purple belt to a brown belt. He was known as one of the better jiu-jitsu players in Peru. We would be competing in submission grappling, as a sort of sideshow during an MMA event. And we were being paid, making it my professional debut in submissions.

As I sat in the locker room waiting for them to call my fight, my hands shook visibly and I couldn't sit still. It had been a week since I had slept well, but I didn't care. After everything I had been through in the past week, this seemed unimportant.

I had spent the last two nights sleeping on Ben's couch. Ben and Fiorella had stayed up watching me until I fell asleep, like concerned parents. When I first arrived at Ben's apartment, he began reading about benzodiazepine withdrawal online. His jaw dropped, "Oh my god, this stuff is legal?" He read everything he could, because I still had trouble reading. That first night, I fell asleep on his couch and I slept for five hours. It was a huge relief because I hadn't been sure if I would ever sleep again.

In the locker room, Ben tried to cheer me up. "You know that thing you always say about the flu or whatever?"

"Flu-Like Symptoms."

"Yes, that. Go out there and do your thing."

"Yeah, well, this is different, I think. I don't know if..." but I just nodded my head and agreed. I didn't want to be there. I wanted nothing to do with this fight.

The announcer called us into the ring. Instead of a cage, this event was being held in a boxing ring with three ropes around the edge of a square canvas. When the match started, Tano ran towards me and tried to pull me into his guard. I stepped to the side and pushed him away. I didn't want to get tied up in his game, so I kept my distance and circled around him. We fought for wrist control.

When we got in a flurry, I tried to stop and breathe. He pulled me into his guard and I tried to pass it, but his defenses were too good. I broke away, but he grabbed my wrist and dragged my arm. He snatched my leg and lifted it into the air. It would be embarrassing if I let him take me down since I was a wrestler. I hopped around on one foot, trying to stay balanced. When he loosened his grip, I pulled my foot out and faced him on our feet.

He returned to the mat, and we resumed the boring game where I attempted to pass his guard. I closed my eyes and took a deep breath. He tried rolling under my legs and I dropped my weight down and pinned his right knee to the mat. I trapped him and reached across to secure his other leg with my hands. I stretched his legs apart and extended my body, but he rolled out of it.

He held me in an unusual half-guard position. I spun back to the outside, but Tano was too quick. Everything I tried, he had an answer for, and everything he tried, I had an answer for.

I bunched his legs together and pushed them over the top. I was now behind him, but he flipped onto his stomach. I spun around to his back. I needed to get both of my legs inside of his in order to get points, but before I could lock anything up, he did a forward roll. I latched onto his back and followed him through.

When we landed, I slipped one of my legs around his and trapped it. I pulled myself on top of him when he recovered to his knees. I had secured one hook, but he had turtled up so much that I couldn't get anything more.

I looked over to Ivan, and he signaled me with hand motions to hit a Twister. Of course! I leaned my weight over the top so that he would try to throw me off of him. He took the bait and turned hard. Instead of fighting the motion, I rolled with him and even gave him an extra shove. I sat up and pulled his arm back over my head and locked my hands around his neck.

Imagine having your neck pulled one way, your hips being pulled the other, and your spine twisting in agony like a sponge being wrung: that is a Twister. Two seconds later, he pounded his hand against the ground and tapped out.

I had submitted a brown belt. Ivan ran into the ring with a big smile on his face and hugged me. I was happy to be alive.

CHAPTER
41

S ometime during the mayhem of the previous few weeks, I had gotten a call from an old friend who was organizing an event in New York City. He asked if I was interested in wrestling in Madison Square Garden. It was just eleven days after my match with Tano.

The Grapple at the Garden was an exhibition that featured MMA fighters who were former wrestlers. We were divided into two teams: Team Joe Warren and Team Renzo Gracie. Even though I had first learned jiu-jitsu in Renzo's gym in New York, I was drafted to Team Joe Warren.

I had no business even being mentioned in the same sentence as the other guys competing. There was Muhammad "King Mo" Lawal, the former Strikeforce champion and Bellator standout; Joe Warren, the Bellator champion and Greco-Roman Olympian; and UFC legend Gray Maynard. The list continued on.

I was booked to face Stephen Abas, a three-time NCAA champion and Olympic silver medalist. He was considered to be one of the greatest collegiate wrestlers of all time. I had gotten his autograph when I was a kid. Unfortunately, a few days before the event, Abas broke his hand and had to back out. As a last-minute replacement, I would be wrestling an Egyptian wrestler who I had never heard of before. Nonetheless, I was happy to be getting the chance to wrestle in such a prestigious event.

I arrived on Friday night and checked into the Wyndham New Yorker across from Madison Square Garden. The room probably cost more than my monthly rent in Peru, but I wasn't paying for it. In fact, they were paying me to compete. Just two weeks after my professional submission debut, I was having my professional wrestling debut. I had wrestled my whole life for free, and it was nice to finally get pampered.

I had told all of my old friends about the event and they were all coming to watch. People had been following my story and I had made fans out of many people who had initially doubted me. Everyone seemed to be on my side. It was my grand homecoming.

This event featured so many MMA stars that it got the attention of the national media. All of the MMA websites and magazines started writing features about the event. The event organizers had billed me as: "Rollie Peterkin, the former Univ. of Penn star and talented freestyle wrestler, who left Wall Street to become an MMA fighter." Websites like mmafighting.com, mmajunkie.com, and bloodyelbow.com began running articles about the event and I was mentioned in all of them. I was riding the coattails of the stars and getting my name out there.

The event was organized to bridge the gap between MMA and wrestling. Many former wrestlers faced a difficult decision after college: whether or not to continue chasing the Olympic dream. With the rise of MMA, a lot of top wrestlers were getting funneled out of the sport and some wrestling purists were angered by this.

The Grapple at the Garden was a reaction to those purists. Just because these competitors were now fighting, the logic went, doesn't mean they couldn't still support wrestling.

The sport of jiu-jitsu faced a different problem. Jiu-jitsu purists often prefer to "pull guard" and bring the match to the ground rather than grapple for a takedown on their feet. This was the strategy that Tano had used against me. It works well within the confines of sport jiu-jitsu, but it makes it more difficult to transition into MMA. To counteract this, the Gracie family was making a push to learn wrestling and stay ahead of the curve. At the Grapple at the Garden, three Gracies would be competing: Gregor Gracie, Igor Gracie, and Rolles Gracie.

At the weigh-ins and press conference. I saw the Gracie family sitting in a corner. I wasn't sure if they would remember me from the relatively short time I had trained with them, but they all greeted me with smiles and teased me for switching teams.

The whole atmosphere was casual and everyone seemed to have brought a sense of humor. Bellator star Mo Lawal was facing Rolles Gracie, who was a whole foot taller than him, so at the weigh-in Mo pulled up a chair and stood on it so that he could look down at Rolles. Everyone had a good laugh, even Rolles.

In the morning, we walked across the street to Madison Square Garden. I was the first match so I began warming up, but the other guys were just goofing around. A camera crew was busy interviewing the more well-known fighters.

We filed out onto the mat and crowded in the corner. I went through and slapped everyone's hands and Joe gave me a quick pep talk. "Go kick his ass!" he screamed.

I met my opponent in the center of the mat and shook his hand. I immediately attacked and snapped his head. He stepped his ankle forward and I trapped it, throwing him to the ground. It almost seemed too easy. I tried to turn him to his back, but my wrestling technique was rusty and the ref stood us back up.

Again, I shot a single leg takedown and he fell to the mat. After another attempt to turn him, the ref stood us up again.

I posted my hand on his shoulder and pulled him towards me. When he stepped forward I dropped to a fireman's carry and threw him to his back for four points. I held him there and squeezed. The ref blew his whistle and called a pin.

It had been an easy match and I was almost disappointed. I had wanted to give a good show to the people who came to watch. After the match, I talked to my opponent. It turned out that he was a Greco-Roman wrestler who wasn't used to defending his legs. That's what you get for a last minute replacement.

Next, Joe Warren faced his friend, Scott Jorgensen. They had trained together and had been playfully talking shit the whole time I had been with them. They had even gone out drinking together in Hoboken just two nights before. Scotty had fallen down and was sporting a large abrasion on his face. All of the talking didn't help Scotty though. Joe got a tight body lock around his waist and pinned him.

Next Shawn Bunch downed Demacio Page. Shawn was a collegiate All-American who now fought in Bellator. The next match featured Oklahoma State's two-time NCAA champion Jordan Oliver on our side and Penn State's NCAA champion Frank Molinaro on the Gracie team. Both of these guys were still competing in wrestling. Oliver edged out Molinaro to keep our undefeated streak alive. Our team's Gray Maynard beat World Series of Fighting champion Ozzy Dugulubgov. Bellator fighter Brennan Ward defeated Igor Gracie.

Our team stayed undefeated until Darryl Christian lost to Gregor Gracie. Darryl was a two-time Greco Roman national champion, and this was definitely an upset. It was impressive that the Gracies had made such strides in wrestling already. But we closed out the dual meet with a decisive win by Mo Lawal over Rolles Gracie.

The match was over, but then Scott Jorgensen ran out to the center of the mat and grabbed the microphone. In a move reminiscent of the WWE, he called out Joe Warren to a rematch right then and there. Joe accepted the challenge, stepping out to the center. Unfortunately for Scotty, this match ended in the same fashion and Joe Warren got his second pin of the night.

After the event, I went to the bar with a large group of my old friends to celebrate. Everyone was excited about my MMA career and expressed their admiration.

"When are you fighting again?"

"I don't know," I said. "My finger is still messed up."

"Do you think you will make it to the UFC eventually?"

"I hope so. That is my goal. I want to be a world champion."

I said it confidently, but it just didn't sound right. I was happy to build my fan base and inspire people. But there was one thing that bothered me: I was beginning to have doubts about my own commitment to MMA.

At the end of the day, I was getting punched in the head for a living. Even in my short time fighting, I had probably received a number of concussions, although I never bothered to get checked out. There was that time sparring with Pinedo when my knees buckled and everything went black and I fell to the mat. After shaking it off, I got back up and finished the sparring session. Ivan had knocked me down a number of times too. After a few minutes of disorientation, I went right back to practice. It just hadn't seemed like a big deal to me.

There was so much research that showed the horrendous effects of traumatic brain injuries, but I had accepted that as a professional hazard.

That all changed after my recent battle with Clonazepam. I had experienced firsthand the effects of an impaired brain. In fact, I began to wonder if the damage I had done would be permanent. Even though I had been through the worst of it, the symptoms still lingered. I had a persistent tremor in my hands. I suffered bouts of hopeless depression followed by episodes of gut-wrenching anxiety. I had trouble sleeping through the night and would often jolt awake in spasms of terror. I had horrific dreams. It got better with each day that passed, but did I really want to risk that again? The brain is a delicate organ, I began to realize, and it's really all that you have on this earth.

I looked around at my friends and fans, and I felt bad. They all wanted to see me succeed, but I wasn't sure if I wanted it anymore. I had inspired them, and now I was starting to feel like I had failed them all. I felt like I was trapped in a cage of my own making.

CHAPTER
42

When I returned to Peru, I found everything in chaos. The Pitbull gym had been on a slow, steady decline since Martin had ceased funding our program. The gym itself was not economically viable on its own merits. Our facilities were amazing: we had eight sets of bunk beds in the back room. Our training mat was large enough to play a game of ten-on-ten dodgeball. We had a full-size octagonal cage at the far end. There was a kitchen on the second floor with a chef. We had a weight room. And the offices for both Pitbull and Inka FC were just underneath.

Apparently Martin owed money for rent on the facilities and they evicted us. I had heard rumors about this before I left, but when I returned from America, it was gone.

Ivan had instructed everyone in the gym not to tell me. He thought it would be funny if I showed up at the gym to find it closed up. When I arrived back to Lima, I called Claudio and he tipped me off.

"We're training in Breña with Hector's guys now."

"No way."

"Yeah, it sucks."

The next morning, Claudio and I went to practice together. We took the Metropolitano bus to the Center of Lima, and then caught a small bus through the streets of Breña.

Everywhere I looked, there were abandoned buildings with crumbling roofs and people idling on street corners. I wouldn't want to be stuck here alone at night. We got off and walked several blocks before arriving at Avenida Aguarico. The street was bordered on both sides by dilapidated brick buildings and empty lots. Street dogs trotted up and down the block. We had arrived at the Team Perros Sarnosos.

There were two cars parked outside that were surrounded by men bent over the open hoods, with metal parts scattered across the pavement. They gave us strange looks as we passed.

We walked in the gym. I've seen public bathrooms that are larger. Speaking of bathrooms, there weren't any. If you had to piss in the middle of practice, you had to put your shoes on and walk down the street to an empty lot and piss on the brick wall. But you had to be careful where you stepped because there were scattered piles of dog shit everywhere. If, god forbid, you had to take a shit, there was a gas station a few blocks away with a disgusting bathroom out back. But you had better bring your own toilet paper.

The roof was made of corrugated metal and riddled with holes. The mat space was about fifteen by fifteen feet. It was difficult training with more than a few people at a time. The shabby concrete walls were painted with camouflage.

Without the bunk beds, it was much more difficult for guys to come train during the week. A lot of them lived far away and didn't have cars. It took Pinedo several hours to get to the gym through a network of busses. Now he would have to do that every morning.

We practiced like the old days, but there were now only a few of us. I still couldn't fully bend my finger so I could only train grappling and wrestling. I taught wrestling to the guys, but it wasn't the same. It wasn't our gym. I felt like a squatter.

I saw Zury one morning, but he wouldn't make eye contact with me. When I went over to say hi, he walked out of the room. He later told Claudio that he still wanted a rematch and that he would "beat my ass." It sounded like poor sportsmanship to me.

When I first arrived in Peru, I would have loved a gym like this. I was filled with a sense of adventure. Everything new and exciting for me.

But now, I was just filled with frustration. To make matters worse, my finger wasn't getting any better, and I knew I had to do something. Kike drove me to a medical clinic where I scheduled an MRI.

I came back to get the results a few days later, and talked to the doctor. He said I had cut my flexor tendon.

"How long ago did it happen?" he asked me.

"Six months," I said.

"Oh well, it's too late to do anything. There is a surgery to fix it but you have to do it in within one or two months. Why didn't you see anyone earlier?"

"I did. They told me to ice it."

He shrugged.

"Will it ever get better?" I asked.

"Maybe."

"Well, what can I do?"

"I would just live with it if I were you."

"There is nothing I can do?" I asked again.

"Well, there is a surgery, but it is very difficult and I wouldn't advise it. After a lot of time passes, the tendon shrivels up and they cannot reattach it. They have to take a tendon from your wrist and cut your entire finger open..."

I shuddered.

"So like I said," he continued, "I would just live with it."

I had come down here to fight, and now I wasn't able to do that. I felt aimless and irritated. Sometimes I didn't leave my apartment for days. I didn't want to go out and I didn't want to talk to anybody. Life abroad is filled with tiny inconveniences that you take for granted, until you feel miserable enough to pay attention to them. When I first came down, I loved the challenge of overcoming these daily obstacles. Now, every little thing drove me over the edge.

"Why don't you come back to the United States?" my dad suggested frequently. My parents hadn't been happy that I was in Peru in the first place, so they took this opportunity to remind me to come home. "No," I replied. "I can't." I didn't want to bail on what I had started. I didn't want to run home with my tail between my legs.

One thing that kept me going was Ashley. I waited eagerly to talk to her every day. We had begun planning a trip to England and each morning I woke up to a countdown from her. "Just 51 days!" she would say.

My life had changed so much since I left New York. I now realized how little I had known about the world. Since leaving, I had become so much more aware of this, but now, I fancied myself a citizen of the world. Ashley had me beat though. She had traveled all over. She could talk first-hand about so many places. She had grown up in Africa! She had lived in France and Spain. She spoke French and Spanish fluently. Together, we could roam the world and have adventures.

As I grew more disillusioned with Peru, I began to cling to the fantasy of my life with her. She and I would carve out a life for ourselves in a foreign country. I couldn't just go back to the United States. I had seen the light. But I didn't know where to go. At the moment, I didn't feel like I had a home. The world was big and I was lost. But when I talked to her, I felt that maybe I had found a home.

Ashley had started looking for jobs teaching English abroad, but she was having a hard time finding any. One day she called me and she sounded nervous.

"So, I am thinking about getting a degree in Education here in England. Because it will help me find work in teaching. There is a program where I can do it in one year."

"Great, that settles it. I'll move to England."

"Really? Oh my God. Are you sure?"

"Absolutely."

I really was sure. She was really the only thing keeping me sane amidst the chaos of my life.

Claudio's family had rented a small beach house in the town of San

Bartolo about an hour south and he invited me down one weekend. We sat on the beach and he played Peruvian rap on his cellphone. He would play a beat and freestyle rap in Spanish. We went surfing and I embarrassed myself.

"Did you know you were voted the best bantamweight in Peru?" he said.

"That's pretty cool."

"Ben was ranked the best pound-for-pound, of course."

At the end of the weekend, Kike came and picked us up. He had just bought a French bulldog puppy and named him Maximus.

"The king of the gladiators," he said. "Maximus Decimus Medirius."

Claudio held his puppy in his lap on the ride home as Kike zipped in and out of cars on the freeway. I loved these guys like brothers. I knew that whatever happened, they would be my friends for life.

Ben was committed to living in Peru for the rest of his life, but now that he was fighting in Bellator he needed to take his training to the next level. In Peru, he would usually spar with Ivan or Claudio, but both of them were much smaller than Ben. He had begun looking for gyms in the United States and finally settled on Jackson's MMA in Albuquerque, New Mexico. Jackson's was ranked as the best MMA gym in the world. The head coach, Greg Jackson, had coached some of the all-time MMA greats like Jon Jones and Georges St. Pierre.

Ben was still going to live in Peru, but would do training camps at Jackson's before each fight. He had just scheduled a fight in California in May so he was headed to New Mexico in a few weeks.

Ben leaving was the final straw for me. Fuerte was training at American Top Team in Florida. We no longer had the Pitbull Center. They had stopped paying us. We had no gym, we had no fights lined up, and even if we did, I still couldn't fight.

I booked a flight back to the United States.

ROLLIE PETERKIN

ROUND
FIVE

" *Life is an adventure of passion, risk, danger, laughter, beauty, love; a burning curiosity to go with the action to see what it is all about, to go search for a pattern of meaning, to burn one's bridges because you're never going to go back anyway, and to live to the end.*

SAUL D. ALINSKY, *REVEILLE FOR RADICALS*

CHAPTER

43

My dad picked me up from the airport and we drove directly to the doctor's office. I saw a hand surgeon who listened to me for a minute and examined my finger.

"You have trigger finger."

"Not a cut tendon?" I asked.

"Maybe, but that's not important. The problem is down here," he pressed his thumb against my palm. "It's like a knot in a rope that has to go through a pulley. That's why it gets stuck closed sometimes."

"So what should I do?"

"I'll give you a cortisone shot and it'll be better in two days."

"How often will I have to get the shots?"

"Just once."

"And it's completely healed?"

"Yes."

Two days later, my finger was back to normal. Who could have known that the months of pain and frustration could have been solved so easily? With that checked off my list, I set my sights on England.

Ashley picked me up at Heathrow Airport, and the following day we went to her sister's wedding. I was honored that she wanted me to meet her whole family. It was a big moment for me. Ashley was the maid of honor and she walked down the aisle behind her sister. She wore a flowing purple dress and looked beautiful. We caught eyes and she smiled. She even played the piano during the ceremony.

At the party, she introduced me to her family, which included a slew of cousins, aunts, and uncles. We all sat down for dinner, but Ashley had to sit at the head table, leaving me with the extended family.

During dinner, Ashley's father gave a speech to the whole party. He told a story about when the groom came to ask his permission for his daughter's hand in marriage. He paused and raised his hand towards me. "Take notes, Rollie."

Everyone in the room turned to me and I laughed quietly. Ashley put her hand across her face in embarrassment. Secretly though, I was proud. He and I were on the same page. I had found the girl that I wanted to be with for the rest of my life.

When I left Peru behind I had felt lost. My teammates had been like family to me and I was sad to leave. Now, as I met everyone, I began to feel like I belonged here. I couldn't wait to begin my new life in England.

The next day, after lunch with her family, Ashley and I caught a train to London. We got a hotel in Southwark.

"It's pronounced Suh-therk," she explained.

"Then why do they spell it South-wark?"

She rolled her eyes.

In the morning, we walked through the rain to London Bridge. Ashley carried an umbrella but I got soaked. We later walked along the Thames ("Why is it pronounced Tems?"). We walked across Tower Bridge. Ashley leaned against the rail to look out at the city beyond, and I wrapped my arms around her in the rain.

"This is just so romantic," I teased.

We took the Underground to Leister Square and walked to Piccadilly Circus. Down Trafalgar Square, past the giant statues of lions in front of the National Gallery. Big Ben and around the Houses of Parliament. Further along the Thames. It began to rain even harder and we turned back. I was completely soaked by the time we returned to the hotel. It was late and we curled up in the hotel bed with a pint of Ben & Jerry's.

"When I come visit America, will you take me to the Ben & Jerry's factory?" she asked.

"Of course, babe."

The next day, we went to Hyde Park to explore. We walked along the swan-filled lake. The rain had subsided and we enjoyed the scenery.

Later that night, we had dinner with an old friend of mine from Wall Street was now working in London. He asked me about Peru and my MMA career.

"So what's next?"

"I don't know."

I usually had a pretty good idea of what I wanted to do with my life, but now I didn't have anything to explain.

"I just got back from a weekend in Prague," he said. He told us stories about the different countries he visited every weekend. I began to wonder if I could get a finance job in London. After we left, I mentioned it her.

"Do you really think you could go back to finance?" she asked.

"I don't know, maybe."

"Wouldn't you be miserable?"

"Maybe."

I had lived so modestly in Peru and I barely spent any money. In that way, I had been able to support myself as a fighter. But as I looked around at London, I grew anxious. Everything was so expensive.

I didn't want to be a loser boyfriend. I wanted to be with Ashley, and if that's what it took, then I could do it. She would insist that I not do it for her, but that was why I loved her so much. She just wanted me to be happy.

CHAPTER

44

Ashley had booked us a tour of Stonehenge at the following afternoon, so we got an early start from London. As we picked up our tickets at the booth, we overheard a girl in the line talking. "You know, on TripAdvisor someone said you should just stop and see it from the road."

Ashley and I giggled to ourselves. We were given a pair of headphones for an audio tour and boarded a tram. Violent gusts of wind whipped across meadows that extended in every direction. We followed a path around the monument and the audio device gave historical tidbits about the site.

After listening to the first two chapters, I took the headphones off. It was painstakingly boring. They described in great detail the mounds of earth that surrounded the site. They speculated on the tools that people used to create it. Ashley, on the other hand, stopped and listened at each placard. I would walk ahead and then wait for her to catch up. I sheltered my face from the strong gusts of wind. Finally, she finished and we walked towards the exit.

"I can't believe that they were able to assemble this thing," I said. "It's mind-boggling."

"Yeah, well, they explained it on the audio guide," she said.

"The stones came from seventeen miles away and they speculate that they used wooden rollers, even though it seems impossible. Right?"

"Something like that," she said.

"I saw a documentary about it once."

While I was impulsive and impatient, Ashley tended to be more studious and deliberate. We had often discussed our differences. She was a model student who did all of her coursework thoroughly, whereas I was a minimalist and a procrastinator. I liked that we were different and I always viewed us as complementary. Maybe I needed someone like that to keep me in check.

"I guess we should have just stopped and seen it from the road," I joked.

From there we drove to Bath, the Roman town famous for its hot springs. Most of the buildings are constructed from a soft white lime- stone, giving it an air of imperial elegance.

We walked through ancient Roman chambers that housed steam rooms and hot baths. There was a large pool in the middle full of stagnant greenish water, which was once a luxurious Roman spa.

Throughout the day, we walked all around the town and I point- ed out various things we passed. I didn't fully realize how different England and America were until that point. I was surrounded by "To Let" signs instead of "For Rent," and I went to the "loo" instead of the "bathroom."

"Oh that looks like a cool pub," I said, looking around. "Oh look another Costa."

"You just point out everything you walk past," she sneered.

"Oh fuck off," I said, releasing the grip on her hand. I was a tourist in this land and everything I was seeing was new and unusual, but she seemed to get annoyed by everything I said.

The following morning we drove through the Cotswolds. Every vil- lage we passed through looked like a time capsule to a bygone era, complete with stone huts and thatched roofs. We passed meadows dotted with sheep, cows, and horses. We stopped in a small town and got lunch at an old style pub.

"Are you super excited?" she said.

"For what?"

"Cadbury World!"

"Yeah, sure."

We were going on a tour of the chocolate factory in Birmingham. Most of people on the tour with us were parents with young kids. It had talking puppets explaining the chocolate making process and cheesy informational videos. We even rode on a small railcar through a sort of amusement park ride. We got free samples of chocolate. In a different context, I could have had a fun time, but for some reason I was annoyed at Ashley for making me sit through it. I had been in a bad mood since Bath.

"Wasn't that the most fun thing we've done so far?" she said after we finished.

"Um, yeah, whatever."

That night we were staying with Ashley's friend Claire in Warwick. She warned me that Claire's parents drank excessively.

"Good, I could use a drink."

When we arrived, they took us to a local pub where we ordered fish and chips. We sat at a table in the back and ordered beers. They then ordered a bottle of white wine and filled my glass up. On the way home, we stopped at a convenience store where I bought two more bottles of wine.

We sat around their kitchen table and began a game of Cards Against Humanity. Each player got seven cards that contained inappropriate phrases, like "Harry Potter erotica" or "Vehicular homicide." One player picks up a black card containing a question and each player submits one answer and the judge decides which is the funniest. I was surprised to learn that the British version contained different cards, although the rules were the same.

"I don't understand these references," I griped. "Can I exchange my cards?"

"No, Rollie. You should learn them," Ashley insisted.

"I just want to exchange them so I can play the game."

"You need to learn these things if you're going to live here in England," she said.

"Can't I just get new cards?"

"Show me."

I laid down a card that said *The Hillsborough Disaster*.

"You really don't know about that?" asked Claire.

"No."

"Well," Ashley explained, "there was a football game and the gates were blocked and a bunch of people crowded and were crushed to death. It was a huge controversy and they are still investigating it."

"Okay."

"What else?"

My next card was *Madeleine McCann*.

"She was a young girl who was kidnapped while on holiday in Portugal. They went to dinner and left her asleep in the room, but when they checked on her, she was gone."

"Okay."

"See Rollie, you are learning things now. That is good."

I poured myself another glass of wine.

"Don't you think you've had enough to drink?"

"No."

She scowled at me each time I filled my glass up, which just encouraged me. In the morning, she made it clear she was unhappy.

"You snored all night, I kept waking you up but you just ignored me. Do you remember getting up and making all that noise?"

"No."

"You drank way too much."

"I did?"

That day, we walked around the town of Warwick. Ashley wanted to go to the cathedral, so we walked inside. She read some signs explaining its history as I dawdled behind staring at the floor.

We drove to Stratford-upon-Avon, the birthplace of William Shakespeare. We had already spent most of the day in Warwick, but we began to walk through the town. When we reached Henley Street, I spied the old Tudor house that was marked as Shakespeare's birthplace. But we didn't have time to go in the museum.

We got back in the car and drove to Liverpool. It was supposed to be a three-hour drive, but it was almost five hours with traffic. When we arrived, I remarked that the city looked fairly industrial.

"See? I told you there is nothing special about Liverpool."

"I just wanted to come here because of the Beatles."

"That's about all there is here. I told you."

"Oh, I don't remember hearing that."

"Well, you don't listen."

"I feel bad. I didn't realize you didn't want to come here."

"It's fine."

It was raining hard when we began walking through the city. Ashley insisted we go to a chicken place called Nando's. It was a chain in England and she had been raving about it since I arrived.

It was a Thursday night and Nando's seemed to be a popular launching pad for the nightlife. I had never seen so many girls wearing faux-fur vests and black fishnet leggings. Their hair puffed out over heavily made-up faces. And they all seemed to have just returned from the spray tan parlor too.

"They look like prostitutes," I said.

"I don't think so. They look normal to me."

"Do you not see what they are wearing? They look so trashy."

"Well I disagree," she glared at me.

Afterward we walked through the rain and descended the stairs to the aptly named Cavern Club, the bar that gave the Beatles their start. The stone walls were covered with Beatles memorabilia. We ordered beers and listened to the live band.

Still, after a few drinks I asked Ashley if she wanted to go back to the hotel and she nodded yes. We walked home through the pouring rain, and when we got back, she immediately went to bed. In the morning we packed up and got the car.

"What do you want to do?" she asked.

"Whatever you want," I replied.

"Well, you wanted to see the Beatles museum, right?"

"Yeah, whatever."

"Well, do you?"

"Yes."

"Okay, let's go."

It was fascinating learning about the Liverpool roots of the band. Strawberry Fields was a real place. Penny Lane was an actual street, and the street sign had been stolen so many times that the exasperated local officials eventually just painted it onto the side of the building. Ashley seemed to enjoy herself too.

The rain poured even harder when we pulled into York. Ashley had made a reservation at Bettys Tea Room, but we arrived early and had to stand in line outside, huddled under her umbrella. Someone in front of us was smoking a cigarette.

"I find it such a turn off when girls smoke," I said.

"I used to smoke."

"Oh, but I mean girls who smoke like a pack a day."

"I did," she said. "When I was in private school."

"Really?"

How much did I even know about her? We had not discussed much about our pasts. The line moved quickly and soon we were seated. It was an old-fashioned restaurant with wood-paneled walls. We talked about a bus tour she had once taken around the United States.

"What's the place in the desert where they believe in aliens?"

"Roswell?"

"I think that was it. It was full of such strange people."

She had also stopped in Las Vegas.

"Did you gamble?" I asked.

"No, I just drank a lot."

"Wild time?"

"Yeah, well I hung out all night with this group of guys who were there on a stag do." A bachelor party, great.

"Oh fun," I said.

"Yeah, they kept buying me drinks all night."

"And then?"

"I got really drunk."

"And then?"

"I don't remember."

"And then?"

She shot me a dirty look and I didn't press it further. But I couldn't shake the image from my head. Was I even the first American she had been with? I didn't know. We had never even talked about it. For some reason, that was important to me. I certainly had no right to be mad at her, but still, I was. I knew I was being a hypocrite: the last time I was in Vegas, I was kicked out of a strip club.

We walked through York in the pouring rain and came to a cathedral. The woman up front gave Ashley a laminated sheet. "This sheet will guide you around the church."

"Rollie, take one too," said Ashley.

"I don't want one."

"Well, I won't let you look at mine, so just get your own."

"That's okay. I'm fine without one."

Ashley stopped in front of each altar and read the inscription. I would have been just about as interested to learn what brand of urinal cakes they used in their toilets.

Finally, we got into the car and drove back to her apartment in Nottingham. It had been a long week and I was looking forward to lying in bed and watching movies. The stress of traveling together had taken a toll on us.

When we got back, it was late and we unpacked. I desperately needed to do laundry so she threw my clothes in the wash. We got ready for bed and put a movie on. About five minutes later, she turned over and said she was going to sleep. She had a ton of schoolwork to catch up on in the morning and she was going to have to spend most of the next week studying.

This wasn't how it was supposed to be. While I had been antagonistic, I was still deeply in love with her. But all week she had been cold and distant. We had talked with excitement about this trip for so long. I had always dreamed of taking a romantic trip through Europe with a girlfriend, and now that I was here it didn't feel right. All of the passion, excitement, and adventure we had talked about—where was it? I grabbed her shoulder and pulled her towards me.

"What's wrong, babe?"

"Nothing," she said, "I'm just tired."

"Something is wrong."

"No, it's nothing."

"What is wrong?" I repeated. "Something is wrong."

She turned to face me, but she wouldn't even look in my direction. I put my hand under her chin and directed her face towards mine. I saw apprehension in her eyes.

"Something is wrong."

"You're right, Rollie," she said. "This doesn't feel right."

"What?"

"This," she repeated. "This doesn't feel right."

"What, I mean, what…"

"Rollie, we barely even know each other."

"What do you mean? We talk every day. I love you."

I waited, but she sat silently.

"I love you," I repeated.

"We talk every day," she said, "but we didn't actually spend any time together." She paused. "Maybe we just don't work."

She had a metallic coolness in her voice, like a prerecorded answering machine message. She really meant it. She didn't want to be with me. I inhaled deeply and held the air in as long as I could. My head began to spin and I rolled onto my back.

A horrified look crossed her face. It seemed like she regretted saying the words, but also she realized that she had spoken the truth.

I still had two weeks before my flight home. And now I was trapped in a house with a girl who—a girl who didn't want to be with me. I didn't know what to do. I couldn't just stay there. Not after that. I turned over and pulled out my computer.

"What are you doing?" she asked.

"Figuring out where I am going to go."

"You can still stay here."

I was confused. How could I stay?

"No, I am going to leave."

She rose from bed and left the room. I had been so caught off guard. I had been prepared to move my entire life to England for her. Now, in a matter of minutes, it all slipped away from me. My life, my plans, my happiness. I no longer had Peru. And now I would not have England.

Maybe she would return and apologize and take it back. Maybe she would jump in bed and we could make up. I spent the next hour in anguish when she didn't return. I couldn't take it anymore and went to find her. I pushed her roommate's door open and found her lying in bed.

"Are you sure about this?" I struggled to formulate the words.

"Rollie..."

I sat down on the floor and leaned forward. I pressed my face against the floor and covered my head with my forearms. "I can't even—I can't believe this is happening."

"Just think," she said, "it's much better that we figured this out now, before you moved here."

"Ahhhhhhh," I let out a slow hiss.

"Rollie, I'm sorry. I didn't mean for this to happen."

"This is not happening."

"Rollie."

"I have to go." I got up and walked out of the room.

I woke up every thirty minutes that night. Each time, I would find peace for a split-second before remembering the reality of the situation and sinking again into despair.

In the morning, I found her doing schoolwork at the kitchen table. We didn't say anything. When my clothes were dry, I walked into the kitchen.

"Bye," I said.

"You don't have to leave. You can stay here."

"No, thanks."

She walked me outside and I turned and walked down the street without looking back.

CHAPTER
45

Several hours later, my bus pulled into Victoria Station in London. I just wanted to go home, but I didn't even know where home was anymore. I was stuck in Europe so I was going to try to make something out of it. I decided to go to Paris.

I walked through the crowded terminal in London and bought a bus ticket for 11:00 p.m. I still had six hours, so I started walking. I had to keep moving. Each step I took—each corner I turned—seemed to keep my mind occupied. As I walked past people I looked down at the ground. I didn't want them to see my face. This was my hell and I was living it, there was no need to share it with others.

From Victoria Station, I walked up along Hyde Park. The sun actually came out from behind the clouds. It was the first time I had seen the sun in London, but everything was dim and grey to me. I walked up Baker Street and counted the building numbers on the left side of the street until I reached 221B. A small crowd stood outside a Sherlock Holmes museum, but I didn't even cross the street.

I turned around and walked back down. When I returned to the station, I stood outside a coffee shop across the street and connected to their wireless internet. Ashley had sent me a message. My heart skipped a beat. Maybe she realized she made a mistake and wanted me back.

"I'm so sorry for what's happened," she said.

Sorry isn't a good emotion.

"It's not your fault, you can't help how you feel," I tried my best to hold it together.

"I had no words yesterday or this morning," she said.

"You're an amazing girl and I wish you the best, I really do."

I was straining to take the high road. I wanted to break down and scream and cry and beg and lie and cheat and steal, but I wouldn't let her see me like that.

"You're taking this very well," she said.

"Nothing I can do to change how you feel. I wish there was."

"I didn't expect you to say you were just going to leave. I was shocked."

"I was in too much pain to stay."

"I still think in two weeks time it wouldn't have worked out," she said. "Sorry for being hostile. And a total bitch."

"You made me very happy while it lasted. I guess I'll just have to live with that." I was clinging to the edge of a cliff with one finger. "I'm leaving for Paris in thirty minutes."

"I'm sorry it wasn't meant to be," she said. It felt like she had jammed a soldering iron through my heart.

"I'm sorry you feel that way."

"I am too."

There was so much I wanted to say.

"I'm still very confused," I said. "But maybe I don't really want to understand."

"What are you confused about?" she asked.

"What I did that changed everything so much."

"I just felt different from spending time with you."

"Alright."

"Don't take it personally," she said.

"Fuck off," I replied. How could I not take it personally? This was about as personal as it gets. "Anyway I'm going to go board the bus. Bye."

"I guess I'll just fuck off then," I couldn't discern her tone through the text. "Have a safe journey and a nice time in Paris. Like you said, I can't help the way I feel. But like I said, I'm very sorry for that."

I didn't have anything else to say, but then, almost as an after-thought, I said what I had been wanting to say all along.

"You broke my fucking heart."

"I know I have. I'm so sorry I broke your heart."

I boarded the bus to Paris and settled in for a ten-hour journey through the night. We pulled away and I fell asleep.

CHAPTER
46

awoke as we came to a stop. I followed the other passengers as they began to file out of the bus. When I got outside, I realized that we were parked aboard a ferry. It was three in the morning and I had no idea where we were. I wanted to figure out what was going on, but I was too apprehensive to ask anyone. I had assumed that we would be taking the tunnel under the English Channel, but as I later learned, the Chunnel was for trains only.

I sat down in a café in the main corridor of the ferry and leaned against the wall. I was surrounded by people, but I had never felt more alone in my life. I spent the next hour and a half on the ferry trying with every ounce of my energy not to think of Ashley.

We arrived in Paris at seven in the morning. I walked around the bus station until I found a ticket window where the woman spoke English.

"How do I get to the center of Paris?" I asked.

"Where do you want to go?"

"I don't know? Where is the Louvre?"

She took out a small map and directed me to take the Metro and get off at the Opéra. When I arrived, I climbed up the stone stairs into a crisp Paris morning. The sun was shining, but there were few people on the streets.

I walked down the Avenue de l'Opéra towards the river. I walked fast and hard, clutching the map in my hand. At the end of the road, I crossed through an arch into a courtyard. Once inside, I spied the large glass pyramid. Hundreds of people were already standing in line to get in.

I would never wait in a line like that. Ashley probably would though. I bet she walked through and looked at every painting. Not me though. Not even if the building was empty. Like I want to see the stupid Mona Lisa anyway. I already know exactly what it looks like. Seeing it in person isn't going to change my life.

I walked along the Seine and crossed a small bridge, edged by a fence covered in padlocks. I had heard about this bridge before. Lovers were supposed to clip their padlocks on and throw the key into the river, symbolizing the eternity of their love. I wished I had a pair of bolt-cutters so I could prove all of them wrong. But still, tears fell down my face.

I kept my head down and plowed forward as I passed happy couples holding hands. Paris. The City of Love. *Fuck.* Every building I passed was ornately decorated with elegant statues and columns. I wished I could've seen this city under different circumstances because I'm sure it could have been really beautiful.

I followed the Seine around a bend until I saw the Eiffel Tower. Throngs of people angled for the perfect photograph, but I just walked through the park and plunged deeper into the city.

The elaborate façades began to fade away and I started to look for a place to stay the night. I found a hotel with one measly star hanging on the sign. I knew right away it was the place for me. I was in a one-star kind of mood.

There was an empty pack of cigarettes in the trashcan in my room. I could almost picture Jim Morrison squatting in the corner, pulling a belt tight around his arm. There was no private toilet and I had to walk down a narrow set of rickety wooden stairs just to take a shower. I wondered if the sheets had even been washed, but I didn't care. I stretched across the bed and passed through the same painful chain of thoughts over and over again.

I spent hours in paralytic despair, lying in bed, sinking deeper into my world of darkness. I finally mustered the energy to walk down to the reception desk with my map. I asked the concierge for a place to go out drinking. I didn't actually want to go out. I didn't know what I wanted.

"There are some places near here, here, and here." He circled sections all over my map.

I took the Metro to Montparnasse where I was greeted by a bronze statue of a lion. The adjacent street was lined with rows of tables selling everything from old records and books to ironing boards and gargoyles.

I followed my map to the Jardin du Luxembourg. It seemed like a good place to stew in my wretched state. I walked north past cafés and tour busses. It was cold and I could see my breath in the air. I entered a long stretch of shrubbery and sand. The trees were barren this time of year.

Why doesn't she want to be with me? Keep walking and ignore it. What did I do to deserve this? Plenty, I'm sure. I was petty and selfish. I couldn't put our relationship ahead of some trivial squabbles. I deserve this. Keep walking.

I crossed the road and passed through a wrought iron gate into the park.

It's not her fault. People just fall out of love sometimes. It just happens. It's nobody's fault. Love isn't a choice. You either feel it or you don't. And she doesn't.

I walked through the park, hanging my head. I passed large rectangular trees on either side with a strip of grass down the middle. I walked past two girls on a park bench and heard them speaking English.

I need to talk to someone. Anyone. I need a friend. A confidante. A kindred spirit. Someone, anyone, please!

"Hey, I heard you speaking English," I said.

They raised their eyebrows and looked up at me.

"Yes?"

"Well, I am all alone in Paris and I know nothing."

"Okay."

"Well, I guess, I was wondering—well, could you, maybe, recommend a place to go out for a drink tonight?" It was a Monday. I didn't care about a stupid bar. I was just trying to make conversation.

The blonde on the right explained something about an arrondisse-ment to the north. Across the river. I wasn't really listening. That wasn't the point. I smiled and nodded.

"Great, that sounds good. Thank you."

Long pause. Why am I still standing here?

"I am traveling alone because, well, my girlfriend left me. So, now I am alone."

Give me pity, please! Oh just a little bit of pity is all I need. Give me a hug and tell me you want to hear the whole story from the begin-ning. Tell me that I can cry on your shoulder. Tell me that you won't leave my side until I feel better.

"That, uh, sucks," she said.

Of course you don't care about my pathetic life. My miserable stupid pathetic excuse for a life.

I dismissed myself and sat alone on a bench nearby. I walked to the edge of the lagoon in the middle of the park and stared at the reflection of the palace. The sun was beginning to set when I left the park and walked along the Seine. It was cold and dark.

I wished a mugger would creep out of the shadows and rob me. Or maybe even stab me. If I went to the hospital, someone would have to talk to me there.

Ashley probably thinks I'm having a great time in Paris. She loves Paris. When she realizes the mistake she made she will want me back. And then we can talk about Paris together. We will laugh about this. She will say that I was silly for coming here.

I crossed the river and walked north to a large obelisk with hiero-glyphics up and down the side. I saw the Arc de Triomphe in the distance and walked the length of the street towards it. I descended a passage beneath the road, but there was a long line to go up into it.

Has she come to her senses yet? Maybe she needs a reminder.

As I walked back down the street, I stopped outside an Italian restaurant and connected to their wireless internet. My fingers shook from the cold as I pressed the keys on my phone and typed out a message.

"You know that scene in romantic comedies where the girl has a revelation and realizes she's made the biggest mistake of her life... has that happened yet?" I tried to mask my infinite misery under the veil of humor.

"I told you that you could stay," she replied. "All I said was that things felt different."

"Okay, well do you think things could go back, or is that it?"

I held my breath as I slouched into an adjacent doorway to avoid the chilly breeze.

"I don't think we communicate very well."

"We are still getting to know each other in many ways," I said. "I think there will always be hurdles to work through. Don't you think we could work things out?"

"It's not cool that you just walked out like that. I'm not sure I want to be with someone who overreacts to any bad situation that he's not in control of. That kind of behavior rings alarm bells in my head."

"You wouldn't even talk to me," I said. "You spoke with such finality."

"I just couldn't believe that you were leaving. Your actions spoke with finality."

"You hurt me so bad."

"So every time it hurts, you run away. Face your problems, don't run away from them."

I'm not running away! No way. I'm a fighter. I face my problems. I would never... but wait, maybe she's right. I literally left the country. And I left Peru when things went sour. Maybe I ran away from New York too. Maybe I couldn't hack it in my job so I fled. But I was always running towards things too—I ran towards life, towards experience, towards passion. And now look where it's gotten me. What am I running towards now? I have nowhere left to run.

We continued arguing, but I knew that I couldn't win. No one ever debated their way into someone's heart.

"Okay," I continued, "this blame game is not getting us anywhere. I guess you're right and it makes me sad."

"It upsets me too," she said. "You see now that we just can't communicate."

"Yeah."

"Which sucks," she said. "Because I love you."

The very words that had once made me so happy now stabbed me through the chest. I had been on the other end of this conversation enough times in my life to know what she meant: "I love you, but..."

"I obviously love you too," I said. "Otherwise I wouldn't go so loco over you."

We chatted about Paris and she gave me some suggestions, but I grew more confused. We were talking amicably like nothing had ever happened. And she said she still loved me. Where did that leave us?

"Can I get a final word on where we stand?"

"Don't come back," she said. "In the long run I don't see this relationship working and I'm very sorry about that."

I remember getting punched hard in my first fight. I felt like it should've hurt, but it didn't. In the flurry of action, it just didn't register. That is how I feel. It doesn't hurt. I feel nothing.

"Alright. I love you anyway and I wish you the best."

"I'm going to feel so guilty for a long time," she lamented. "I'm sorry for what I've done to you."

"It's gonna hurt for a long time but I'll survive."

"I still hope you enjoyed spending time with me and my family and seeing a bit of England."

"I did. Okay I'm gonna go. Goodnight."

"Okay Rollie. Goodnight."

CHAPTER

47

T he next morning, I decided to leave Paris but I didn't know where to go. I had never planned on even being here. I sat in a café and looked up the route Hemingway had traveled in *The Sun Also Rises*. After some deliberation, I booked an overnight bus to San Sebastián in Spain. As I waited, I found a bar where I ordered a whiskey and toasted to my loneliness.

After four whiskeys, I left for the bus terminal. When I arrived, I handed my ticket to the woman behind the window. She gasped and wagged her finger at me.

"English?" I asked.

"No," she said with a scowl.

"What?" I asked, but she didn't say anything.

"*Español?*" she asked me.

"*Sí,*" I said. "Tell me what's going on."

"You are late! I don't know if you can still get on the bus."

It was 6:45 and the bus wasn't scheduled to leave until 7:30. The ticket said to check-in one hour early, but I couldn't believe that they wouldn't let me on because I was late for check-in.

"I still have forty-five minutes," I said.

"No, you do not," she pointed to the large clock on the wall that read 7:45.

"No," I pressed my cellphone against the glass to show her that it was actually 6:45.

"No, incorrect," she pointed to the clock again. "The bus already left."

She picked up the phone and muttered some words in French and listened for a reply. The she nodded her head and looked up.

"Go. Now. Run!"

I sprinted through the station and arrived at the bus. A moment later we pulled away. I asked the woman across the aisle what time it was.

"Seven fifty."

There had been a time zone change between London and Paris. For my entire two days in Paris, my clock had been off by an hour and I hadn't even noticed.

I arrived in San Sebastián at six in the morning. It was completely dark and the streets were deserted. I pulled my jacket tight under the glow of the streetlights.

I started walking down the street until I came across a small café. A woman was wiping the counter with a rag and all of the chairs were still upturned on the tables. I knocked on the glass and she unlocked the door and brought me a cup of coffee.

I noticed that the menu was written in two languages. It was my first time reading Basque. I hadn't even realized that San Sebastián was in Basque Country. I had always imagined that Basque would be similar to Spanish, but it may as well have been Russian to me. They used the letters k, x, and z excessively.

When I connected to their wireless, I got a message from Ashley saying, "Eurgh why did you leave." Maybe she was starting to come around, but now I was even further away.

I left the café and followed the river out to the ocean. The sky was beginning to show the first signs of light and I crossed the bridge to the far riverbank. The beach curved along the coast in an arc and the sea air filled my lungs. The bright blue water seemed to clash with the retreating darkness. A rocky jetty extended out into the ocean and I walked to the end. I sat on the edge and looked back towards town, which lay before a backdrop of mountains.

I watched the sun begin to rise over the mountains. It ascended slowly until it illuminated the whole beach. I knew that I would re-member this moment for the rest of my life.

I walked along the beach and through the town until I found the Surfing Etxea Hostel. Ashley had recommended it to me the day before. She had stayed here on a previous trip. I rang the buzzer and a slender angular man answered the door. I had woken him up, but he was polite.

"Do you have any rooms available?" I asked.

He rubbed his eyes.

"Maybe. Can you return at eleven?"

"Of course."

I walked back along the beach and crossed to the other side of the river. On top of a small mountain in front of me I saw a castle. I cut through the cobblestone streets and narrow alleys until I found the path up the mountain.

It was still early but the sunrays shone through the trees. I climbed higher up the trail. Even though it was a brisk morning, I began to sweat. I was still carrying my backpack. As I passed to the other side of the mountain, I saw an aquamarine bay full of moored sailboats.

I climbed up a final set of stone steps and through a tunnel. I fol-lowed the parapet along the edge and to a small tower. The morning sun was now well above the mountain peaks. I walked to the edge of the cliff where a red, green, and white Basque flag fluttered in the wind. Today had barely started but already I was feeling better.

Later that morning, I was welcomed into the hostel by Aritz. When I commented about his name, he explained, "It means 'oak' in Basque." After showing me around, he looked me up and down.

"You are a fighter, no?"

"How did you know?"

"Your ears."

He had a good friend from Australia who was also an MMA fighter.

"That is very cool, brother. Welcome to San Sebastián." I told him about my morning and he suggested another hike. "You hike about two hours through the mountains and come down the other side to a small town called San Pedro. It's really beautiful. From there, you can take a boat across to the other side."

He took out a map and sketched the route for me. It wasn't even noon yet when I set out for my second hike of the day. I began climbing the mountain on the other side of San Sebastián. It began with long narrow steps. I passed goats on my right and ponies on my left. My legs were burning already, but the pain felt good.

One step at a time, one foot over the other. The stairs steepened and lush bamboo groves formed a natural canopy. I was sweating and I rolled up my jeans. I hadn't even packed shorts because I had been expecting to be in England the whole time. When I reached a road, I followed it several miles along the mountainside, looking down over San Sebastián.

I arrived at a parking lot and asked an elderly man for directions to San Pedro. "Up that way," he said.

"Is it close?" I asked.

"No." He shook his head.

The road snaked through the forest and the only sound I heard was chirping birds. When I reached the top, I crossed a wide lawn on the other side and looked out onto the ocean. The blue water was serene, interrupted only by the few sailboats that bobbed peacefully in its wake.

As I continued through the woods, the path became smaller and less defined. Every five minutes or so I would pass a person and ask if I was taking the correct route to San Pedro.

Slowly, the traces of society slipped away and I found myself completely alone. Just when I thought I was lost, I came to a field with a rusty barbed wire fence. There were cows grazing inside the fence. And bulls. Huge, muscular bulls.

I must have veered off the path, I thought. I was supposed to be going towards San Pedro, but I kept getting further away from people. I was on a farmer's land now. I could almost picture an angry rancher coming out with a shotgun. There was barely any path to follow anymore.

I walked to a small clearing where I could see the water below. A narrow dirt path cut down through the steep cliff and I began to follow it down. I spied a ghost-white castle down the hill ahead of me. I began to descend the path and got closer. There was no one around. No other buildings or humans in sight except for this eerie white castle.

Just as I was about to leave the path and head towards the ominous structure, I heard a car's horn in the distance. I followed sound of the horn and looked down to a paved road ran about a hundred feet below me. I slid down the embankment until I reached the road.

I followed the road along the coast and it slowly began to descend towards the water. A stunningly beautiful cove opened up in front of me. There was a small pier with a lighthouse at the end. I climbed down the final stone steps and walked to the end to the lighthouse. Three teenagers were casting fishing poles out into the bay. We were surrounded on three sides by mountains and one side by crystal clear water. I followed the shore around the bend into an estuary and arrived at the town of San Pedro. I walked down the metal dock where a man in a small motorboat charged 0.70 euros to shuttle me across the water.

Most restaurants were closed, the boatman explained, because they had just had a fiesta for Easter, which had come and gone in Paris without me even noticing.

I thanked him and walked around the seaside town. I found a restaurant and sat down on the porch that overlooked the water. I ordered a glass of white wine and a plate of *arroz con mariscos* that came doused in black squid ink. I was the only person in the whole restaurant. The wind whipped the canvas roof above me as I sipped my wine and enjoyed my food. Given everything that happened, life was as good as it could be.

When I arrived back at the hostel, I sat in the common area. A set of double doors opened into a patio where a half dozen surfboards leaned against the railing and wet clothes hung from cords. The Europeans gathered outside with their cigarettes. I talked with two girls from the United States who were doing a semester abroad. We were soon joined by three Australians who had just returned from surfing. I sat on the couch as people came and went all day. This was the haven that I had so desired in Paris. I had people to talk to.

We all swapped stories from the road. Even just a few hours of conversation yielded enough stories and advice to fill a travel guide for all of Europe. They talked of Amsterdam, Monaco, Munich. Everyone had been everywhere. Need a hostel recommendation in Venice or Barcelona? Someone had a suggestion. They taught me which apps to use to find hostels and transportation. They opened my eyes.

I couldn't help but message the one person I wished was there. I told Ashley about what a great time I was having. I sent her pictures of all of the sights I had seen. Everything changed from that point forward.

"I don't need constant reminders that my boyfriend left me and is swanning around the world doing all the things on his bucket list. If you ask me, it seems like that's what you wanted to do all along."

I was appalled that she could ever think that I had wanted this. I had been a train wreck in Paris and she had told me not to come back. Now that I was having a better time, I thought she would have been happy for me. Maybe she wouldn't have to feel so guilty anymore. But now, suddenly, it was all my fault?

"I wish I hadn't left," I said. "But I did."

"Yeah you did," she replied. "It's not me who has to live with that for the rest of my life."

"Ouch."

I was going to move to England for her. Now what would I do?

Where would I go? Back to Peru? I was swimming in a sea of uncertainty and regret.

I never again had a pleasant conversation with Ashley. Every time I reached out, we reverted to accusations and name calling. I was devastated and disillusioned. I still loved her, but I also hated her. I hated her so much for what she had done to me. But I loved her more. I just couldn't accept that the relationship was dead. Heartbreak is a bit like being hungover. Everyone has their little remedies and distractions, but at the end of the day, time is the only thing that will actually cure it. I knew this as I sat there, but still, I didn't give a damn about time, and my academic knowledge of its passing did nothing to alleviate my suffering.

When dinnertime came, I slipped away from the hostel and wandered into the cobblestone streets of the Parte Vieja. It was still early but people mingled in cafés and spilled out into the streets. I found a small café with an array of *pintxos* that stretched across the bar. The bartender told me to pile them on my plate and he would tell me how much I owed.

All over my plate were little pieces of bread piled with the most delicious items: fish, sausages, cheese, salami, and ham. When I finished, I filled my plate again. I took a sip from my wine glass and looked out into the street. The warm breeze carried the murmurs of strangers' conversations and hints of cigarette smoke.

CHAPTER
48

I
n the morning I caught a bus to Pamplona for the day. I walked
to the Plaza de Toros and through the Plaza del Castillo. The sil-
houette of Hemingway's face was splashed everywhere I looked. I
walked through the streets and got a sandwich in a small café.

Back in Sab Sebastián, I sat on the beach and watched my new
friends surf. That night, we all went out together one last time. I
didn't want to leave, but the road beckoned me. In the morning, I
was hungover and heartbroken as I caught a bus to Madrid.

I found a hostel in the Malasaña district and immediately started
exploring the city. I walked down to the Puerta del Sol where tourists
flocked around the central fountain armed with cameras. I walked
to the Plaza Mayor and arrived in the large quadrangle of red brick
buildings. A group of young American students approached me.

"Puedes, uh, tomar...un foto...?"

"You want me to take a picture?" I replied and they laughed.

I made my way to the Mercado de San Miguel and got tapas and
a glass of wine at one of the booths. I walked west until I reached a
cluster of fancy buildings and architecture. I passed the Catedral de la
Almudena, Palacio Real de Madrid, and Plaza de Oriente. They were
all rather beautiful, but I didn't even bother to stop.

I walked all the way back across the city to the Parque del Retiro.
I started in the northwest corner and cut down through the massive
park. I came to a large lagoon where people paddled blue rowboats in
front of a large multi-layered statue capped by a soldier on horseback.

When I came out the southern end of the park, I walked down a side street lined with bookstalls. I stopped and browsed the books, but they were all in Spanish. I made my way past the Museo del Prado and passed the Fuente de Neptuno and walked through the Barrio de las Letras.

When I got back to my hostel, I was sweaty and dusty from the day's wanderings. There was a pub-crawl scheduled to leave from the hostel at ten o'clock, so I had time to relax for a bit before going out. I drank sangria in the common area with a group of Germans. We walked to the Puerta del Sol to meet the pub-crawl. At every bar we got a free shot, and it became a hazy night. I chatted with a Spanish guy who was a teacher in Salamanca. He insisted that I had to go to Lisbon because it was his favorite city in Europe. "I would stay there forever if I could. I never want to leave when I visit," he said. "And maybe you go to Seville on the way." I liked his idea, even though I would have to rush if I wanted to make it to Barcelona. There would be some extremely long bus rides involved, but I was up for the task.

I snuck out of the bar around two o'clock and set my alarm. In the morning, I went to the bus station and purchased a ticket to Seville.

When I arrived, I ambled down the maze of cobblestone streets, each bordered by bright houses of red, yellow, and pink. Some even had stripes or small domes affixed to the top. Clothes hung on lines stretched over the street and people sat in front of small cafés sipping coffee. The city was so colorful it seemed to come alive with each step. I stopped at an information center and the man recommended a hostel near the Cathedral of Seville. The Gothic cathedral, which dominated the landscape near my hostel, was the largest in the world.

Seville, in the providence of Andalusia, was occupied by the Moors for 800 years and developed an unmatched synthesis of styles. It is the origin of flamenco dancing and bull fighting. The rich fusion of cultures over the years has produced an identity unique to the region.

That night, I met a group of travelers on the roof of the hostel for drinks. There was a boisterous Australian, a quiet English girl traveling with her Italian boyfriend (who spoke five languages fluently), and three American girls. The Italian insisted I try the concoction he had mixed.

"It's called *kalimotxo*," he explained. "It's a popular drink with the Basques."

"What is it?"

He chuckled, "Coca-Cola and cheap red wine." He even held up the flimsy carton of red wine as proof. After some encouragement, I tried a glass and actually enjoyed it.

We went out to a nightclub called Bandalai. After a round of drinks, the Australian guy was eager to meet girls so I followed him to the dance floor. He approached a group of Spanish girls but walked away when they didn't speak English. I moved in after him.

"*Hola me llamo Rollie.*"

The girl on the end giggled lightly and introduced herself as Estefani. Just twenty years old, she was a Mediterranean beauty with a radiant olive complexion and dark, expressive eyes. She had studied English before, but didn't have much confidence as she tried to squeeze out a few sentences.

I told her about my travels, but I left out the sad parts of the story. "*Que envidia,*" she said. We went to the bar and I bought her a drink. "Baileys," she said. "I don't really drink and that is the only thing I like." She sipped it slowly and wouldn't accept another drink after that. We stood by the bar talking as her friends danced on the floor below. Two in the morning came and went. Three. Four.

I leaned in and kissed her. It was a sweet, innocent kiss—more appropriate for a fancy date than a dance club at four in the morning.

"Do you always stay out this late?" I asked.

"Sure," she shrugged.

"How do you do it?"

"*Es normal.* We eat dinner at ten, and then go out."

"When do you sleep until?"

"Three?" she said again with a giggle.

I was exhausted from my travels and wanted to go home, but I didn't dare leave my sweet Andalusian beauty. I stayed until six in the morning when she regrouped with her friends and we all walked out. She still lived with her parents, which seemed to fit her perfectly.

"Do you know how to get back to your hostel?" she asked outside the club.

"*Sí*," I assured her.

She smiled and waved goodbye.

"Wait," I said before she walked away. "Do you want to get dinner tomorrow?"

She smiled and nodded and then walked off. I had been planning on leaving for Lisbon in the morning, but I decided to stay another day.

The next evening we met at the Metropol Parasol at seven. While the rest of Seville was cloaked in a mysterious tapestry of Moorish and medieval influences, the Parasol stood out in its stark modernism. Six large mushroom-like structures stretched towards the sky. The umbrella-like canopies joined each other almost a hundred feet above where I stood. Each parasol was a grid of wavy lattices that connected to each other at right angles. I met Estefani on the steps in front.

"*Quieres subir*?" she asked with a smile.

"All the way up there?" I asked, pointing to towering canopies.

She nodded and smiled again. She was always smiling. We walked inside and took the elevator to the roof. A walkway swooped and banked over the surreal framework like a serpentine vertebrae. If Dr. Seuss had been an architect, he may have dreamt this up.

When we reached a viewing platform, I pressed her against the railing and kissed her. The city sparkled in the background. She pointed out various buildings in the distance, "That is the Giralda, where you are staying." I oriented myself and saw the Cathedral.

We walked back through the narrow streets and talked the whole time. She explained history of Andalusia to me. She even knew how to dance flamenco and had participated in some ceremonies during the ferias. When I mentioned an ex-girlfriend, her face suddenly dropped its natural cheerfulness.

"My boyfriend and I broke up a few months ago. Around Christmas," she forced the words out. She looked down at the ground as we walked.

"How long were you together?" I asked.

"Three years," there was so much sorrow in her voice. Months had passed and she still suffered. I wanted to grab her and hug her.

"I had a relationship end too, recently," I said.

"When?"

"Well," I laughed, "last week. It's a long story and I don't want to talk about it." She understood. I reached out and grabbed her hand, interlocking our fingers as we continued down the street.

We did a loop around the Cathedral and passed a queue of horse-drawn buggies waiting on the corner. I joked about taking one and she blushed. "You are joking, no?"

"*Vamos*," I said.

She giggled when I walked over to a driver and asked about a ride. She followed behind. "*Sube*," I told her. "Get up."

We started down the street and the driver pointed out passing attractions, but I couldn't hear him above the clippety-clop of the hooves on the road. We passed the Torre de Oro and followed the river south before turning into the Parque Maria Luisa, an enormous expanse of exotic gardens, fountains, and gazebos. It was starting to grow dark and the palm trees were mere silhouettes against the dusk sky. Inside the park, we came to the Plaza de España. The central fountain was surrounded by an extravagant building that stretched in an enormous semi-circle. The vaulted archways sat behind a moat, in which a few people were rowing small boats. The driver asked if we wanted him to take our picture. We both laughed but agreed. He snapped photos of us as we stood in front of the fountain at dusk. I was living in a Woody Allen movie.

After the driver dropped us off back by the Cathedral, we found a small tapas restaurant. I ordered a glass of wine but she didn't want one. "Like I told you, I don't drink that much. Alcohol tastes gross to me." She was so cute and so innocent.

It was late when we finished eating and she had class the next day, so I walked her to the bus station and kissed her goodbye.

CHAPTER
49

I remember hearing that sharks can never stop swimming or they will die. They even swim when they are sleeping. That was how I felt. I knew I had to keep moving. I wanted to stay another day with Estefani, but I had to keep moving on.

The bus ride to Valencia was supposed to be twelve hours, but I was disheartened when the bus sputtered into a gas station and the driver said something about the motor being broken. The driver wouldn't tell us how long we would have to wait. I don't think he knew. Maybe another bus would come, or maybe they would fix it. I sat down in the café across the street and ordered food.

It was late when we finally arrived in Valencia and I checked into my hostel. When I handed the guy my passport, his eyes darted up: "Happy birthday!" He was the only one who had said it to me in person all day. It wasn't exactly what I had imagined my birthday would be like—stuck on a bus all day. Ashley had talked eagerly about baking me a birthday cake. Now I was more alone than ever.

The next morning, I walked around the city, but didn't feel particularly inspired. I was anxious to get to Barcelona for my last days in Spain. I went back to the bus station after spending less than twelve hours in Valencia. I hadn't even gotten to try their famous paella.

In Barcelona, the man at the front desk of my hostel took out a tourist map and began explaining the city. He gasped when I had never heard of Antoni Gaudí.

"The Sagrada Familia...?" he probed.

"No, sorry."

He looked horrified. It was just a few blocks away, he said, and

I could still see it in daylight if I went now. I hesitated. I had been sprinting through Europe for almost ten days now and I was exhausted. But he eventually persuaded me to go.

Before I even reached it, I saw four conical spires pointing towards the heavens. Slowly, the rest of the structure revealed itself. I had never seen such unique architecture before. The spires looked like termite hills, and the façade was festooned with the most elaborate and strange imagery carved into stone. A bundle of purple grapes blossomed atop one of the spires. Nativity scenes and infernal demons adorned the exterior. A large archway opened in the front with rib-like columns. A logjam of tour busses blocked the adjacent street, and the sidewalk was so congested with tourists that it was impassable. I didn't care to go inside.

The next morning, I joined a walking tour of the city. We met in the southwest corner of the Plaça de Catalunya. Our guide was a British expat and we followed him out of the park and down La Rambla, the famous tree-lined street. We stopped at a small fountain called the Font de Canaletes. It was a drinking fountain, our guide explained, and the legend was that anyone who drank the water was fated to return to Barcelona. I took a big slug of water from the spigot and the rest of the group followed.

Barcelona is the capital of the region of Catalonia in eastern Spain. They traditionally spoke Catalan, a language distinct from Castilian Spanish. Unlike Basque however, Catalan is a Romance language, and to me it looked like a hybrid of Spanish, French, and Italian.

We began to cut down side streets and through narrow alleys until we arrived at a small plaza enclosed by stone buildings.

"This is one of my favorite spots in Barcelona," explained our guide, "The Plaça de Sant Felip Neri." We walked over to the front of the church that formed one wall and he touched the façade. "See how it is damaged? During the Spanish Civil War, a bomb exploded here and the shrapnel tore these chunks out."

One of the guys in our tour group spoke up. "Can you recommend any books about the Spanish Civil War?"

"*For Whom the Bell Tolls* by Hemingway," I suggested.

"Yes, that's a great book," said our guide. "It was the reason I wanted to move to Spain in the first place."

"What about *The Sun Also Rises*?" I said.

"Another great one. I even went to San Fermín a few years ago."

"Did you run with the bulls?"

"Of course. I went with my girlfriend and I wasn't going to back out in front of her."

We were seated around the fountain in the center of the plaza.

"And *A Moveable Feast*?" I asked.

"That one inspired me to move to Paris."

"You lived in Paris?"

"Yeah, for six months."

"Man, I want to move to Spain so badly," I said. "I need to figure out how to live here. I love this place."

"Life is amazing here," he nodded in agreement.

We continued down La Rambla, occasionally stopping to view an old church or ancient ruins. At the end of the tour he invited us to lunch in the neighborhood of Barceloneta.

"Man, I need to live here," I repeated over tapas. "I wonder if I could coach wrestling or something. I would even teach English. I would do just about anything to live here."

"You know what? I heard about this program the other day where they are looking for native English speakers to teach in the public schools. Maybe you could apply to that. What's your e-mail? I'll send you the info."

I spent the remainder of the day at the computer in the hostel applying to jobs in Spain. I downloaded my old résumé and began slashing and rewriting it. No one in Spain would care if I worked on the New York Stock Exchange for the summer. Gone. I wondered if they even knew what a mutual fund was, or a bond trader for that matter. Gone and gone. Did they care if I had taken classes like Financial Derivatives or Portfolio Management? Gone. I was slashing away things that had once seemed so important to me. An aspiring professional would kill for the things I was deleting.

I highlighted all of the coaching I had done over the years. I wrote cover letters. I wrote personal statements. I spoke of my passion for learning Spanish. I wanted "new challenges" and "enriching experiences." I had to get two letters of recommendation from college professors. I applied to dozens of teaching jobs. I recreated myself in a matter of minutes. Within hours, I was a whole new person.

CHAPTER
50

As I write this sentence, I am sitting in a café in the neighborhood of Lavapiés in Madrid. I have been living here for four months now. Out of all of the jobs I applied to, I heard back from only one of them: the one that my tour guide had recommended.

In the weeks that followed my trip to Europe, I sent Ashley several sappy messages begging her to take me back, but she didn't relent. As I sit here writing, I struggle to remember what I saw in her in the first place. I don't blame her for anything, we both did the best we could under the circumstances. Life can be a confusing mess at times, and it's always easier to judge your actions in hindsight. All we can do is hope to learn from our mistakes. And I made plenty of them.

After I returned from Europe, I spent the summer back in the United States before packing my things and moving to Madrid. I was excited and not even a little bit nervous for the big change that lay ahead of me. How could I be? After everything else I had been through, this was a cakewalk.

I like to do an exercise daily in which I reminisce on the inflection points in my life, as I had done on the floor of the Cuzco airport on San Pedro. I like to think about the bad things that happened to me. I think back to the NCAAs my senior year. It left me upset and unsatisfied. It left me wanting more. So I moved to Peru. I think about cutting my finger. It more or less ended my MMA career. But the Clonazepam was what put the final nail in the coffin. After that, I knew I had to leave Peru. And I met Ashley.

I would have given it all up for her. But she didn't see it the same way. And so I ran across Europe and shared my misery with each new place I visited. I ran away, but I also ran towards. I followed that childish impulse in me that begs to run off to faraway lands in search of adventure.

I currently teach English to Spanish children between the ages of six and nine at a public school. It's a far cry from the world of MMA that I left behind, but it's scary in a different way. I try to look at it as a new challenge.

I train daily with the Spanish national team in wrestling. I even wrestled at a tournament in Barcelona last month. I got third place after losing to an Armenian wrestler in the semifinals. I wasn't happy about losing, but in the grand scheme of things, I was grateful. Who else can go wrestle in Barcelona on a whim?

One weekend before I left for Spain, Ben and I met in New York City. We went out to dinner with some old friends and had a great time. Many of them worked on Wall Street and I chatted with them about the industry. It had been so long since I had talked about finance. I knew that I had changed a lot in the past year, but the contrast really hit me as I talked with them.

As I walked around the city that weekend, I felt like a stranger. All of the skyscrapers that had once been so impressive, now seemed excessive and obstructive. I had thought that I would spend the rest of my life in New York, but now it didn't feel the same.

Ben and I sat down to get a slice of New York pizza and he asked me, "Do you think you'll regret that you never discovered your true potential in MMA?"

"No," I said. I didn't even need to think about it. "I think I would've regretted if I'd never moved to Peru, but I did it. And I loved it. I never have to look back as an old man and ask what would have happened if I had moved to Peru. I know what happened."

In the end, I wouldn't change a single thing about the experience. Everything that happened—good or bad—brought me here to this. It was a fight at every step of the way, and it was never easy, but in the end it was worth it.

During my first days in Peru, Ivan taught me a lesson about mentality that I will never forget. When you get punched in the face, he said, the most important thing is that you keep moving forward. And so I keep pressing forward, awaiting the next punch.

AFTERWORD

Ben won his next fight in Bellator, but then lost the following match. It pained me as if I myself had lost. Fuerte was featured on the UFC's reality show, The Ultimate Fighter: Latin America. The show is formatted as a tournament with rounds each week. The winner gets a valuable UFC contract. When he made it to the finals, all of Peru was watching. When he won, he made all of us at Pitbull proud. Not bad for a kid from the barrio.

I found an MMA gym in Madrid and trained intermittently. I began wrestling daily with the Spanish national team. I even wrestled at a tournament in Barcelona with them. I placed third after losing to an Armenian wrestler. I had a lot of fun with the experience.

I have been back to San Sebastian. I was walking on the street and ran into Aritz, the guy from the Surfing Etxea Hostel. "You're Rollie, right?" I was blown away that he had remembered my name.

I went back to Seville too, but Estefani was busy that weekend. I went out with a group of people from the hostel and wound up swimming in the Guadalquivir River at five in the morning.

I've been to Portugal, Ireland, Germany, Belgium, and Hungary. I have friends in many European countries. The amount of interesting people I have met over the past two years could fill a whole other book. I wouldn't trade these friendships for all the money in the world.

I was in the center of Madrid recently and a guy pickpocketed me. I confronted him, but he denied it even though I could see my wallet in his hands. I punched him in the face and it fell to the ground as he ran away. My life is never boring.

I put my heart and soul into writing this book and it feels like I carved out a chunk of my flesh and slapped it down on the table. Part of my journey was about overcoming my deepest fears, but in the end, I realize the futility of this approach. All you can do is accept them and continue living.

I am nervous as hell about this book. Will people like it? Is that even important? I didn't write it for people to like it. I wrote it because I had to. I had no choice. I had all these experiences that were so amazing, so meaningful, and so painful that I couldn't keep them bottled up in my own head. I needed to put them on paper.

I wanted people to see what I had seen. To feel what I had felt. I don't care if I don't make a dollar on this book. In fact, I'm expecting to lose money, especially considering the countless hours I've put into it, and what economists would refer to as the "opportunity cost" of my time. I wrote this for me.

I sometimes think of how writing this book has changed me. Can I call myself an author now? I don't know, nor do I particularly care. At different points, I identified myself as a wrestler, a bond trader, and MMA fighter. Am I still any of those things? Labels are temporary.

Wrestling has given me a sense of purpose, and for that I am forever grateful. My parents still define the day I started wrestling as a watershed moment that changed everything. I have to thank them for being so supportive of me over the years.

Mom, I can't even begin to thank you for all you have done for me. If you are reading this, that means you have read the rest of the book. I want you to know that I'm sorry. All of those dangerous things I did are entirely made up, I promise. To everyone else: ignore that, they are entirely true.

And dad, thank you for your infinite patience. I know it couldn't have been easy witnessing this journey, but you never once tried to change me. You somehow had faith in me throughout everything.

I obviously have to thank the people who played a role in the events that led to this book. Clinton Matter for always believing in me and inspiring me to be the best version of myself. Brian and Bellini for teaching me infinite small lessons that I still dwell on to this day. To Ed McBride for having my back. To Rich Tavoso for always supporting me and being a great mentor.

I shouldn't even need to thank Ivan at this point. The whole book is a giant thank you card. Few people have had such a outsized impact on my life as he has.

My teammates Claudio, Pinedo, and Fuerte. You guys are all champions. I wouldn't have made it without you guys. Thank you Kike "The Boss" Franco. You have been an amazing friend and an amazing person.

Ben Reiter. Words escape me. You are the most kind, considerate, and compassionate person I know. You have done a million small things that helped me on my journey. I don't know what I would have done without you and Fiorella. No matter what happens, you guys will remain family for life.

When I sat down to write the book, I had to learn as I went. I never studied writing. It was a battle the whole time, but I had so much fun. Writing is a very lonely process, and staring at the blank page all day can drive you insane. But thankfully I have amazing friends who listened to me and gave me input at every step of the way.

No single person has helped me more in writing this book than Chris Palmisano. Not even close. During the process, I would call Chris just about every day. He listened patiently as I discussed some problem I was stuck on, and almost always, he offered sound advice. We would bounce ideas back and forth until we had viewed the book from every angle imaginable. His knowledge of MMA and jiu-jitsu was also invaluable. And he did two full rounds of edits. Simply put, this book would be much worse if not for him.

My brother, Kenny Peterkin also helped me immensely in the editing process. He has a special gift for narrative that I am grateful for.

Many other people were also invaluable to this book. Thank you Jordan Michelson, Harrison Cook, Mike Steltenkamp, Thomas Shovlin, Andrew Coles, Scott Giffin, Sara Peterkin, Dan Zander, Neil Cisper, Tyler Blakely, Scott Jones, Doug Witzenbocker, John Witzenbocker, Dave Hagel, Lorenzo Valterza, David Azzolina, Marty Borowsky, Wayne Catan. Special thanks to Hudson Collins and Jana Hirsch, for being there when I needed you most. Thanks to Ali Wasiutynski and Bill Cotter. Thanks to Josh Pickell. Thank you Jalil and Wayra. Gracias a Jorge Allegre, Fernando Calero, Rodrigo Quevedo, Hector Iberico, Luigi Dapello, Zaid Rojas, Luis Mayta, Jordan Gambini. Thank you to my wrestling coaches: Dave Paltrineri, Sean Bilodeau, Chris Gelinas, Matt Wassel, Kendall Cross, Jeff Buxton, Matt Valenti, Kyle Cerminara, and Rob Eiter.

Thank you to Ann Maynard and Nils Parker at Command+Z for doing a fantastic job editing this book. Thank you to Erin Tyler for blowing my mind with your creative abilities. The cover and the layout are better than I could have imagined.

Special thanks to James Altucher, who has always been an inspiration to me since I first read his work as a teenager. His prolific writings have almost single-handedly inspired me to write this book. And his dictum that writers should "bleed" on the page has served as my guiding beacon.

I put everything into the book, because, who knows if I will ever write another one? I have no plans at the moment, and I am just focusing on living my life. If I had one piece of advice, it would be this: try to lead a life that is worthy of a book. That is what I have tried to do and will continue trying. Thank you all!

ROLLIE PETERKIN
LAVAPIÉS, MADRID
1/15/2016

Made in the USA
Middletown, DE
05 July 2023